Comparative Legislative Studies

Malcolm E. Jewell, Editor

CONGRESSIONAL COMMITTEE CHAIRMEN

Three Who Made an Evolution

Andrée E. Reeves

THE UNIVERSITY PRESS OF KENTUCKY

Library of Congress Cataloging-in-Publication Data

Reeves, Andrée E., 1958-
  Congressional committee chairmen : three who made an evolution /
Andrée E. Reeves.
    p.   cm. — (Comparative legislative studies)
  Includes bibliographical references and index.
  ISBN 0-8131-1816-6
  1. United States. Congress. House. Committee on Education and
Labor—History. 2. Barden, Graham Arthur, 1896-1967. 3. Powell,
Adam Clayton, 1908-1984. 4. Perkins, Carl Dewey, 1912-1984.
5. Legislators—United States—Biography. 6. United States.
Congress. House. Committee on Education and Labor—Biography.
I. Title. II. Series.
JK1430.E352R44   1993
328.73'07658—dc20   92-34812

Contents

Tables

Acknowledgments

Although each of us likes to think of herself or himself as the sole author of a book, each author is dependent on a host of others. Many people made this book possible. The faculty of the Department of Political Science at Rice University afforded me the opportunity to study with a dedicated group of scholars and provided me with a graduate fellowship to attend Rice.

I particularly appreciate the assistance of Joseph Cooper, now vice president and provost at Johns Hopkins University, and Rick K. Wilson of Rice University. Mark A. Morgan also provided invaluable technical assistance at all stages of this research.

Without the help of the many people connected with the Committee on Education and Labor when this research was undertaken, it could not have been completed. They tolerated my presence cheerfully and were exceptionally helpful and supportive of my project. First and foremost, Benjamin F. Reeves gave me the benefit of years of experience in dealing with members of Congress and this committee in particular. Louise Wright provided access to all committee roll calls taken since 1951 and to other committee documents. I am especially grateful for her superb record-keeping. Lelia Beall also often came to my aid. Others currently or previously connected with Education and Labor provided assistance, including Donald Baker, Donald Berens, Patricia Bowley, Katherine Clark, Louise Maxienne Dargans, Cindy Fox, Jim Harrison, Jack Jennings, Dick Johnson, Susan Maguire, Barbara Morrison, Charles Radcliffe, Hartwell Reed, Peter Schott, Gene Sofer, Ivan Swift, Gene Thomson, Robert Vagley, Thomas Wolanin, and Marian Wyman. In Chairman Perkins's office, Charlotte Welch, David Whalen, Ruth Epperson, and Connie Frederick Crosby provided assistance.

I appreciate the time and insights provided by members of the House, including Chairman Perkins and his son, Carl C. Perkins. Their willingness to share information contributed to the depth of this research. The other members interviewed, who shall remain nameless because of a promise of anonymity, deserve wholehearted thanks, gratefully given. Nextdoor neighbor James L. Oberstar of Minnesota and his wife, Jo, put up with my questions about Congress at inconvenient times.

Scholars who provided helpful comments at various stages of this research include Roger H. Davidson, Richard L. Hall, Robert L. Peabody, and Mavis Mann Reeves. At the University of Alabama in Huntsville, Fiona Rae cheerfully helped me proofread the final copy.

The data and tabulations utilized in this book were made available in part by the Inter-University Consortium for Political and Social Research. The data for Roster of United States Congressional Officeholders and Biographical Characteristics of Members of the United States Congress, 1789-1985 Merged Data were originally collected by Carroll McKibbin and the Inter-University Consortium for Political and Social Research. Neither the collector of the original data nor the consortium bears any responsibility for analyses or interpretations presented here.

I especially appreciate the faith offered by Malcolm E. Jewell and Christopher J. Deering that this manuscript was publishable, although I absolve them from any blame that might arise.

Finally, my greatest debt is to my parents, Benjamin F. and Mavis Mann Reeves, who provided sustenance, maintenance, encouragement, and editorial assistance.

I appreciate the help of all these people, without whom this study could not have been completed. Thank you, one and all. Despite all of their help, none of these individuals was willing to accept responsibility for the final product, which remains with me. Unfortunately, I have been unable to find anyone foolish enough to accept blame for any mistakes it may contain.

A Note on the Interviews

Some of the data for this study were collected through observation of the committee in action. Other information came from scheduled, semistructured interviews. Additional material was gathered informally, by asking staff members and occasionally committee members questions as they arose.

I conducted semistructured interviews with eight current and former House members: Chairman Carl D. Perkins, six others who were on the Committee on Education and Labor, and one other member. In addition, I interviewed the chairman's son, Carl C. Perkins, who was elected to fill his father's seat in 1984 and who sat on Education and Labor until his retirement in 1992. Several other House members told me personally that they could remember little about the periods under study or that they were reluctant to talk about their colleagues. As a result of this reluctance, the persons who were interviewed were guaranteed anonymity.

I also conducted semistructured interviews with eight high-ranking professional staff members who had worked on or around the committee during the chairmanships of Carl D. Perkins and Adam Clayton Powell, Jr., and were close to the chairmen or to other key members. Several were interviewed two or three times. One person interviewed had worked for Powell during the chairmanships of both Graham Barden and Powell and later worked for Perkins. I also conducted formal interviews with at least three of the support staff who worked for the committee during at least two of the three periods. The semistructured interviews lasted between forty-five minutes and two and a half hours each.

Informal interviews were conducted on an irregular basis with at least thirty-five different staff members in addition to one or two committee members and some of Chairman Perkins's office staff. Several of his constituents also were questioned. I returned to the staff frequently to ask more questions, since one person's comments usually led to further questions or to the need for verification. Many of the top staff members and some of the support staff on the committee since 1982 were questioned numerous times. On a few occasions group discussions added to insights into committee operations and leadership. The informal interviews lasted from five minutes to two hours.

As a result of my father's employment as a top staff member of the committee and adviser to the chairman, Mr. Perkins and the committee staff were unusually helpful in my endeavors and tolerant of my frequent presence. My internships on Capitol Hill gave me a prime opportunity to view the committee and to discuss it with the staff and committee members.

Introduction

Scene 1: After a roll-call vote on the floor of the U.S. House of Representatives that had interrupted a committee meeting, a prominent chairman hurries, almost at a trot, to get back to the committee chamber ahead of his colleagues. He beats them by a furlong. Finding no other members present in the committee room, the chairman exercises his prerogative, declares the absence of a quorum, and adjourns the meeting. The major legislative proposal under consideration is put off—again. The same chairman, on several occasions, lines up with the opposition party on his committee to defeat a major federal aid to education bill sponsored by fellow party members.

Scene 2: Another chairman, newly designated, begins his tenure by delegating substantial authority to his subcommittee chairmen, thus facilitating passage of major legislation. Later he pockets a bill ordered reported by his committee and holds it hostage until the House and Senate act on other measures.

Scene 3: A third chairman finds himself stymied by minority party members on his committee who block a vote on major legislation by staying holed up in their lounge—twenty feet away from the main committee chamber, where the majority members are waiting for the executive session to begin. The chairman declares the meeting open to the media and the public. When the doors open and reporters and photographers swarm into the chamber, they are followed in short order by the minority members, who file in like little gentlemen to take their places on the dais. It is the beginning of the open meeting policy, which soon spreads throughout the other congressional committees.

Strangely enough, all of these chairmen headed the same committee—the U.S. House of Representatives Committee on Education and Labor. Each chaired the committee at a different stage of its organizational development and in his own way left a lasting impression on the committee, the House, and education and labor policy.

The first of these chairmen, Graham Arthur Barden, Democrat of the Third District of North Carolina, was almost a caricature of the southern conservative committee chairman. By virtue of the powers concentrated in the hands of the chairman, he had the power to strangle any legislation that could be considered liberal or progressive. Although he was a strong advocate of education, he feared federal involvement because he saw it as federal interference in state and local control of the school system. Taking the traditional southern position, he also opposed organized labor and set about to rein it in at every opportunity. Many committee members, particularly those in the Democratic party, were frustrated by these actions. Under Barden's leadership members had little opportunity to exercise their creativity, and some found themselves denied chances to influence public policy. In a rare display of unity, Democrats forced the adoption of committee rules diminishing Barden's power.

The second chairman was Adam Clayton Powell, Jr., Democrat of New York's Twenty-second District. A Baptist preacher from Harlem, he had been denied a subcommittee chairmanship by Barden despite his position as the second-ranking Democrat. When he became chairman, he encouraged participation by his fellow Democrats, rewarding them with subcommittee chairmanships and making sure their names appeared as sponsors of important committee bills. He facilitated the passage of landmark federal aid to education legislation requested by the Kennedy and Johnson administrations. Initially, his colleagues regarded him as a good chairman. Later, however, his personal conduct interfered with the conduct of committee and House business and embarrassed his colleagues. Ultimately, the committee acted to restrict his discretion. The House went so far as to strip him of his chairmanship and subsequently to deny him his seat in Congress, an action that later was overturned by the U.S. Supreme Court.

Carl Dewey Perkins, the third chairman, represented the generally poor, mountainous Seventh District of Kentucky. He inherited a fully developed set of committee rules governing the conduct of the committee and limiting the power of the chairman. Nevertheless, his calculated use of personal resources ensured that he made a lasting impact on federal social policy. By pleading, bargaining, and dogged, unembarrassed persistence, Perkins was able to overcome the obstacles in House and committee rules and to steer major measures through the committee and through Congress. Faced with a less favorable environment than his predecessor, who chaired the committee under conditions ripe for big social welfare programs, Perkins was able to preserve much of Powell's legacy by his tenacity and skillful manipulation of opportunities.

The conduct of these chairmen during various periods of the committee's history changed not only the committee's operations and output but its function and development. Moreover, some of their maneuvers resulted in changes in both House and committee procedures. The actions of these men as chairmen influenced the path national education policy and labor policy took for years to come. The contrasts in the ways these chairmen conducted the business of the committee raise important questions for those interested in how governments operate. What have been the effects of disparate committee leadership on the structure, operations, and output of the committee? How did each chairman operate in the context of the committee? How did he lead? How did the committee evolve? What factors have been important in its evolution? Have committee functions remained constant over the years? Have the amount and character of committee output changed?

This study will argue that the chairmen made a difference in the structure, operations, output, and function of the committee, each leading in a different way. While institutional environment influences leadership, the way the chairman uses the resources at hand—both institutional prerogatives and personal resources—also has an impact on the institution and its outputs. In large part as a result of the differences in leadership, the committee was a different organization under each chairman.

In recent decades, political scientists have considered leadership as a function of its institutional context (e.g., Fenno 1978; Cooper and Brady 1981a; Jones 1981; Sinclair 1983). The current study regards leadership as influenced by institutional context but also as proactive: leadership is also an independent variable. The chairman's orientation determines, to a large extent, how he operates the committee and how he treats the issues that come before it. His ideological proclivities affect the content and form of legislation reported by the committee and often determine its outcome. His orientation and his use of resources help determine committee operations and outputs, thus leaving their mark on public policy. Examining three chairmen of a single committee reduces variations in external influences so the effects of the chairmen can be highlighted.

The Committee on Education and Labor

The House of Representatives Committee on Education and Labor was created by the Legislative Reorganization Act of 1946 (P.L. 79-601), which combined the Committee on Education and the Committee on Labor that

had operated separately since 1883 (House Rules, 96th Cong.). Mc-
Conachie reported that efforts to combine the two committees earlier had
met with "quick and angry opposition from the dominant Southerners"
(1898, 41n).

In the 80th Congress (1947-48), when the reorganization act took
effect, the Republicans had control of the Congress. Fred A. Hartley of
New Jersey became the first chairman of the new Committee on Education
and Labor. MacNeil referred to him as "one of the seniority system's
failures" and alleged that the previous chairman of the Education Committee, Mary T. Norton (D-NJ), resigned because of Hartley's neglect of the
committee (1963, 168; see Goodwin 1970, 120). Hartley's tenure, however,
was short-lived, because in the next Congress (81st, 1949-50) the Democrats regained control. John Lesinski, Sr., of Michigan became the chairman. His reign was cut short when he died in May 1950. Graham A.
Barden (D-NC) assumed the chairmanship until 1953, when the Republicans again ruled Congress, promoting Samuel K. McConnell, Jr., (PA) to
the chairmanship. He held the post for only one term, since in the 84th
Congress (1955-56) the Democrats once again were in power. Barden took
up where he left off and stayed until his retirement at the end of 1960.
Adam Clayton Powell, Jr., (D-NY) became chairman of the committee at
the beginning of the 87th Congress (1961-62), where he remained until he
was deposed and then excluded from membership in the House at the
beginning of the 90th Congress, in February 1967. Carl Dewey Perkins, a
Kentucky Democrat, became chairman and stayed until his death in August 1984. Augustus F. Hawkins, Democrat of California, succeeded
Perkins as chairman, followed by William D. Ford, Democrat of Michigan,
in 1991.

Of all the committees in the U.S. Congress, the House Committee on
Education and Labor is one of the most fascinating. It is important in the
policy process as the authorizing committee for major legislative programs
involving issues such as labor, manpower, poverty, school lunch, and other
aid to education. Its style, along with its importance, intrigues the student
of congressional committees. It is fractious. It is raucous. It has had colorful
leadership throughout its history. It authorizes big-money programs and
subscribes least to Sam Rayburn's philosophy of "to get along, go along."
Education and Labor epitomizes not only the fundamental party and
liberal-conservative dichotomies but those aspects of the legislative process
that reflect the divisions in society. It is never dull. It might be described as
the naughty child of Congress. Some committees conform and act in the
prescribed fashion. They are concerned with their images in Congress
(Fenno 1973; Manley 1970). But Education and Labor tends to be rebellious
and sometimes rambunctious. Neither the committee nor its membership is
House-broken. It acts unconventionally, and this unconventional behavior

has come to be expected of it. Perhaps it is even institutionalized. The consensus among scholars who have studied Education and Labor is that it is a highly partisan "policy-oriented" panel that exhibits little integration. Education and Labor probably is the most frequently employed example when these characteristics are discussed.

Cross-committee studies, such as Fenno's (1973), have shown that because of the loyalties and linkages based on ideological interests that most members have, the Education and Labor Committee is unusual in the extent to which it is divided along partisan and interest group lines. Fenno treated Education and Labor in his exploration of member goals, environmental constraints, strategic premises, decision-making processes, and decisions of six House committees. He found the Education and Labor Committee to be characterized by the member goal of making good public policy, high partisanship, and a high degree of conflict and as being pluralistic and party-led. It is the type of committee identified by "its extra–House-oriented decision rules, the permeability of its decision-making processes, the de-emphasis on committee expertise, its lack of success on the House floor, the absence of any feeling of group identification, and the relatively higher ratio of non-member to member satisfaction with its performance" (Fenno 1973, 278-79). Munger and Fenno (1962), Fenno (1973), and Manley (1965, 1970) began the tradition of depicting Education and Labor as the model of partisan conflict and low integration when an example of the antithesis of a well-integrated committee was needed. Feig's mathematical models (1979, 1981) substantiated Manley's and Fenno's findings concerning integration and partisanship on this committee.

Smith and Deering (1984), like Fenno (1973), characterized Education and Labor as a policy committee in their cross-sectional analysis of the significance of changes in committee environments and in formal structures and procedures. Members were motivated by their interests in the policies under the committee's jurisdiction. The authors noted that the committee's appeal among members diminished after the 1960s, a decade when its programs were at the top of presidential agendas. The protection of established programs became the committee's focus. Unekis and Rieselbach (1984) studied Education and Labor as part of their study of the politics of congressional committees based on committee roll calls. Researching participation-specialization, partisanship, and leadership, they depicted Education and Labor as the epitome of a policy-oriented committee. Parker and Parker (1985) used Education and Labor in their investigation of factions in committees as exhibited by voting behavior on committee roll calls taken between 1973 and 1980. They characterized the committee as having a bipolar factional alignment and as being dominated by party-led policy coalitions. They identified organized labor as one of the most important constituency groups operating in Education and Labor's environment.

If committees and subcommittees are the most influential decision makers, as has been posited for years in the literature on Congress (see Wilson 1885; Galloway 1953a; Goodwin 1970; Fenno 1973; Davidson 1981b; Smith and Deering 1984), why is so little "known about the ways that committee leaders operate and the effects that their actions generate?" (Unekis and Rieselbach 1983, 251). Although a number of scholars have examined the seniority system and the acquisition of leadership positions (Follett 1896; Brown 1922; Peabody 1966, 1976; Hinckley 1969, 1970, 1971; Parker 1977; Parker and Parker 1979; Bach 1984), only a few have addressed the exercise of committee leadership directly (Jones 1968; Manley 1969; Parker 1977; Berg 1978; Unekis and Rieselbach 1983; McCormick 1985; Evans 1986; Strahan 1990; Evans 1991). Their studies have focused on a number of leadership facets—power, style, voting patterns, and the impact of reform. Some have examined a single chairman; others have done comparative studies.

Huitt (1965), Jones (1968), Manley (1969) and Evans (1986) concentrated on the exercise of power. Huitt, in discussing "ideal types of chairmen," noted the importance of committee leaders in the internal distribution of power in the Senate. Jones used the examples of Speaker Joseph Cannon (R-IL) and Rules Committee chairman Howard W. Smith (D-VA) to analyze excessive use of leadership power and its consequences when such power was independent of the leader's procedural majorities. Manley examined the influence of Wilbur Mills, chairman of the Committee on Ways and Means, conceptualizing leadership via the chairman's relationship to his committee colleagues. Drawing on literature from psychology, he studied five bases of a chairman's influence—expertise, legitimacy, rewards, reference, and sanctions—and determined that Mills was effective in all five areas. Evans compared leadership in four Senate committees to determine whether influence over legislation was widely dispersed or concentrated in the hands of formal leaders. He found senators in leadership positions more likely to influence the process and outcome, particularly at the bill-drafting stage.

Bibby and Davidson (1967), Evans (1986, 1991), and Burns (1978) looked at leadership styles. Comparing the styles of two chairmen, Bibby and Davidson argued that "the legislative styles of chairmen are varied, but they dramatically affect the capacity of committees to perform legislative functions such as oversight" (173). They concluded that the styles of the two chairmen gave credence to the dictum that "committee functioning depends heavily on the chairman's style of leadership" (179). In comparative studies of leadership styles, Evans examined the role of formal leadership in Senate committees to determine how leadership influences the outcome of bills. He studied the behavior of committee leaders, the effects of their actions, and how and why their tactics varied in an effort to determine whether influence over legislation was widely dispersed or concentrated in the hands of chairmen and ranking minority members. Although Burns paid tribute to committee leaders in his landmark study of leadership, he dealt with them only peripherally.

In an effort to construct a theory of committee leadership and to explain the causes and consequences of leadership patterns, Unekis and Rieselbach (1983) scrutinized committee roll calls for nine committees to identify patterns of committee leadership in voting alignments. They found leadership stances to be related to the committee's partisanship, integration, and success on the House floor. They determined that the chairman's exercise of authority must be consistent with the goals of committee members and the committee's decision-making premises and structures.

Parker (1977), Berg (1978), Rieselbach and Unekis (1981-82), and Strahan (1990) studied the relation of congressional reforms to committee leadership. In the aftermath of the automatic election of chairmen by the House Democratic Caucus, Parker looked at the criteria members used in evaluating their committee leaders. He determined that concern for the functioning of the committee, not personal factors, was the underlying basis for the election of committee leaders. Berg questioned how different the new chairmen were from the ones they replaced and asked if the changes affected committee performance. Studying committee outputs from the 93d (1973-74) to the 94th (1975-76) Congress, he found little difference, suggesting that the new chairmen were not markedly different from those they replaced. Rieselbach and Unekis, studying the same four committees as Berg, examined formal committee leaders to see how they fit into the voting structure of the committee. They used roll call votes to determine if leadership style had changed and if that made any difference in the committee's performance. On three of the four committees, they found that leadership change was symbolic. On the Committee on Ways and Means, however, committee politics shifted somewhat. But the effects of the chairmanship change were mediated by external factors, such as enlargement and turnover, changes in House Democratic Caucus rules, and a shift in the committee's agenda. Strahan's case study of the Committee on Ways and Means assessed the effects of reforms on the committee and compared the leadership styles of Al Ullman (D-OR) and Dan Rostenkowski (D-IL). He concluded that "leadership proved to be a more important factor than one might have anticipated from the emphasis that has been placed in recent years on contextual factors as the primary determinants of leaders' styles and their effectiveness" (171).

Purpose and Theory of This Study

With the hope of contributing to the understanding of Congress and its committees, especially their leadership and development, this study examines the Committee on Education and Labor as an organization as well as a component of the Congress. The study focuses particularly on committee leadership. Political scientists have yet to develop an accepted theory of political leadership. As Cooper and Brady noted, "It remains a topic in which our intellectual grasp falls far short of our pragmatic sense of the impacts leaders have on organizational operations and performance" (1981a, 411). The best characterization to date is Neustadt's argument (1960, 1990) that presidential power is the power to persuade. This statement can be extrapolated to apply to all political leadership, including congressional committee leadership. After the 1910 revolt against Speaker Cannon, congressional leaders were left with few ways to compel compliance with their wishes. Over the years several sets of reforms in the House stripped committee chairmen of many of their institutional resources, leaving them to rely largely on their own persuasive abilities. As Burns (1978) emphasized in discussing the transactional nature of legislative leadership, they have had to depend on reciprocity, brokerage, and exchange. As the current study shows, to play this game committee chairmen have had to replace or augment a diminished set of institutional prerogatives with whatever personal resources they could bring to the job. They have been most successful when they relied on their personal abilities to persuade rather than on techniques of control.

The other focus of this study is committee development via its composition, structure and operations, and function. On the theory that congressional committees develop much as do other organizations and that the operations of their leaders are important to their functioning, the present study chronicles the evolution of the committee and the leadership of three chairmen over three decades. It is the study of three who made an evolution. It examines the committee's major characteristics, delves into its development, and analyzes the changes in its setting, composition, voting patterns, structure and operations, work load, functions, and leadership under the respective chairmen.

To advance understanding of congressional committees and committee leadership, specific findings must be subsumed under more general statements. One way of doing so is to draw questions and variables from established theory, such as organization theory. A number of scholars have approached the study of Congress from this perspective (Polsby 1968; Froman 1968; Cooper 1977, 1981; Cooper and Brady 1981a, 1981b; and Davidson and Oleszek 1976). The current study will draw questions and some variables from organization theory but will not rely on it exclusively.

Congressional committees are not business organizations, but democratic institutions that cannot be controlled in the same manner as private entities. They have to rely on democratic values precluding anything but a limited tolerance for hierarchy; an inability to control the size or character of the work force, the work load, or output goals; little ability to base decision making on technology; and constraints on identifying or merging institutional and individual interests (Cooper and Brady 1981b, 998). What is more, they have no "bottom line" in the economic sense.

In recent years some political scientists have viewed leadership as being molded by the institutional context and having little independent influence on the institution. This view plays up organizational context and downplays the influence of personal factors (Cooper and Brady 1981a; Jones 1981; Sinclair 1983; Rohde and Shepsle 1987; Little 1991).

The present author disagrees with organization theory on this view of leadership and argues that committee leaders often determine how the committee operates and in some cases its structure, its function, and the character of its outputs. Anyone who has worked or participated in an organization knows that who is at the helm can make a great difference in the operation of the organization, its relations with its internal and external environments, and its success. Of course institutional context constrains committee leadership, but other elements are influential also. A chairman brings his personality and background with all its prejudices to bear on a committee. How he sees his job and how (or whether) he behaves within those limits affect the committee—and sometimes the House.

Although congressional committees are parts of larger organizations— the Congress itself and either the House of Representatives or the Senate— there can be little doubt that they themselves fall into the general category of organizations. Every committee has a formal structure. Every committee has a set of operating procedures, well defined or not. Every committee has a formal leader and at least a minimal hierarchy. And every committee has some standard by which it can be judged.

A congressional standing committee is much more an organization than just a group. It is more formal. It has statutory standing. It has continuity and formal powers. It has boundaries. If, as Miles defined it, an organization is a "coalition of interest groups, sharing a common resource base, paying homage to a common mission, and depending upon a larger context for its legitimacy and development" (1980, 5), then congressional committees certainly fit the bill. They also conform to Haas and Drabek's characterization of an organization as "a relatively permanent and relatively complex discernible interaction system" (1973, 2). Certainly standing congressional committees are relatively permanent and relatively complex, and they are interaction systems. Cooper (1977, 140) broadly conceptualizes organizations as rational, goal-oriented entities created and structured to perform certain functions or tasks. As such, committees are vehicles set up to satisfy Congress's needs for division of labor; each is designed to deal in a particular area of legislation, although many of these jurisdictions overlap.

Considering the Committee on Education and Labor as an organization does not deny its uniqueness. There is only one such committee in the House of Representatives or in all of Congress. It has had a distinct set of members over the years. No other committee has had exactly (or even approximately) the same membership. No other committee has had the same leaders. No other committee in the House, with the possible exception of the Rules Committee, has had to deal with the issues under this committee's jurisdiction. Over the years education and labor issues have proved to be some of the most controversial matters handled in Congress, although certainly other committees have jurisdiction over divisive legislation. Because of its composition and the issues under its jurisdiction, this committee has had to endure a unique set of pressures and internal turmoil.

More important for theory building, however, are the elements that this committee shares with other standing committees. All congressional standing committees are creatures of the Congress and would not exist without the statutory approval of Congress. They all have similar structures, with defined leadership consisting of a majority party chairman and a ranking member from the minority party. For purposes of organizing the committee and distributing power, committees are administered by and mainly composed of members of the political party holding the majority of seats in the appropriate chamber, with the remaining vacancies filled by members of the minority. All committees have some kind of operating procedures. They are all subject to the rules, procedures, norms, and reforms of the parent chamber, and all abide by some semblance of the seniority system. As part of the larger organization of the Congress, committees share with it an institutional context or environment. They are subject to the same constraints that the Congress faces, though these limitations are exaggerated in committees. In many ways, this institutional context affects developmental patterns in committees, as environment does in other organizations, although individual committee leaders have been responsible for a great deal of change in committee structure, operations, and output.

Committee development is influenced by a number of factors, including committee leadership, the committee's environment, the way the committee adapts to environmental demands, the composition of the committee, the salience of the issues under the committee's jurisdiction, and the committee's function. This study addresses the influence of these factors on development.

Neither political science nor organization theory has paid much attention to the role of the chairman in determining changes in congressional committees. But by virtue of his official position, the chairman is more important than any other member of the committee. His visibility, his seniority, his influence with both members and the House leadership, his orientation, his perquisites, his control of the agenda, and his experience contribute to his dominance. Only a few studies have investigated the relationship between the chairman and his committee (Manley 1969; Rieselbach and Unekis 1981-82; Unekis and Rieselbach 1983, 1984; Bibby and Davidson 1967, 1972; Evans 1986; Strahan 1990). The current study examines the role of the chairman in shaping the structure and operations, function, and output of the committee. It seeks to rectify the previous neglect of the chairman as an important actor in committee politics. It tries to determine to what extent each chairman was a unique leader and had a different impact. It attempts to examine leadership within an institutional context by considering the chairman in conjunction with his committee and in light of developments internal to and external to the committee.

From organization theory comes an emphasis on the environment as an independent variable or catalyst in determining changes in an institution. Cooper and Brady (1981a) argued that institutional context determines leadership style. Sinclair maintained that "the context of environment shapes and constrains leadership styles and strategies" (1983, 3). Downs (1967) emphasized that exogenous factors rather than internal developments are the primary agents of change in organizations. He proposed that in early life, all bureaus must seek external sources of support to survive. Cooper (1977) discussed the environment of the House as having two primary segments, the electorate and the executive establishment. They overlap to form the functional environment to which Congress must answer in action and consent or else face loss of its domain, which is defined by its actual outputs. Little (1991) viewed the nature of legislative leadership as a function of the particular environment in which that leadership is performed. The present study considers the environment as a major factor in changes in the Committee on Education and Labor over the years, but not the only determinant.

Another contributor to the way committees develop is the manner in which they adapt to demands from the environment. Davidson and Oleszek (1976, 39) argued that the roles of both internal and external environments are sources of stimuli for change and that an organization must adapt to both to survive. This study addresses the question of how the Committee on Education and Labor adapted to internal and external pressures. Did it develop in stages or by a smooth, incremental evolution? Did its structure become more complex, its operations more decentralized, and its members more reliant on formal rules to govern its procedures, as organization theory would posit? Did all aspects of the committee—such as procedures, work load, and voting behavior—change, or did some remain stable? This study argues that the committee developed in stages, roughly concurrent with the tenures of various chairmen. Its structure became more complex and more decentralized, and its members relied increasingly on formal rules to govern committee procedures. Procedures changed as the committee adapted to its internal and external environments and, particularly, to the behavior of its chairmen. Its work load shifted both in quantity and importance, and its voting behavior varied from chairman to chairman.

Committee composition is another variable affecting committee development. In his studies on linkages between elections and policy changes, Brady noted that critical elections, which replace large segments of both houses with members not wedded to the old ways of doing business, provide the conditions necessary for "clusters of policy changes" (1978, 81). They diminish the two most important impediments to party government in the House: party-constituency cross-pressuring and the nature of the committee system. Critical elections enable the building of partisan majorities capable of enacting clusters of policy change. They also disrupt the continuity of committees by drastic turnovers in membership and leadership. Majority party voting and cohesion rise as a result of a realignment, enabling the new majority to enact major policy changes. Subsequently, Brady and Sinclair (1984) discussed whether replacement of members, conversion of their issue positions, or both allowed the passage of nonincremental legislation in the early to mid-1960s. For some issues, such as federal aid to education, replacement was clearly responsible. For others, such as the poverty program, conversion was important. They also found that both replacement and conversion played roles in the building of majorities to pass major legislation.

Elements of the Brady and the Brady and Sinclair theories are relevant to committee development; however, there need not be a critical election to change committee composition. It is true that policy output and operations of a congressional committee may change only incrementally unless the composition of the committee shifts and the issues before it become salient enough to allow these changes to occur. Nevertheless, a shift in committee composition does not necessarily have to be the result of a party realignment. There only has to be a replacement of old members seeking to maintain the status quo by new members wanting change or an augmentation of the committee by the addition of new members. This can be accomplished by "packing" or "stacking" a committee with members predisposed to change in one direction or another or by attrition of members opposing change and their replacement with members in favor of change. During the periods under consideration, the regional and ideological composition of the Committee on Education and Labor altered significantly, contributing to the policy shifts that occurred. For example, membership changes in the early to mid-1960s helped alter the character and scope of committee policy outputs from the Barden to the Powell years. In addition, a chairmanship change enabled previously bottled up major legislation to reach the floor.

The salience of the issues in a committee's dominion also affects a committee's development. Salience could be the result of increasing unease in the electorate over a particular problem, or it could be dramatized by an event, such as an enemy satellite launch, a Supreme Court decision, a coal mine disaster, a strike, or a war. Other events or developments may redirect public attention, highlighting issues whose salience supersedes those before a particular committee. These external developments largely determine the pool of issues from which the committee selects its agenda. Whether that agenda is pursued actively, ignored, or blocked is determined, to a large degree, by the chairman.

Congressional committees, like other organizations, seek to increase or alter their jurisdictions to make up for slack in the salience of existing markets. They diversify. They adapt to shifts in the importance of the issues under their jurisdictions in attempts to maintain their domains. If the major issues under their jurisdiction are decided or are no longer salient, the committees are in danger of being reorganized or possibly eliminated. Education and Labor essentially followed the pattern outlined by organization theory in diversifying its jurisdiction. The salience of the issues before it ebbed and flowed, and the committee responded accordingly.

One of the coping mechanisms organizations use is a change in function. The function of Education and Labor changed concurrently with each chairman and as the salience of issues under its jurisdiction waxed and waned. It responded to internal and external pressures, particularly the president's agenda, the increasing budget deficit, the interests of the chairmen, and the goals of the committee's membership, which all affected the salience of matters under the committee's jurisdiction and the committee's function.

Approach and Methods

This study employs both a historical and a comparative analysis of the Committee on Education and Labor from 1951 to 1984. The historical approach provides an opportunity for assessing the impacts of certain external and internal developments—reforms, changes in leadership, and changes in membership—on the committee. The longitudinal comparison of the development of the committee during various periods of its existence facilitates comparison of committee development with what scholars ascribe to organizations generally. Although not pretending to be the firm basis for general theories, the case study can offer important contributions to the formation of general propositions and thus to theory building (Lijphart 1971). Its details supply the foundation for later, broader generalizations and analysis of committee similarities and differences. It also can furnish warning signals for avoiding miscalculations in future work.

Several characteristics drawn from the study of organizations and of Congress will form the analytical framework for this study: setting, composition, voting patterns, structure, work load, function, and leadership. Changes in each of these characteristics are examined from the 1950s to the 1980s, with the time periods divided according to the tenures of the chairmen. Only those chairmen who served at least two consecutive terms in that position will be considered; thus the chairmanships of Fred Hartley (R-NJ), 1947-48; John Lesinski, Sr. (D-MI), 1949-50; and Samuel McConnell, Jr. (R-PA), 1953-54, will be omitted. Only the legacies they left the committee are discussed, such as major labor legislation coming out of the committee during Republican-controlled Congresses. These men were not chairmen long enough to establish discernible patterns of leadership or differences in functions and structure. In short, there are not enough data for these periods. Analysis in this study begins with the period from 1951 to 1960, when Graham Arthur Barden (D-NC) served as chairman, with the exception of 1953-54. The second period covers the years between 1960 and 1967, when Adam Clayton Powell, Jr. (D-NY) chaired the committee. The era of Carl Dewey Perkins (D-KY) from 1967 to 1984 constitutes the third time period.

Several questions derived from the literature on organizations, committees, leadership, and Education and Labor in particular are asked: What was the role of the chairmen in shaping the structure, operations, function, and output of the committee? To what extent did each employ a unique leadership and have a different impact? Did the committee change dramatically from Barden to Powell to Perkins? How did each chairman get the committee to do what he wanted? What was it about each chairman that made him effective or ineffective? To what extent did the committee reflect the chairman's leadership?

The discussion of committee leadership is aimed at showing how the chairman related to the rest of the committee and how well he fit the needs of the committee at the appropriate time. In an attempt to answer the questions, this study will treat the orientation of the chairman and his leadership. The chairman's orientation, or the way he thought about the committee and its legislation, is inferred from examination of several aspects of each chairman: background, constituencies, reputation among his constituents, ideological leanings, partisanship, predisposition on certain controversial issues, voting behavior in committee, and victories in the committee. Each chairman's ideological leanings are gleaned by his scores on measures compiled by the Americans for Democratic Action (ADA), Americans for Constitutional Action (ACA), and the AFL-CIO's Committee on Political Education (COPE), as well as various labor union measures available in the 1950s when others were not. His partisanship is measured by his party-unity scores compared with those of the other committee members and by how often he voted with his party. The chairman's predisposition on controversial issues is taken from interviews, biographies, and scholarly or newspaper articles. Constituency characteristics are drawn from data in Congressional Quarterly publications, interviews, biographies, and letters and articles on each chairman. Other information concerning his orientation was gleaned from interviews with fellow members and committee personnel.

The chairman's leadership is a different matter. The study is concerned with how he operated—the way he used his resources. Burns (1978, 361) who defined leadership as a form of power, characterized the position of the chairman as providing a bank of resources that could be used as political currency. This currency is valuable in the committee as well as in the House. The chairman's leadership is in part based on his power, which Burns depicted as having two essentials: motive and resource. Motive is almost impossible to measure, since often it is not announced and must be inferred from other sources. In the present study, the discussions of the chairmen's backgrounds and orientations provide hints about their motivations, as do some of their actions (e.g., Barden's blocking techniques).

A chairman's resources are both institutional and personal. As Wilson and Jillson noted, "Legislative leadership must be rooted in institutional rules and procedures if it is to be sustained over time" (1989, 5). While each chairman's personal resources are unique and presumably long-lasting, his institutional resources may change over time. The present study considers the chairman's reliance on both types of resources. In that sense, it employs both the personal and the contextual perspectives of leadership. Institutional prerogatives include the chairman's use of subcommittees, conduct of meetings and hearings, influence over the committee's agenda, treatment of the minority, dispensation of rewards and sanctions, and control over the budget. Personal resources include the chairman's expertise on the rules and subject matter of the committee, his reputation among his peers, his political acumen, and whatever other assets he may have brought to the office. Institutional and personal resources then are considered together in terms of which were used more frequently and effectively. Much of the data concerning leadership come from interviews with members and staff as well as books and articles about these men. Chairman Powell wrote an autobiography, and Chairman Perkins was interviewed personally for this study. Consistent data on each chairman were not always available.

In considering the degree to which the committee reflected the chairman's leadership, committee function is examined. A word of explanation is appropriate about the use of the term *function*. It is difficult to pin down as applied to congressional committees. Huitt (1954) discussed a committee's function as guardian of the public interest in the face of competing interests. He also noted the committee's fact-finding function, its role as a court used to judge which special interest will prevail. He mentioned the committee as a public forum for debate from which the general interest will derive. Other functions include serving as a podium for the dissemination of information, a "propaganda channel," and a "catharsis for frustrations and grievances" (Truman 1951, 372-77). The most obvious function of a committee is the consideration of legislative matters that come under its jurisdiction.

In the present study the term *function* is interpreted broadly. The committee's function is determined by the external and internal environments of the committee, depending on whose view of the general interest prevails. The prevailing sense of what is in the public interest is considered to be the committee's function. It is a general gauge of why the committee acted as it did. The function can be gleaned from what the committee does, whether it blocks or facilitates certain kinds of legislation, disseminates information, reinforces existing opinions, or provides a stage for propaganda. It is determined by the actions of the committee chairman, in particular, and also by the membership. How influential factions on the committee regard the committee's agenda is, in a sense, its function. To investigate changes in function, this study will determine whether the committee's purpose and actions were different under each chairman.

What is the relationship, if any, between any shift in the regional and ideological composition of the committee and policy outputs? If Brady's critical election theory (1978) is correct as it relates to this committee, substantial evidence of regional and ideological shifts should lead to changes in the policy output of the committee. Other variables include the committee leadership, the party ratios, executive interest, and public opinion. The composition of the membership will be gauged by the patterns of regional representation of the members, by their ideological leanings, by their seniority, and in terms of where members went after service on Education and Labor (i.e., whether they transferred to other committees or served their entire congressional careers on this committee). Regional representation is shown by comparing the geographic makeup of the committee with that of the House. Seniority is discussed by examining the amount of time members had spent in Congress and on the committee, including the proportions of new committee members and freshmen.

The ideological makeup of the committee is measured by interest group scores. This study takes advantage of ADA scores, COPE scores or other labor support scores, and ACA scores. These ratings were available regularly after 1960 and irregularly during the 1950s. In the Barden years, the ratings were published as the number of votes each member cast in accordance with the group's position. During the Powell and Perkins years, these interest groups changed their reporting procedures to the percentage of votes each member cast in accordance with each group's stance.

In its adaptation to both external and internal pressures, how did the committee develop—in stages or through smooth, incremental transitions? Did the structure become more complex, more reliant on formal rules, and more decentralized, as organization theory would posit? How did the structure differ from chairman to chairman? How did reforms imposed by the House and by the Democratic Caucus in the 1970s affect the committee's structure? Did all aspects of the committee's structure and operations change, or did some remain stable? Did procedures become more democratic? Did work load increase or decrease? Did voting patterns—cohesion and partisanship—change? If so, how? To answer these questions, several variables will be examined: structure, work load, and voting patterns.

Structural features of committees can be derived from measures of salient structural characteristics applied to the House (Cooper 1981). In the present study, committee structure is examined by exploring the existence of, changes in, and reliance on the written rules, which denote formalism; measures of the physical configuration of components, which illustrate the degree of organizational elaboration; and the reliance on subcommittees with specified jurisdictions. Committee structure then is discussed in relation to its degree of centralization. The relevant aspects of structure are examined for each chairman's tenure.

The work load of Congress and its committees is hard to pin down because there are so many aspects of it, many of them not easily measurable, quantitatively or not. In this study, it is gauged by the number of hearings held in full committee and in subcommittees and by the number of bills the committee reports. Other bills considered but not successfully reported also are discussed on occasion. In addition, the numbers of bills referred to the committee are discussed. Despite frequent use (Galloway 1953a, 1956; Mackenzie 1981; Davidson 1986), this measure has a number of problems. It might be effective after the 1969 advent of multiple sponsorship, but not for those years when only one sponsor per bill was allowed, unless duplicates are counted. From 1969 to 1978, up to twenty-five members could cosponsor a bill (House *Rules*, 96th Cong., sec. 854, rule 22, p. 549). In a 1978 rules change, the House allowed unlimited sponsorship, effectively reducing the number of measures introduced (Davidson 1986, 8).

The Committee on Education and Labor has had the reputation of being noncohesive and highly partisan for most of its existence (see Masters 1961; Fenno 1962; Munger and Fenno 1962; Manley 1965; Pressman 1966; Bolling 1968; Morrow 1969; Dyson and Soule 1970; Fenno 1973; Ripley

1978; Ostrom 1979; Harris and Hain 1983; Unekis and Rieselbach 1984; Smith and Deering 1984; Parker and Parker 1985; Smith 1986). With the exception of a few scholars who have taken advantage of committee roll calls beginning in the 1970s (Unekis and Rieselbach 1984; Parker and Parker 1985), no one has been able to show conclusively that the committee in fact was partisan and that it lacked cohesion or "integration," as it is often called in the literature.

The present study examines all recorded roll calls taken in Education and Labor between 1951 and 1984, with a few exceptions. Roll calls and minutes for the Republican-controlled 83rd Congress (1953-54) and for 1957 were not available. Rice Index of Cohesion Scores (Rice 1928), which are the percentage of yea votes minus the percentage of nay votes cast on each roll call, are calculated for every roll call and averaged by term. The average Rice Index Scores show the extent to which members actually voted together in committee—whether they voted cohesively or not, as has been alleged but not proven in previous research. When at least 70 percent of the committee votes together, minimal cohesion is deemed to be present. The 70-percent minimum yields a Rice Index Score of 40 or above.

The degree of partisanship, often seen as another important variable in the operation of committees (e.g., Matthews 1973; Manley 1965, 1970; Dyson and Soule 1970; Fenno 1973; Parker and Parker 1979; Feig 1981; Unekis and Rieselbach 1984), is measured as well. Scholars often relate it to the degree of integration (Fenno 1962, 1973; Manley 1965; Feig 1981). In the present study, the degree of partisanship is determined by three measures: the percentage of party votes in committee, House party-unity scores, and Rice Index Scores applied to committee roll calls and controlled for party.

Partisanship frequently has been conceived of as the proportion of times that Democrats vote with Democrats and Republicans vote with Republicans, though the 90-percent criterion has been used also (Brady, Cooper, and Hurley 1979). In the present study, the degree of partisanship is measured by the percentage of committee roll calls on which at least 70 percent of Democrats voting opposed at least 70 percent of the voting Republicans. A simple majority measure is not adequate because on many occasions a bare majority of Democrats opposes a bare majority of Republicans, thereby appearing as a party split but in reality being nonpartisan. The 90-percent benchmark is too high for this committee, particularly in its early days when one or two Democrats voted consistently with the Republicans against the rest of their own party.

Party-unity scores for committee members are examined to provide some measure of party support outside of committee. These scores measure the percentage of House party-unity roll calls on which each member voted in agreement with a majority of his party. Party-unity roll calls are those on which a majority of one party opposes a majority of the other party. Failure to vote lowers party-unity scores. Not only do political scientists make use of these scores (e.g., Matthews 1973; Sinclair 1983; Hinckley 1971), but members of Congress use them to determine which members supported the party on votes the party leadership deemed important. In the late 1980s the House Democratic Caucus relied on party-unity scores in judging whom to support in the contest for chairman of the Committee on Armed Services. One candidate, the sitting chairman, had more seniority, and the other had a far better record of party support. In the end, after threat of deposition, the sitting chairman prevailed (interview, member).

The Rice Index of Cohesion applied to committee roll calls and controlled for party is another measure of partisanship. As is the case for the determination of party votes, minimal partisan cohesion is present when at least 70 percent of the members of one party vote together, thus yielding a minimum Rice Index Score of 40.

Although committee evolution is a continuous process, this framework allows comparisons of the committee's setting, composition, voting patterns, structure and operations, jurisdiction, work load, functions, and leadership at different periods. It is useful for comparing the committee of the 1950s with the committee of the 1960s, 1970s, and 1980s. Moreover, these questions and variables could prove useful for comparing a cross section of committees. By examining these variables at different times, one can make inferences about the committee's organizational development and, possibly, what will be the case in the future. The study includes an analysis of the overall pattern of development of the committee.

1

The Committee during the Barden Years

A successful congressional committee chairmanship depends, in part, on the cards that the chairman was dealt in the game of leadership. These include the committee's environment, its membership, and the rules under which it operates. The chairman's own leadership skills are his ace in the hole. When Graham Barden, a conservative North Carolina Democrat, picked up his cards as chairman in 1950, the game of the modern committee on Education and Labor was just under way.

Setting

National security issues, particularly involving the Korean War and its aftermath, dominated much of the politics of the 1950s. Communist fear inspired by traumatic foreign affairs events carried over into the domestic arena. As a result of the convictions of eleven leaders of the U.S. Communist party for conspiracy to teach and to advocate the violent overthrow of the U.S. government (*Congress and the Nation* 1965, 1656), the Alger Hiss treason affair, and McCarthyism, which prospered until Senator Joseph McCarthy (R-WI) was censured by the Senate in 1954, public and congressional attention converged on the Communist threat.[1] The country suffered repercussions of the "Red scare" for years. The Soviet launch of *Sputnik* in 1957 intensified the fear of communism. Americans were shocked and chagrined that such a "backward" nation had beat them into space. *Sputnik* highlighted educational deficiencies in U.S. public schools.

Labor issues also charged the environment. President Harry Truman's 1952 seizure of the steel mills to thwart a strike that he believed threatened national defense heightened public awareness of labor difficulties (executive order 10340, April 8, 1952). And in the early 1950s television emerged as a prominent factor in congressional activities and in national politics. First used in the Senate, it provided a basis for later Education and Labor investigations. Throughout 1951 Senator Estes Kefauver's (D-TN) subcommittee held televised hearings on organized crime, exposing national criminal organizations that made immense illegal profits, influenced local politicians, and bought protection. The Kefauver hearings were the first opportunity for most Americans to witness congressional activities, and the hearings attracted widespread attention. So did subsequent hearings by Senator John McClellan (D-AR) in 1957-60 that revealed growing evidence of widespread abuse of union funds, accelerating the clamor for labor reform.

Racial discrimination also made headlines, particularly after the Supreme Court handed down its *Brown* v. *Board of Education of Topeka* decisions. The 1954 decision, which sparked widespread protests and debates, declared unconstitutional racial segregation in public schools as a denial of equal protection under the Fourteenth Amendment. Previously sanctioned under the separate but equal doctrine of the 1896 *Plessy* v. *Ferguson* decision, dealing with transportation, separate but equal school facilities were declared by the Court to be "inherently unequal." A year later, after hearing further arguments about the relief to be granted, the Court ordered local authorities to "make a prompt and reasonable start" and local courts to "proceed with all deliberate speed" to end segregation in the public schools (*Brown* v. *Board of Education of Topeka, II*).

Congress argued federal aid to education issues repeatedly throughout the decade, but most proposals failed because of race-related issues. The 1957 crisis at Little Rock, Arkansas, intensified the conflict, particularly in education, although other areas in which discrimination existed, such as housing, also were in the limelight. President Dwight Eisenhower's action to enforce a federal court order desegregating Little Rock's Central High School incited a long-lasting conflict pitting states rights against the federal government.

At the onset of the decade, Democrat Harry S Truman was in the White House; however, he did not run again in 1952. With former supreme Allied commander in Europe Dwight D. Eisenhower as their candidate, the Republicans held the presidency from 1952 to 1960, and they controlled the 83d Congress (1953-54) as well. Democrats managed to regain control of both houses of Congress in the 1954 elections, although by small margins. They won in increasingly large numbers in both the 1956 and 1958 elections, setting the stage for a return to prominence of the social welfare issues traditionally emphasized by liberals. The Democratic platform in the 1960 election brought the social issues under the jurisdiction of the Committee on Education and Labor to a top spot on the agenda.

While much of the country was attentive to events in the international arena, the members of Education and Labor were faced with a number of important and controversial issues that were often so divisive that no agreement was possible or, in the eyes of some, desirable. The focus of both education and labor legislation changed over the decade. In the context of outside events that both hindered and helped their resolution, the 1950s Committee on Education and Labor haggled over two major education issues, school construction and general aid to education. The latter had been stifled for years because of a continuing controversy over whether the federal government should provide aid to religious and segregated schools.

School construction, one of the few issues on which members could compromise, occupied much of the committee's time throughout the decade. Proposals focused primarily on aid to areas overly burdened by increased enrollments resulting from defense-related federal activities. In 1950 Congress passed two Education and Labor bills, Public Laws 81-815 and 81-874, known as "impacted areas" legislation, that authorized funds for the construction of elementary and secondary schools and for operating expenses to local educational agencies in federally impacted areas, such as those with large federal installations that detracted from the local tax base. In following years the committee amended and reauthorized this legislation. These two laws became models for subsequent proposals by the National Education Association (NEA) for general aid that would provide substantial assistance to public schools with no federal control provisions attached (Thomas 1975, 23).

Nearly all of the efforts for general aid to education met with resistance in the 1950s. From 1951 to 1953 federal aid was considered as an offshoot of a long-standing argument between the states and the federal government over "tidelands." At issue was whether the federal government or the coastal states owned the submerged lands between the low-tide mark and the continental shelf. Several members, including Carl Perkins (D-KY), proposed applying revenues from offshore oil to general aid to education. Groups interested in guaranteeing that the coastal states controlled the oil deposits adjacent to their shores opposed these amendments. The House resolved the issue in favor of the states and omitted oil-for-education provisions.

The Supreme Court's 1954 decision in *Brown* v. *Board of Education* affected aid to education deliberations for years to come. With its prohibition against segregation, *Brown* removed the question of whether Congress should provide aid to segregated schools as an issue, although southerners still opposed attaching strings to disbursements of federal money. The Court's decision fueled the rancorous debate over federal aid to education, especially in the Education and Labor Committee. Several members refused to vote for aid that did not include segregated schools, and others refused to support aid to school districts that had not followed the decree. Eisenhower's sending of federal troops to Little Rock and his nationalization of the Arkansas National Guard in 1957 also hampered efforts at enacting federal aid to education. The events bolstered Chairman Graham Barden's arguments that federal aid would result in federal government interference in local affairs.

Not until federal aid funds could be tied to the national defense was there any hope of a general aid program passing. *Sputnik* provided that link, and as a direct result, Congress enacted the National Defense Education Act of 1958 (NDEA, P.L. 85-864), a one-billion-dollar school aid program to improve the teaching of science, mathematics, and foreign languages at all levels. Proponents capitalized on the widespread impression that American education was inadequate compared with that of the Soviets. By including the reference to defense in the title, they made it difficult for even the staunchest opponents of federal aid to vote against the act, because it was a national security matter.

In sum, external events changed the issues facing the Committee on Education and Labor throughout the decade of the 1950s. The question of aid to religious schools that had been so prominent in the 1940s was eclipsed by the problem of aid to segregated schools. Later, the integration issues, although not completely dormant, gave way to national security concerns. Supporters hitched general aid to education to the bandwagon of national defense in response to perceived Soviet dominance in space. School construction remained a prominent topic throughout the decade.

Although the labor issues facing the committee during the 1950s were less prominent than those concerning education, they proved fertile turf for committee efforts and were equally contentious. The most visible issues involved labor reform, including pleas for repeal of the Taft-Hartley Act, threatened strikes, and the corruption of labor unions exposed during the Kefauver and McClellan hearings in the Senate.[2] President Truman's seizure of the steel mills contributed to the public awareness of labor problems. As pressure for reform gathered steam from televised hearings and strike threats, conservatives and prounion Democrats in the House joined forces to kill a Senate labor reform bill in the 85th Congress (1957-58), but the coalition dissolved in the 86th. In addition, proponents of a fair employment practices committee kept up the heat, but their efforts were fruitless. Minimum-wage increases frequently were proposed and occasionally passed. Little labor legislation of consequence came out of the committee, however, until 1959, when, after considerable dickering and maneuvering, Congress passed a significant and stringent labor reform law, known as the Landrum-Griffin Act, named for two proponents on the Education and Labor Committee.[3]

The decade of the 1950s thus seemed to be a pressure cooker for education and labor issues. The education laws enacted toward the latter part of the decade were merely the first trickle of steam escaping through a valve, before the cover blew off the whole pot.Education issues rolled to a full boil before additional legislative remedies were enacted in the early to mid-1960s.

Composition of the Committee

When Graham Barden picked up his cards as chairman, he appeared to have every right to suppose that his incumbency guaranteed his domination of the game. But his luck eroded as the years went by, and the House leadership, hearing a different call, simply stacked his own deck against him. Barden became a leader of a committee majority that would play his game no longer.

The political culture of each state helps mold the political behavior of its voters (Elazar 1984). Although regions are less unified in political culture than are states, the geographic constituencies committee members represent are important determinants of their political philosophies. For example, as a southern state, North Carolina had been Democratic since the Civil War, and its citizens' attitudes about racial equality were bound to influence Barden. While other areas may not have political cultures as distinct as that of the South, their cultures can influence representatives' philosophies and voting behavior and ostensibly, committee policies. The regional makeup of the Education and Labor Committee during the 1950s differs from that of the later periods, although the urban Middle Atlantic states enjoyed a predominant proportion of the membership throughout all three periods (see table 1.1). From 1951 through 1960, when committee size ranged from twenty-four to thirty, these states averaged over a third of the committee's membership. On average, almost a third of the Democrats and more than 40 percent of the Republicans represented Middle Atlantic states, especially New York, New Jersey, and Pennsylvania. The increase in the proportion of Middle Atlantic representation from the 82d to the 85th Congresses primarily resulted from the Democratic leadership's efforts to populate the committee with more liberal Democrats, the reputed influence of organized labor in the selection of committee Democrats, the Republicans' response to those efforts, and the increasing salience of committee issues to large urban areas.

The East North Central region, a Republican stronghold during the 1950s, boasted the next-highest representation. A fourth of the Republicans, a conservative group, came from this area. Illinois, Indiana, Michigan, Ohio, and Wisconsin all claimed Republican representation on the committee. Most of the time, few committee Democrats came from the East North

Table 1.1. Regional Composition of the Committee in 1950s (in percentages)

Region	Congress				
	82d	83d	84th	85th	86th
	Full Committee				
New England	4.1	0.0	0.0	3.4	3.3
Middle Atlantic	29.1	32.1	40.0	44.8	36.7
East North Central	16.6	14.3	10.0	10.3	20.0
West North Central	12.5	14.3	6.7	3.4	6.7
South	20.8	14.3	10.0	10.3	10.0
Border	12.5	7.1	6.7	6.9	6.7
Mountain	0.0	14.3	13.3	10.3	3.3
Pacific	4.1	3.6	13.3	10.3	13.3
External	—	—	—	—	0.0
	E & L Democrats				
New England	7.1	0.0	0.0	0.0	5.0
Middle Atlantic	28.6	23.1	35.3	37.5	35.0
East North Central	0.0	7.7	5.9	0.0	15.0
West North Central	14.3	14.3	5.9	6.3	5.0
South	35.7	30.8	17.6	18.8	15.0
Border	14.3	15.4	11.8	12.5	10.0
Mountain	0.0	7.7	11.8	12.5	5.0
Pacific	0.0	0.0	11.8	12.5	10.0
External	—	—	—	—	0.0
	E & L Republicans				
New England	0.0	0.0	0.0	7.7	0.0
Middle Atlantic	30.0	40.0	46.2	53.8	40.0
East North Central	40.0	20.0	15.4	23.1	30.0
West North Central	10.0	13.3	7.7	0.0	10.0
South	0.0	0.0	0.0	0.0	0.0
Border	10.0	0.0	0.0	0.0	0.0
Mountain	0.0	20.0	15.4	7.7	0.0
Pacific	10.0	6.7	15.4	7.7	20.0
External	—	—	—	—	0.0

Source: Author's calculations from data in Inter-University Consortium for Political and Social Research. The sums of some columns are not exactly 100.0 percent because of rounding.

Central states. In later years, however, several Democrats who represented some of the urban areas, such as Chicago and Detroit, and who tended to be labor union advocates secured assignments to Education and Labor.

During the 1950s the South sent only Democrats to the committee and few Republicans at all to Congress. Members from Alabama, Georgia, North Carolina, Texas, and Arkansas held over a fifth of the Democratic committee seats during the decade but constituted less than a sixth of the full committee's membership. As it happened, southerners did control some of the more powerful seats on Education and Labor, including the chairmanship. The percentage of southerners on the committee dwindled from 20 percent (over a third of the Democrats) to 10 percent by the close of the decade. The other areas of the country had smaller proportions of Education and Labor membership. The West North Central, Border, Mountain, and Pacific regions each was represented, on average, by less than 10 percent of the committee's membership. New Englanders had few seats on this committee in the 1950s.

The regional makeup of Education and Labor shifted toward the urban areas during the 1950s. Although the Middle Atlantic states maintained a substantial edge in representation on the committee throughout the decade, the balance between the East North Central states and the South was reversed: As southern and border state representation decreased by about half over the period, the proportion of East North Central and Pacific members increased. During the later years of the decade few southerners either wanted or were appointed to seats on this committee. The Democratic leadership refused to give the recalcitrant North Carolina chairman more ammunition than he already had in his war against progressive legislation.

Committee membership turnover is also important because it can, and usually does, change the ideological composition of the committee and thus the chairman's power base. In the case of Education and Labor under Barden, turnover and new assignments as the result of an enlarged committee realigned the ideological composition, changing a rather conservative committee in the early 1950s into one dominated by "liberals" largely committed to supporting legislation favorable to labor interests and to federal aid to education, contrary to the wishes of the chairman (interviews; Bolling 1966, 97).

The changing face of the committee significantly altered the chairman's power base over the course of the decade. Nearly a third of the membership of Education and Labor was new to the committee in the 1950s. Over a third of the Republicans were first-time appointees in the 1950s, as were about 28 percent of the Democrats (see table 1.2). Not surprisingly, the highest proportion of new members came in the Republican 83d Congress, with half of the committee members either freshmen or new additions (either transfers or members with dual assignments).

First-term representatives filled two-thirds of the vacant seats on the committee during the 1950s, comprising over 80 percent of the new Democrats and 54 percent of the new Republicans. About a fifth of all committee members were freshmen each term. Only 10 percent of the 142 committee seats were taken by nonfreshman members not previously assigned to the committee; these were split fairly evenly between Democrats and Republi-

Table 1.2. Seats, New Members, and Freshmen, 1950s

		Number								
		All members			New members			Freshmen		
Congress	Year	Full	Dems	Reps	Full	Dems	Reps	Full	Dems	Reps
82d	1951-52	24	14	10	5	3	2	2	1	1
83d	1953-54	28	13	15	14	4	10	10	4	6
84th	1955-56	30	17	13	9	7	2	7	6	1
85th	1957-58	30	17	13	9	4	5	6	3	3
86th	1959-60	30	20	10	8	5	3	6	5	1
	Total	142	81	61	45	23	22	31	19	12
	Mean	28.4	16.2	12.2	9.0	4.6	4.4	6.2	3.8	2.5

		Percentage					
		New members			Freshmen		
		Full	Dems	Reps	Full	Dems	Reps
82d	1951-52	20.7	21.4	20.0	8.3	7.1	10.0
83d	1953-54	50.0	30.8	66.7	35.7	30.8	40.0
84th	1955-56	30.0	41.2	15.4	23.3	35.3	7.7
85th	1957-58	30.0	23.5	38.5	20.0	17.6	23.1
86th	1959-60	26.7	25.0	30.0	20.0	25.0	10.0
	Percentage of total	31.7	28.4	36.1	21.8	26.8	23.5

Source: Author's calculations from *Congressional Directory*, 1951-60.

cans. The nonfreshmen new members assigned to the committee in the 1950s either transferred from other committees or were given Education and Labor in addition to other assignments. All three new nonfreshman members in the 82d Congress transferred, giving up seats on other committees—Judiciary and Veterans Affairs for the two Democrats, and Merchant Marine and Fisheries for the Republican. Republicans had to draft members from other committees to fill vacancies on Education and Labor, particularly in the 83d Congress (and in many subsequent sessions).[4] For several reasons, including the chairman's recalcitrance and the nature of the issues under the committee's jurisdiction, Democrats had similar difficulty in attracting members, a major reason that over 80 percent of their vacancies went to freshmen (interviews). Only three Democrats newly assigned to Education and Labor between 1951 and 1960 were not freshmen—two in 1951 and one in 1955.

It appears that few members voluntarily gave up assignments on other committees to serve on Education and Labor; there were few out-and-out transfers to the committee. Most new members either were freshmen or

Table 1.3. Percentage of Members Who Left after Each Congress, 1951-1960

Congress	Year	Full	Dems	Reps
82d	1951-51	42.0	36.0	50.0
83d	1953-54	25.0	23.1	26.7
84th	1955-56	30.0	23.5	38.5
85th	1957-58	23.3	23.3	38.5
86th	1959-60	26.7	25.0	30.0

Source: Compiled from Committee on Education and Labor, Calendar 1951-60.

had multiple assignments. Republican membership on this committee offered few constituency or power benefits. Members were forced to consider issues that few could capitalize on and that might even be harmful to them back home. The preponderance of new Democrats were freshmen. They were not assigned to the committee unless they were supported by organized labor or held particularly safe seats (interviews; Masters 1961, 245). Using data on committee transfers, Goodwin (1970, 114-15) and Ripley (1975, 102) show that Education and Labor ranked twelfth in attractiveness out of the nineteen House committees from 1949 to 1968.

Electoral defeat proved to be the predominant reason for members' leaving Education and Labor (see table 1.3). Moreover, not a few members decided not to stand for reelection to Congress; some retired, and some pursued other careers. Although a number of members served out their careers on Education and Labor, seven transferred to other committees, some taking chairmanships and others just moving to a more desirable assignment. A few ran for the Senate or for other public offices, and occasionally a member received a cabinet-level position.

The ideological leanings of members of the Committee on Education and Labor during the 1950s cannot always be supported by "hard" data. To show how representative the committee was of its parent body, surrogate measures based on agreement with several interest groups are used in an attempt to derive some judgment of the degree of liberalism or conservatism of committee members relative to all House members. A number of interest groups identified their congressional supporters and opponents. In the 1950s these groups included the Americans for Democratic Action (ADA), the Americans for Constitutional Action (ACA), the American Federation of Labor (AFL), the Congress of Industrial Organizations (CIO), and the Committee for Political Education (COPE). Several sets of preselected votes from which measures could be calculated to gauge the ideological leanings of members of Congress are available for the decade of the 1950s, albeit somewhat sporadically.[5] Since no interest group published "right" and "wrong" votes for each year, no one type of score was calculated for every session, necessitating the use in this study of a variety of group ratings. The ratings are based on the percentage of "right" votes cast by

Table 1.4. Interest Group Scores for 1950s

	AFL 1947-52	CIO 1951-52	ADA 1951-52	Labor 1953-54	ACA 1957-59	ADA 1960	COPE 1959-60	AFL 1947-56	
Full HR	35.0	40.1	39.2	41.6	43.6	56.3	54.6	35.2	Mean
	31.9	34.0	33.6	41.5	34.0	37.4	40.0	29.8	SD
	429	430	421	428	428	430	431	428	N
Full E & L	34.6	38.3	37.7	41.5	39.8	68.0	65.2	34.0	Mean
	34.3	38.2	38.7	34.2	36.7	37.7	41.3	43.0	SD
	24	24	24	28	30	30	30	30	N
HR Dems	54.2	56.1	56.3	66.2	22.0	72.2	71.8	52.4	Mean
	29.3	35.0	33.5	37.7	18.1	34.6	36.4	27.9	SD
	228	229	227	214	278	279	280	230	N
E & L Dems	54.5	57.6	59.3	72.6	15.9	88.9	88.7	55.1	Mean
	31.4	38.3	37.0	24.3	13.7	26.6	28.0	31.3	SD
	14	14	14	13	20	20	20	17	N
HR Reps	13.1	21.7	19.1	17.0	83.5	26.9	22.5	15.3	Mean
	17.5	21.4	19.8	27.7	15.0	21.1	22.7	16.6	SD
	200	201	193	217	150	151	151	198	N
E & L Reps	6.6	11.2	7.3	14.5	87.6	26.4	18.1	6.5	Mean
	10.3	14.7	9.7	8.5	11.2	13.9	12.2	6.8	SD
	10	10	10	15	10	10	10	13	N

Source: Author's calculations from Congressional Quarterly Weekly Reports 1951-60.

N is the number of members whose votes were included in the calculations.

each member out of the total number of possible votes, in accordance with the measuring group's point of view.[6] The higher the score on votes chosen by ADA, COPE, AFL, AFL-CIO, and CIO, the more liberal a member is assumed to be, since labor union support generally is regarded as the liberal position. Members with higher ACA scores are considered to lean toward the conservative end of the ideological spectrum.

Table 1.4 shows the average interest group ratings for House members and committee members, Democrats and Republicans. For every available rating, committee Democrats on average ranked as more liberal than did all House Democrats, with similar degrees of variation until about 1960, when the committee showed less variation than did the House. By the same token, committee Republicans averaged more conservative scores than did all House Republicans, with substantially less variation. During the early years of the decade, the differences between average scores of House and committee Democrats were modest. As time passed, the magnitude of the differences generally increased, as did the size of the Democratic advantage on the committee, leading to the conclusions that the committee was becoming more liberal than its parent body and that liberals were represented disproportionately on the committee. This deduction is reinforced by the 1960 ADA and 1959-60 COPE scores, on which committee members averaged about seventeen points higher than did all House Democrats.

On all the positions deemed to be favorable by liberal interest groups, committee Republicans scored lower and thus are considered to have been more conservative than were House Republicans. It is interesting to note that committee Republicans' scores were most conservative relative to their House colleagues' on votes taken in the early part of the decade, just before they won control of the 83d Congress (1953-54). This difference could have been caused by several factors. It could have been a function of the issues chosen by the liberal-oriented ADA and COPE or of the prominence of Korea and communism as issues. Alternatively, it could have resulted from the influences of conservative party leaders, such as Senator Robert Taft (R-OH) and Representative Charles Halleck (R-IN). The more moderate Eisenhower forces had not yet come to power. Or it could have been a result of Democratic control of both houses and the Republican response of assigning the most conservative Republicans to the committee that dealt with provocative labor issues—the Taft-Hartley Act, Truman's seizure of the steel mills, and federal aid to education proposals. To many Republicans and other conservatives, the latter represented federal interference in a state domain. Over the years, as determined by their average interest group scores, the committee Republicans generally became more representative of their parent House population, while the opposite was true for the Democrats. The high average ACA scores for both committee and House Republicans on votes cast between 1957 and 1959 indicate that the average Republican in the House, whether or not on the committee, tended to vote the conservative position on issues chosen by the ACA.

In the first decade or so of the committee's existence, the Democrats seemed to reflect fairly closely the overall ideological picture of House Democrats. On the other hand, Republicans were more extreme, thereby pulling the whole committee to the right. Until 1959 and 1960 the entire Education and Labor committee membership, as reflected by all the interest group ratings, mirrored relatively closely the ideological leanings of the entire House. Except for the 1959-1960 scores, the differences between average House and committee interest group ratings were small.

The magnitude of the 1959-1960 differences can be attributed to the House leadership's stacking of Education and Labor with liberal Democrats to overpower the conservative chairman.[7] Beginning in the mid-1950s the leadership conspired to fill vacant seats that had been held by conservative committee Democrats with more liberal members. Allegedly the labor unions had some influence over the selection of Democrats assigned to the committee. For several years, only those who were reputed to have strong labor sympathies were assigned (interviews). As Clapp noted, "In 1959 no one unwilling to take a certain position on labor legislation was permitted to gain a seat on the Committee on Education and Labor, though five vacancies existed" (1963, 229). When the southerners retired or were defeated, more progressive northern members filled the vacancies. The House leadership refused to give the conservative chairman any more natural allies. In addition, during the late 1950s the leadership increased the size of the committee, and more liberals were added to accommodate the desire of House members to facilitate the passage of liberal social legislation, such as federal aid to education. [8]

Interest group ratings have shown that conservatives dominated Education and Labor in the early part of the decade and that subsequently the committee was transformed into a bastion of liberalism. Additional data, research done by other scholars, and interviews with members and staffs support this characterization. Early COPE and AFL scores reflect that as a rule Education and Labor members in the early 1950s were no more disposed to vote for proposals deemed beneficial to organized labor than was the House as a whole. During the late 1940s and the early to mid-1950s committee members' labor ratings fairly well represented those of the entire House, a condition still not overwhelmingly favorable to organized labor.

The situation, which changed after the mid-1950s, was described by one member: "The AFL-CIO got the committee stacked against Barden, who was staunchly antilabor. Bolling and Rayburn stacked the committee. The Speaker controlled Ways and Means, which controlled committee assignments. In '54, '56, and '58, no one who wasn't solid prolabor was appointed to the committee. This also was the first time that organized labor got into the structural process of the committee" (interview). Another longtime student of Washington politics described the complexion of the committee as follows: "Only after six years of carefully planned appointments did the Democratic leadership in the House manage to build a majority within the Education and Labor Committee that did not share the anti-labor and anti-education bias of its then chairman" (Cater 1964, 160). Former Rules Committee chairman Richard Bolling said: "By 1958, the Democrats so preponderantly controlled the House that the bipartisan conservative grip on the committee was broken, and a majority was assembled that was favorable to federal aid to education and to unorganized and organized labor" (1966, 97).

In addition to, and possibly contributing to, its leverage over assignments, organized labor held some powerful purse strings over committee members. According to the *Congressional Quarterly*, thirteen out of twenty Education and Labor Democrats in the 86th Congress received contributions from labor organizations in 1958 (*Weekly Report*, April 19, 1959, pp. 512-15). Comparable data for earlier years are not available. Labor also gave campaign money to Lee Metcalf (D-MT), who was on the committee in 1958 but transferred to Ways and Means the next year. Three New

Yorkers, Adam Powell, Ludwig Teller, and Herbert Zelenko, did not receive union funds, nor did New Jersey's Dominick Daniels. Of these northerners, only Powell faced an opponent who got financial contributions from labor, and they were minimal. The three southerners, Chairman Barden (D-NC), Carl Elliott (D-AL), and Phil Landrum (D-GA), also received no support from labor unions, nor did they offer any to labor at voting time. All the other Democrats on the committee benefited from union contributions in the 1958 elections. Labor supported no committee Republicans and few others.

Scholars also noted that the Democrats shifted toward the liberal wing of their party while the Republicans still recruited committee members from the conservative extreme of theirs. Masters wrote that, with a few exceptions, "Democrats have felt that only members who can afford politically to take an outright pro-labor position—i.e., who get union support for election—should be assigned to this committee" (1961, 245). Other members were steered in other directions: "Members from farm or middle-class suburban districts are discouraged from applying. Service on this committee by a member whose district is relatively free of labor-management or segregation conflicts would only result in raising issues in his district that could prove embarrassing and even politically fatal to the member" (Masters 1961, 245). Republicans, on the other hand, also discouraged most members from applying. An assignment on this committee in the 1950s, and to some extent in the 1980s, was a hardship post, somewhere Republicans did their time and then moved on to more politically lucrative assignments (interviews). Masters (1961, 245-47) noted that the Republicans were hard-pressed to take a moderate stance on labor-management issues. They were likely to take promanagement, antilabor positions and have close ties to management groups.

Fenno (1969) provided a vivid description of assignment to Education and Labor. He noted that freshmen Republicans were discouraged by their leadership from choosing this committee unless "their convictions are firm, their talents for combat considerable, and their districts reasonably safe" (289). Those who ended up with this assignment, either by draft or by choice, usually represented the conservative end of the spectrum. Of committee Democrats, Fenno wrote: "Members are strongly issue-oriented, personally contentious, and vigorously committed. They tend to represent the more liberal elements of their party. Party leaders produce this result both by encouraging the appointment of labor-oriented congressmen and by discouraging the appointment of southerners. To an individual representing a manufacturing or mining constituency, a place on the committee dealing with labor matters will have positive electoral advantages" (290). The Democrats appeased organized labor by assigning prounion members, and Republicans catered to the National Association of Manufacturers by placing promanagement members on Education and Labor. Masters pointed out that "this assignment is no place for a neutral when there are so many belligerents around" (1961, 245).

Looking at Education and Labor through the eyes of its chairman, Puryear's descriptions of committee activity (1979) reinforce the idea of the contentiousness of members that has surfaced in the work of many other scholars, including Munger and Fenno (1962), Fenno (1969), Eidenberg and Morey (1969), Brenner (1974), and Ostrom (1979), and in this author's interviews with committee and staff members. Puryear characterized the committee as having severe ideological differences, noting that in the 1940s "the religious issue had caused the 25 members of the House Committee on Education and Labor to become so badly divided on Federal aid to education that the Democratic leadership was doubtful as [to] how to proceed. One congressional leader characterized the situation as 'things are in a mess'" (1979, 89, quoting the *New York Times*, July 7, 1949).

As a result of the strong ideological divisions and the committee's control by conservatives until the 86th Congress, no federal aid bills stood even a slight chance of passing, especially during the Republican-controlled Congress. The odds were little better under the Democrats, particularly in light of the feuds over aid to segregated or parochial schools. These divergent attitudes on school aid are reflected in Frank Thompson, Jr.'s (D-NJ) recollections of Barden's comments at a committee meeting in early 1959 at which five new committee Democrats made their first appearance:

Chairman Barden motioned me to sit by him and asked in his old-boy voice, "Frank, what about these boys? Who are they?"

"Well, that first fellow there on the end is Roman Pucinski—that's spelled P-u-c-i-n-s-k-i. He's from Chicago, and he's a Roman Catholic. Then the next fellow there is Bob Giaimo, spelled G-i-a-i-m-o. He's an Italian-American from Connecticut. And he's a Roman Catholic. The next one is Dominick Daniels."

Barden brightened and said, "Daniels. That sounds like a good Anglo-Saxon name."

"No," I said, "He's of Italian background, too. And he's a Roman Catholic from New Jersey. And that last young fellow there, that's John Brademas, spelled B-r-a-d-e-m-a-s, from Indiana. He's the first Greek-American ever elected to Congress. And he used to teach at St. Mary's College."

By this time, Barden's face was a vivid red, and the arteries were standing out above his shirt collar. It looked like apoplexy was on the point of overtaking him.

"Goddammit," growled Barden. "It looks like they've given me the whole goddamned League of Nations and the Pope of Rome, too."

With that, I got up and went back to my seat, doing my best to disguise the look of satisfaction on my face. [Interview]

According to Fenno, "until the Eighty-sixth Congress in January, 1959, the Republicans plus the southern Democrats constituted a majority—hence a controlling influence whenever they could agree" (1969, 292). The alliance of conservative Chairman Barden and Phil Landrum (D-GA) with committee Republicans effectively created a standoff and stifled most efforts at enacting any bills on federal aid to education, or any other "liberal" legislation. The few not defeated in Education and Labor were thwarted by Judge Howard Smith (D-VA), the chairman of the Committee on Rules.

The interest group data, this author's interview findings, and the interpretations drawn by other scholars support the impression that members of the Committee on Education and Labor reasonably reflected the ideological leanings of the House, at least until the late 1950s. The data buttress Masters's and Fenno's conclusions that, in the late 1950s and early 1960s, the committee attracted extremists from both parties. That was not the rule during the early years of the committee, although some members were interested in either restraining or catering to organized labor and in either promoting or destroying opportunities for federal aid to education. By all accounts, during the latter part of the 1950s the committee was contentious, disputatious, and bitterly divided. As a result, brute force was the only way to get legislation out of committee and passed.

Voting Patterns

Throughout much of the literature on congressional committees, Education and Labor frequently has been the example of a conflictual, non-cohesive, and extremely partisan committee (Masters 1961; Manley 1965; Pressman 1966; Bolling 1968; Morrow 1969; Fenno 1973; Ripley 1978; Ostrom 1979; Harris and Hain 1983; Parker and Parker 1985; and Smith 1986). Studies have shown and interviews with former members and staff have confirmed the committee's high degree of discord. Archival committee roll-call votes, only recently available, finally substantiate these observations.[9]

Education and Labor voting records show that in the early 1950s the committee was not as partisan or liberal as its reputation would have one believe. In fact, as MacNeil (1963, 159-60) argued, it was decidedly conservative. Beginning in the mid-1950s, however, the House leadership's strategic assignments to the committee decreased full committee cohesion and increased party cohesion on committee roll calls. By the end of the decade Education and Labor was transformed into a unit that voted primarily along partisan lines when the parties were divided.

A comparison of House and committee member party-unity scores yields a measure of partisanship as well as some indication of how represen-

Table 1.5. Party-Unity Scores, 1951-1960

	Congress					
	82d	83d	84th	85th	86th	
HR Dems	77.0	76.6	71.0	68.3	70.7	Mean
	22.5	11.8	15.0	14.5	17.0	SD
	68.8	76.8	54.6	59.5	57.2	% > 70
E & L Dems	77.0	76.9	75.0	72.6	76.2	Mean
	26.0	12.2	16.0	16.0	15.1	SD
	71.4	84.6	64.7	77.8	72.2	% > 70
HR Reps	80.7	83.8	69.7	66.1	74.5	Mean
	17.4	10.7	11.1	14.9	14.0	SD
	75.5	91.7	52.5	43.5	69.6	% > 70
E & L Reps	90.2	84.9	70.3	63.8	73.9	Mean
	9.7	6.8	8.3	9.8	12.4	SD
	90.0	100.0	38.5	16.7	75.0	% > 70

Source: Congressional Quarterly Almanac 1951-61.

tative committee members were of their party in the parent body. On the whole, Education and Labor Democrats supported their party on about three-fourths of the votes reflecting party unity (see table 1.5)[10] Given the reputation of this committee for being more partisan than the House, committee scores should have been substantially higher than average House scores, but for the most part they were only slightly higher. The degree of difference between House and committee Democrats' scores, however, increased throughout the decade. As committee Republicans became less supportive of their party relative to House Republicans, committee Democrats became more partisan relative to House Democrats. Moreover, the committee boasted larger proportions of Democrats with party-unity scores greater than 70 percent than did the House. After 1954 the opposite was true for the Republicans; there were higher proportions of party loyalists in the House. These phenomena give credence to the allegations that the House Democratic leadership assigned only liberals to the committee beginning in the mid-1950s.

Given the committee's reputation for conflict, it would be surprising if committee members voted together with any degree of regularity. Fenno (1962, 1969, 1973) discussed the lack of integration on this committee, writing: "The most basic fact about the House Committee on Education and Labor is that, unlike its counterpart in the Senate, it exhibits an almost classic incapacity as a consensus-building institution" (1969, 286). Based on research conducted on House roll-call votes, Dyson and Soule (1970) found Education and Labor to be one of the least integrated committees in

Congress in the period 1955-64. And highlighting the committee's reputation for a lack of full committee agreement, Ostrom (1972) based his dissertation on the conflict present in this committee.

An examination of committee voting records corroborates these assessments. Committee roll calls, as reflected in Rice Index Scores, where a score of 40 indicates minimum cohesion of 70 percent, showed relatively low rates of cohesion.[11] Members apparently were unable or did not try to minimize conflict. High cohesion scores, on the other hand, would have meant that members played down conflict sufficiently to be able to vote together to make policy decisions. The 1950s full committee Rice Index Scores averaged on the low end of the 0 to 100 scale, indicating a relatively high degree of conflict (see table 1.6). The average Rice Index for all available roll calls in the decade was 29.0, well below the minimum standard of 40. An index score of 29 means that, on average, approximately 65 percent of those voting lined up against 35 percent. During the last two years of the decade, when the number of recorded votes increased, the degree of full committee cohesion declined, indicating more conflict. The committee reached the Rice Index of 40 benchmark for minimum cohesion on only 23.9 percent of the votes taken in 1959-60 (when a relatively large number of recorded votes were taken) and on 29 percent of its roll calls for the ten-year period, supporting assertions that the committee was wrought with conflict.

Full committee cohesion levels may have been higher in the Republican 83d Congress (1953-54) or in 1957, the years for which voting records are not available, but it is doubtful. The ratio of Democrats to Republicans in the 83d Congress was almost 50:50, and there is no reason why it or the 1957 session should be deviant with respect to committee cohesion. In fact, the committee was particularly antagonistic in 1957, the year members staged a revolt against the chairman. Most of the Democrats were unified against the chairman, and the Republicans, under threat from the chairman, were allied with him.

The degree of full committee cohesive voting dropped sharply in Chairman Barden's last term, after the House leadership, over a period of years, had assigned more liberal Democrats to the committee. Barden voted with the Republicans, who generally voted together. Moreover, the primary legislation considered by this committee during the 86th Congress was the hotly contested Landrum-Griffin Act, which exacerbated interparty controversies as well as intraparty differences among the Democrats.

Given that full committee cohesion was low, that the subject matter represented the fundamental differences between the two parties, and that high concentrations of partisan members were assigned to the committee, one would expect conflict to divide primarily along party lines, particularly in the late 1950s. Partisanship and a lack of full committee cohesion should

Table 1.6. Committee Roll Calls Meeting Minimum Cohesion and Mean Rice
Index Scores, 1951-1960

Congress	Year	N	Rice Index			Full E & L RI>40	
			Full E & L	Dems	Reps	%	N
82d	1951-52	27	33.0	35.8	65.9	29.6	8
84th	1955-56	20	35.9	65.5	61.4	35.0	7
85th	1958	30	32.9	72.5	73.0	40.0	12
86th	1959-60	92	25.1	52.1	85.1	23.9	22
	Total	169				29.0	49
	Mean		29.0	54.7	77.1		

Source: Compiled from Committee on Education and Labor, Minutes 1951-60. Data for 1953-54
    (83d Cong.) and 1957 are missing.

yield high Rice Index Scores for each party on committee roll-call votes.
Confirming this expectation, Republican cohesion scores should be higher
than Democrats', since minorities traditionally band together to protect
their interests from being overrun by the majority. Moreover, Democrats
were (and are) not known for agreeing among themselves.

These expectations generally are borne out by the data. With the exception of 1955, Republicans voted more cohesively than did Democrats
during the 1950s. In 1955 the Republicans split on several issues, including
minimum wage; the "Powell Amendment" (antidiscrimination), even when
offered by one of their own; library services; and the Davis-Bacon Act.
On two occasions, in the 82d Congress (1951-52) and the 86th Congress
(1959-60), their cohesion scores substantially exceeded (by more than 30
points) those of the Democrats. In the 82d Congress, the issues divisive to
the Democrats were an investigation of the Wage Stabilization Board (six
roll calls) and the prevention of major disasters in coal mines (fifteen roll
calls). A major sticking point on coal mine safety was the size of small mines
that were to be exempt from safety regulations.

The high Republican cohesion in the 86th Congress may have been, in
part, a response to Chairman Barden, who reputedly told Republicans to
support his position or they would never get anything from him again
(interviews). Moreover, labor reform issues dominated committee life and
roll calls in 1959, and the Republicans united in their dislike of organized
labor and in their preference for management views. Democrats, however,
had no such coherent philosophy, and Barden worked to promote divisions. The few southerners disliked labor unions and vowed to impose
strict regulations. Organized labor, on the other hand, had played a role in
selecting the Democratic committee members, and by 1959 the committee
was stacked heavily in its favor. What is more, Democrats did not always
agree on the best ways to achieve common ends. Some were out to stop

labor reform completely, while others tried to minimize the inevitable damage.

The index scores show that throughout the 1950s members of the Committee on Education and Labor deserved their reputation as being highly partisan, although Democrats were less partisan generally than Republicans. At the outset of the decade, Democrats lagged Republicans substantially; however, in the mid-1950s the gap narrowed, only to widen again during Barden's last term when the committee size and political ideology changed. Republicans averaged 77.1 and Democrats 54.7 on the index for the years counted, showing that they voted together on about 89 percent and 77 percent, respectively, of the roll calls throughout the decade. If the southern Democrats, including the chairman, who traditionally strayed to vote with the Republicans, had not been among the ranks or had not bolted, Democratic cohesion scores would have been higher.

Voting together was in the Republicans' best interest. If they voted together and were joined by the chairman and one or two of his Democratic allies, as was likely, they had the votes to defeat anything that the Democrats put forth. In addition, they had the advantage because it was easier to maintain the status quo and stop legislation from being enacted than it was to get a law rewritten once it had passed. As a result, the Republicans were able to stymie advances by more progressive-minded Democrats. The Democrats, on the other hand, may have agreed on the ends, but not on the means. Since they could not agree on how to achieve their goals, it was easy for the Republicans and their allies to divide and conquer. Moreover, until the end of the decade, the liberal Democrats did not have sufficient votes to predominate over the conservative coalition.

The percentage of committee roll calls classified as "party votes" illustrates the degree of competition between the Democrats and Republicans on Education and Labor. Although the 70-percent criterion is the level of choice in this study, statistics on voting at four levels are presented for comparison with other investigations. Table 1.7 shows the percentages of party votes meeting four criteria (50 percent, 70 percent, 75 percent, and 90 percent). By the 70-percent party vote benchmark, the roll calls themselves lend only moderate support to the supposition that the committee was excessively partisan, until 1960, when the percentage of party votes nearly doubled (from 35.2 percent in 1959 to 66.7 percent in 1960). Over the decade, an average of about 38 percent of the committee's roll calls could be considered party votes.

The degree of party competition generally increased from 1951 to 1960. From 1955 on, more than 40 percent of the roll calls taken in Education and Labor could be classified as party votes. Possibly the degree of party voting has been obscured by the small sample size and by the lack

Table 1.7. Percentage of Party Votes in Committee by 50-, 70-, 75-, and 90-
            Percent Criteria, 1951-1960

Congress	Year	N	(number of qualifying roll calls in parentheses) > 50%	> 70%	> 75%	> 90%
82d	1951-52	27	48.1 (13)	14.8 (4)	11.1 (3)	0.0 (0)
84th	1955-56	20	65.0 (13)	40.0 (8)	25.0 (5)	15.0 (3)
85th	1958	30	60.0 (18)	46.7 (14)	43.3 (13)	26.7 (8)
86th	1959-60	92	70.7 (65)	42.4 (39)	39.1 (36)	16.3 (15)
	Total	169	(109)	(65)	(57)	(26)
	Percentage of total		64.5	38.5	33.7	15.4

Source: Author's calculations from Committee on Education and Labor, *Minutes* 1951-60. Votes
         for 1953-54 (83d Cong.) and 1957 were not available.

of statistics on voice votes, although one could argue that the fact that roll
calls were taken instead of voice votes shows more conflict and thus more
partisanship. Or perhaps the committee was not as partisan as it was
reputed to be until the latter part of the decade, when the Democratic
leadership had succeeded in saturating the committee majority with liberals. Either way, by the 86th Congress, the conservative coalition no longer
had a lock on Education and Labor.

A number of factors contributing to the committee's lack of cohesion
and its relatively high degree of partisanship during the 1950s exacerbated
the problems of coordination on Education and Labor. The most important
were the nature of the subject matter it considered, its original focus on
labor matters, the activity of its chairman, the temperament of its members,
the party ratio on the committee, and its operations. First, and most
important, the nature of the subject matter under this committee's jurisdiction accounted for a good deal of the friction. On many issues no compromises were possible. They embodied the fundamental differences in
philosophy of the two main political parties: the questions of whether, how
much, and in what direction the federal government should be involved.
Members also considered issues that surfaced in most congressional campaigns in one form or another during the 1950s: minimum wage, labor-
management relations, and aid to education. Liberal Democrats supported
unions and fought to keep conservative and antiunion Republicans and
southern Democrats from trying to diminish organized labor's clout. Not
only did the nature of the issues encourage the lack of full committee
cohesion, it fostered partisan conflict.

Federal aid to education, too, posed a divisive threat to organizational
unity on the Committee on Education and Labor. Republicans opposed
any form of federal interference in what they considered to be the domain of

state and local governments. Chairman Barden, too, remained suspicious of federal control; to him, federal money meant federal control. He held the firm conviction that "with Federal Dollars came Federal regulators to interfere in the operation of the local schools" (Puryear 1979, 108). A legacy of disputes in the 1940s over aid to private or segregated schools also beset the committee. The segregation issue particularly plagued the committee after the Supreme Court case *Brown* v. *Board of Education of Topeka*, dividing both Democrats and Republicans. Formulas for the allocation of federal aid funds created further dissension. Some proposals allotted money on the basis of need, whereas others based the distribution of funds on school-age population. Other plans took into account a combination of state resources, state financial contributions to education, and the school-age population.

Labor, as the primary focus of the modern committee when it was established in 1947, also aggravated full committee unity. Because most committee members maintained major interests in labor and only minor interests in education, the House leadership referred many education programs to other committees, thus weakening and fragmenting efforts to enact education legislation (Fenno 1969, 287-88). Education and labor issues also generated conflicting forces. While members were able to agree on some issues, especially in the field of labor, their constituencies pulled them in different directions on education legislation, particularly concerning religious and racial issues. According to Fenno, "Internal conflict would doubtless be harsh in a single education committee, but the tradition of charge and countercharge accompanying labor-management legislation has certainly made it more difficult to build a consensus among the same people in the area of education" (1969, 288).

The chairman was a third factor inhibiting committee harmony and contributing to the air of partisanship. Discussed in greater detail in the next chapter, Barden's ability to thwart legislation on federal aid to education and anything favorable to organized labor undermined committee unity. He skillfully created opposing coalitions in the committee, purposely keeping the committee split to prevent progressive legislation from being enacted or even from getting to the floor. In fact, one of his last efforts was aimed at splitting the committee into a separate Committee on Education and a Committee on Labor.

The feisty nature of committee members offered a fourth barrier to committee accord. Fenno (1969) argued that the committee conflict was not really over issues but among individual members. Ostrom described some of the members as "issue-oriented crusaders" (1972, 85). Members from both sides of the aisle were committed to their positions on education and labor issues, having been assigned to the committee for just that reason. In other words, these were the true believers, a difficult group in which to work out compromises.

A fifth factor, the party ratio on the committee, also contributed to the lack of interparty consensus. Until 1959 the Republicans combined with the southern Democrats to constitute a majority in direct opposition to the liberal Democrats on the committee. In 1959, at the urging of several members, the Speaker recommended a new party ratio, increasing the Democratic portion to twenty out of thirty seats. Against the wishes of the conservative chairman, the Democratic leadership then added six new liberals. The new additions further divorced the chairman from the rest of his party and necessitated alliances between conservative Democrats and Republicans to fight liberal advances.

The committee's operations also interfered with compatibility. On other committees, such as Appropriations or Ways and Means, procedures and norms developed that accommodated members whenever possible (Fenno 1966; Manley 1965, 1970). Education and Labor never spawned these practices and, instead, fostered competition and filibuster. During the Barden years, nothing was done to minimize the suspicions of Democrats about Republicans and vice versa. Nothing fostered cohesion across party lines, while several elements operated to enhance party voting on the committee.

Committee Structure

Chairman Barden wielded more influence over the structure of the committee than did his successors, who operated in a more institutionalized setting. In the absence of committee rules, he determined committee structure by and large. During his tenure, what had been a relatively small and uncomplicated organization grew in size and complexity. The configuration of committee units became more elaborate, and the staff size increased. The newly adopted rules led to the establishment of standing subcommittees, and as the committee developed, it became more decentralized, albeit not to the degree it would be under subsequent chairmen.

Before the adoption of committee rules, House committees operated within the rather vague guidelines set out in the 1946 reorganization act, which allowed the chairmen a great deal of discretion. The act required that each standing committee fix regular meeting days, keep a complete record of actions and votes, report bills approved by its members, require written testimony in advance from hearing witnesses, and open its hearings to the public. The chairman determined other more important matters.

Committee rules came about because of need, not as a result of regularized committee procedure. The old adage "if it ain't broke, don't fix it" applies to congressional committees as well as to a variety of other entities. Education and Labor, like other organizations, did not institute rules until something failed to work. This action demonstrated that the system as created by the 1946 act was not working to the satisfaction of a majority of members. The procedures delineated in the House rules were not sufficient to ensure that Education and Labor operated democratically, as the majority of its members thought it should. Additional interference by forces external to the committee indicated that the committee was also not conducting its business to the satisfaction of the House leadership.

When Education and Labor instituted specialized rules in 1957, it was one of the pioneer committees to do so. Only two committees had adopted rules previously: Government Operations in the 83d Congress and Interior in the 84th. An Education and Labor staff member commented that "the excesses of the chairmen of this committee are largely responsible for the committee rules and for some of the House rules." These excesses were exactly what precipitated the revolts against Barden and later against Powell. In a rare occurrence, Education and Labor members joined forces to create a new committee in structure, leadership, and operations. After several years of Barden's rather autocratic committee leadership, the committee boiled with controversy over procedure in 1957. The Democrats resented the chairman's delaying and obstructing tactics, including his failure to call meetings in accordance with the reorganization act and his alliance with committee Republicans. Bolling reported: "[Stewart] Udall [D-AZ] hit upon what was to be the coup de grace—the drafting of a set of committee rules, meeting majority approval, that when adopted would constrict the chairman so that his dictatorial scepter could be knocked from his hand" (1966, 97). After years of dissatisfaction, Democrats revolted, demanding weekly meetings, the appointment of standing subcommittees, and majority approval of the hiring of professional staff members. To forestall a crippling fight, Barden cleverly proposed several similar, less restrictive measures. He maneuvered to avoid more stringent rules by having his Republican allies move to take up his proposals en masse, thus preventing consideration of each proposal separately. Barden's version was approved with Republican support. Some Democrats, notably Powell, still were unhappy, but they did not have the votes to amend the new rules until the next Congress (see Powell 1971, 200; Puryear 1979, 116-17; and Mac-Neil 1963, 172-73).

The committee's new 1957 rules incorporated regular bimonthly meetings and standing subcommittees. Another important correlate in the rules was the requirement that the chairman refer all legislation to the appropriate subcommittee, a provision aimed at preventing him from sitting on bills he opposed or referring them to unsympathetic subcommittees. It enabled bills to go to hearings without the chairman's consent. Under the new rules, the chairman had the power to appoint subcommittees and their chairmen, although not necessarily on the basis of seniority, after consultation with the ranking minority member. The chairman and ranking minority member had ex officio membership on all subcommittees. Any committee member could attend and participate in any subcommittee meeting, although he could not vote unless he was a member of that subcommittee. The new rules also allowed written proxies to be accepted in committee meetings if a majority of the members were present physically. The chairman maintained his control over the hiring and discharge of committee majority staff members.

Even after the rules were imposed, the committee still was not working to its members' satisfaction. Committee Democrats revolted again in 1959. Aided by the Speaker and the Committee on Ways and Means (acting as the Democratic Committee on Committees), who stacked the committee in their favor, members pushed for and won additional limitations on the chairman in the committee rules.[12] One new provision required that the chairman appoint every member to one or more subcommittees, with due regard to individual preferences to avoid skipping some members in the assignment process. In the past, some had been passed over while others received multiple subcommittee assignments. A second new provision diluted the chairman's ability to prevent the official receipt of testimony by declaring the absence of a quorum. Another rule stipulated that two subcommittee members, rather than the majority required for transaction of other business, constituted a quorum for the purpose of taking testimony. This rule made it more difficult for the chairman and his allies to avoid taking testimony contrary to their views by boycotting hearings. Ostensibly to prevent the chairman from referring bills not to his liking to subcommittees he knew would oblige him and bury the legislation, a third rules change enabled the committee, as well as the chairman, to recall a bill from a subcommittee for the full committee's direct consideration or for referral to another subcommittee.

Nevertheless, Barden salvaged a few remnants of his authority during the 1959 revolt. Much to the chagrin of Adam Clayton Powell, the ranking Democrat, Barden and his allies defeated a provision requiring the chairman to rely on seniority in naming subcommittees and chairmen, thus enabling Barden to skip over Powell in doling out subcommittee chairmanships. The 1957 and 1959 changes proved monumental for the structure of the committee. The institution of committee rules effectively realigned the power structure and the configuration of the committee, formalized committee procedures, and decentralized the decision-making process.

Committee size and party ratio were used by both House Democrats and Republicans when they were in the majority to control the decisions of the committee. Leadership actions enlarged the committee's membership under Barden from twenty-four to thirty and diluted his control. Both parties overrepresented themselves when in the majority. Republicans took advantage of their majority status in the 83d Congress and overrepresented themselves slightly compared with the party ratio of the House. The Democrats generally had about one more seat per term than this ratio would seem to dictate. The extra seat enabled them to put an additional liberal on the committee, a useful addition in efforts to override the conservative chairman's maneuvers and, later, to undermine his effectiveness at stalling. Overrepresentation of the majority party members proved to be particularly important in the late 1950s, when the Democratic party leaders had trouble getting Chairman Barden to accommodate their wishes. As a result of the Democrats' sweep in the 1958 elections, they had twice as many seats on Education and Labor in the 86th Congress as did the Republicans. The large Democratic majority, with its influx of liberals, set the stage for upcoming liberal policy victories in the early 1960s.

The number and jurisdictions of subcommittees fluctuated during the 1950s. In his first full term as chairman in 1951-52, Barden created ten ad hoc subcommittees for various studies or investigations. The committee accomplished little, however, and held relatively few meetings (only four roll call votes were taken in 1951). Republicans, who had a majority of members on the committee in the 83d Congress (1953-54), replaced the subcommittees with ten special subcommittees focusing on the most prominent issues under the committee's jurisdiction, such as aid to schools in federally impacted areas, aid for school construction, and handicapped rehabilitation. Another subcommittee investigated federal activities in education. Given their anti–organized labor sentiments and the mood of the country, it is not surprising that the Republicans established several labor subcommittees in the 83d Congress to investigate dubious aspects of union behavior, such as abuses in labor union welfare and pension funds or strikes and racketeering. The subcommittees established by the Democrats when they regained their majority in the 84th Congress (1955-56) had a different focus. Most related to education, although others focused on facets of the labor acts under the committee's jurisdiction, mine safety, and allegations of misuse of union funds. Several of the fourteen subcommittees existed only for one session.

The 1957 rules enabled committee members to transform the committee structure from a relatively simple one based on temporary ad hoc subunits to a more complex arrangement with permanent subcommittees with fixed jurisdictions spelled out in the rules. In addition, the rules required that the chairman automatically refer legislation to the appropriate subcommittee as determined by the subject matter. Nonetheless, Barden managed to bypass the process and have his House or committee allies pigeonhole most of the bills he opposed.

The committee set up five new standing subcommittees—two on

education, two on labor, and one on safety and compensation—with jurisdictions delineated in the committee rules. The chairman also created a special subcommittee in 1957 to handle the volatile issue of welfare and pension plan matters. Later, in the 86th Congress (1959-60), the chairman combined the Subcommittee on Labor-Management Relations, headed by Carl Perkins (D-KY), with the Labor Standards Subcommittee, chaired by Phil Landrum (D-GA) to create a special joint labor subcommittee with cochairmen. This move was part of a broader plan to prevent the bill that would become the Landrum-Griffin Act from being pigeonholed in the subcommittee chaired by labor ally Carl Perkins (Puryear 1979, 198). As the 1950s ended, Education and Labor had five standing and two ad hoc subcommittees.

Not only did subcommittee structure change during the decade, but reliance on it shifted. At the beginning of Barden's tenure, in 1951 and 1952, subcommittees held rather extensive hearings. They conducted over 70 percent of the 82d Congress committee hearings and almost half of those in the Republican-controlled 83d Congress. By the time Barden resumed his chairmanship in the 84th, however, subcommittee hearings had dropped precipitously, to less than 5 percent of the total committee hearings. Federal aid for school construction and the minimum wage accounted for most of the 1955 and 1956 hearings, which were held by the full committee. Only two subcommittees heard testimony that term, one on extending the Fair Labor Standards Act to cover certain retail employees, and the other to investigate the Performance Trust Fund of the American Federation of Musicians (committee *Calendar*, 84th Cong.). All other committee business was conducted in full committee. Table 1.8 shows the proportion of full committee versus subcommittee hearings. After the 1957 rules allowed for standing subcommittees with fixed jurisdictions, both the number of hearings and the proportion held in subcommittees increased dramatically. The number of hearings grew by more than one hundred and the proportion in subcommittees skyrocketed from under 5 percent to almost 92 percent. The full committee held only a few hearings in the 85th Congress, and none in the 86th. All 166 hearings in 1959 and 1960 were before subcommittees, including the many pertaining to the Landrum-Griffin Act.

The committee staff grew markedly during the Barden years, doubling between 1951 and 1960 and culminating in the employment of eight professional and ten support staff members for the full committee by 1960. The minority was shortchanged, however, with only one employee in each category. Apparently this also was the case in regard to subcommittee staff, although ostensibly subcommittees had both majority and minority staff members after the rules were established. A minority staff director complained in later years that there was little Republican subcommittee staff

Table 1.8. Full Committee and Subcommittee Hearings, 1950s

Congress	Year	Days of full committee hearings	Days of subcommittee hearings	Total days of hearings	Percentage of subcommittee hearings
82d	1951-52	25	62	87	71.3
83d	1953-54	54	50	104	48.1
84th	1955-56	88	4	92	4.3
85th	1957-58	16	180	196	91.8
86th	1959-60	0	166	166	100.0
	Total	183	462	645	
	Mean	36.6	92.4	129.0	63.1
	Percentage of total	28.4	71.6		

Source: Compiled from Committee on Education and Labor, Calendar 1951-60.

under Barden: full committee minority personnel were assigned to assist subcommittees (interview).

In part, the chairman complied with the Legislative Reorganization Act of 1946 requiring that staff members be selected "on a permanent basis without regard to political affiliations" (P.L. 79-601). Some of the staff members appeared to have been appointed on a partisan basis, while others were not. During the 82d Congress, Fred G. Hussey served as chief clerk of the committee, and John O. Graham served as minority clerk. When the Republicans took control of the 83d Congress, the two clerks switched places. Had the staff been assigned on a nonpartisan or nonpolitical basis, these two men would have remained in their respective jobs. On the other hand, Russell Derrickson may have been one of the few truly nonpolitical, nonpatronage staff appointments on this committee, or at least he maintained friends on both sides of the aisle. He served as the committee's investigator in the 82d Congress and as the chief investigator from the 83d until 1961, when he became staff director under Chairman Powell. Edward A. McCabe, who did not stay nearly as long, served as the general counsel for both the Republican majority in the 83d Congress and the Democratic majority in the 84th. Subsequent chairmen and ranking minority members made few nonpartisan or nonpolitical staff appointments, although a few staff members endured several chairmen.

The structure of Education and Labor changed dramatically over the decade of the 1950s. At the outset, it was centralized: the chairman had discretion over almost every aspect of committee operations. His abuse of this discretion in opposition to his fellow Democrats led to the institution of rules that decentralized the chairman's power, decentralizing the committee. Although the resources still were not distributed equitably among the majority members, for the first time they had at their disposal the means to circumvent the chairman and to enforce their will. Concurrent with the institution of standing subcommittees and the mandatory referral of legislation to the proper subcommittee came increased use of subcommittees for hearings and legislative consideration. Subcommittees had a better chance of getting their legislation reviewed in full committee, too, because the chairman was required to call meetings. In addition, at the end of the decade, staff members were assigned to subcommittees for the first time. The enlargement of the committee and the Democratic leadership's interference in the assignment process to circumvent Barden's obstructionist tactics changed the compositional picture of Education and Labor, setting the stage for the progressive programs of the 1960s. Education and Labor metamorphosed into a larger, more liberal, more conflictual, and more partisan committee during Graham Barden's chairmanship. It also evolved into a more universalistic, permanent organization.

Jurisdiction, Work Load, and Function

In its establishment of the Committee on Education and Labor, the Legislative Reorganization Act of 1946 specified its jurisdiction and outlined a set of general operating procedures. Neither changed much during Barden's chairmanship. In addition to general responsibility for measures relating to education and labor, the reorganization act gave the committee responsibility for all proposed legislation relating to child labor, convict labor and the entry of goods made by convicts into interstate commerce, labor standards, labor statistics, mediation and arbitration of labor disputes, regulation and prevention of importation of foreign laborers under contract, and the wages and hours of labor. Issues of school lunch, vocational rehabilitation, the U.S. Employees' Compensation Commission, Columbia Institution for the Deaf, Dumb, and Blind (now Gallaudet University), Howard University, Freedmen's Hospital (now Howard University Hospital), Saint Elizabeth's Hospital, and the welfare of miners also came under the committee's jurisdiction (P.L. 79-601, as amended).

The House charged each committee with the review of all legislation under, and the tax policies affecting, its jurisdiction. In addition, committees oversee the activities of federal agencies within their purview. The House rules gave the committee additional responsibility for reviewing, studying, and coordinating all laws, programs, and government activities concerning domestic educational programs and institutions, including student assistance programs under the jurisdiction of other committees (House *Rules*, rule 10, sec. 693, cl. 3[c]).

An examination of the committee's work load provides the basis for showing what the committee accomplished during the period that Barden

Table 1.9. Bills Referred to Education and Labor, 1951-1960

Congress	Year	Number referred	Number reported	Number passed HR	Number public laws
82d	1951-52	232	8	7	4
83d	1953-54	268	15	14	12
84th	1955-56	462	12	11	10
85th	1957-58	601	18	14	14
86th	1959-60	720	17	10	8

Source: Compiled from Committee on Education and Labor, *Calendar* 1951-60.

was the chairman. The work load is gauged from the number of days of hearings held by the full committee and by subcommittees, and the number of bills reported to the House (table 1.9). The sheer numbers of bills on which action was taken are not used because they do not reflect accurately the amount of work; this period predated multiple sponsorship of legislation, and many bills were duplicates. Moreover, the bills referred differ in their level of importance and in the amount of work they require. To compensate for this problem, this section includes some discussion on the relative importance of the bills considered and some individual proposals that took up a disproportionate amount of the committee's time.

Although an important gauge of committee success, the measure of the number of bills reported, used by itself, obscures a great deal of the work done; consequently, hearings are expressed by the number of days devoted to that activity. Several days could be spent holding hearings on legislation that never cleared the committee, such as some of the federal aid to education legislation. Members oftentimes were thwarted by the chairman in their efforts to get particular legislation considered by the full committee. The number of days of hearings held in subcommittee and in full committee fluctuated dramatically over the decade. Full committee hearing days ranged from 88 days in the 84th Congress to 0 in the 86th. Subcommittee hearings ranged from a low of 4 days in the 84th to a high of 180 days in the 85th. A large number of hearings in the 85th and 86th Congresses concerned particularly controversial bills. The committee spent numerous days in the 85th Congress considering aid to education to promote the national defense, and a substantial proportion of the 86th Congress hearings concerned the Landrum-Griffin Act proposals.

The number of bills reported by the committee grew more than twofold from the early to the late 1950s. As reflected in table 1.9, the number of bills reported increased by 50 percent from the 82d Congress (1951-52), which reported eight bills, to the 84th Congress (1955-56), which reported twelve bills. The number of bills reported peaked in the 1957-58 with eighteen and stayed relatively high in 1959-60, when the committee completed work on seventeen bills, for a total of seventy reported for the decade.

With the exception of a few bills, most of the legislation reported by the Committee on Education and Labor during the chairmanship of Graham Barden was of narrow scope and of little national significance. Many of these bills were important to small groups of beneficiaries, such as longshoremen, agricultural workers, and people with various handicaps, but few had earth-shaking, widespread impact. That assessment is not to belittle the accomplishments of the committee, but just to note that much legislation of broader scope was blocked somewhere in the process to prevent its enactment. Not inconsequential time was spent on the proposals that never had a chance of being considered by the full House—namely, those bills favorable to labor unions. Most of the legislation that survived obstacles in the committee either amended previously existing laws or helped a narrow subset of the country.

By the end of the decade the picture had changed. In particular, four rather significant pieces of legislation, two education and two labor, emerged from the committee during Barden's tenure as chairman, all in the late 1950s. All consumed a considerable amount of the committee's time and effort. The two education bills were landmarks. The critical need for increased national defense provided members with a vehicle for a general aid to education bill. The National Defense Education Act (NDEA, P.L. 85-864), the first major aid to education program to pass in years, opened the door for an increased federal role in education. Another important bill, Representative Frank Thompson's general aid bill emphasizing the need for school construction, passed the House in 1960 (86th Cong., H. R. 10128). After Senate adoption of a similar measure, the Thompson bill died because the Rules Committee refused to authorize a conference. Nevertheless, the school construction bill did overcome a significant obstacle: it passed the House with the inclusion of Powell's antidiscrimination amendment, heretofore an impossibility. These two bills were the precursors to the advancements in federal funding to education enacted in the 1960s.

The committee also reported landmark labor legislation concerning welfare and pension benefit plans (P.L. 85-836) and labor-management reporting and disclosure (the Landrum-Griffin Act, P.L. 86-257). Members capitalized on the negative publicity accorded to organized labor and, after extensive hearings and mark-up sessions, passed two bills increasing the already harsh provisions (from the union standpoint) of the 1947 Taft-Hartley Act, the main law governing the behavior of labor and management (other than minimum-wage laws). The 1959 Landrum-Griffin Act, in particular, increased the regulations and penalties for labor unions and changed the face of labor-management relations.

Several factors account for the committee's general trend toward increased work load and productivity. Some changes were the result of external variables, such as a surge in the number of bills introduced in the House and referred to the committee. Others are attributable to committee-specific factors. Environmental influences, including the growth of the population, the changing role of the federal government, the expansion in interest group activity, communications advances, and the complexity of issues, contributed to the sharp rise in the number of bills and resolutions introduced in Congress (Mackenzie 1981, 3-10). In addition to the sheer volume of legislation, a shift in the committee's agenda increased the work load and output. Growing interest in labor legislation, stemming both from the desire to protect the rights of workers and the desire to regulate labor unions, resulted in a larger number of bills referred to the committee and more action taken. Moreover, *Sputnik* and defense concerns prompted a greater interest in education, necessitating action by the committee.

In large part, several overlapping, committee-specific factors contributed to the greater activity and productivity. The new liberal emphasis in the committee partially was responsible for the rise in the number of hearings, the proportion of hearings held in subcommittees, and the number of bills reported. By the end of the decade liberals had built enough support within the committee to override the chairman's wishes, aiding their pursuit of an activist agenda in education matters. The expanded number of liberals on the committee facilitated the 1957 adoption of committee rules, which, in turn, significantly enhanced the reliance on subcommittees for much of the committee's work. Mandatory subcommittee creation diverted the work to smaller groups and diluted the chairman's influence. The requirement that every bill referred to the full committee in turn should be referred to its respective subcommittee contributed to the increase in the number of hearings.

Although Barden had made substantial use of subcommittees in his first term as chairman, he slacked off in his second term, probably partly as a result of the 1954 *Brown* decision. The Supreme Court case marked a turning point in his views on federal aid to education (Puryear 1979, 106-7) and coincided with his reduced reliance on subcommittees, especially those that dealt with education matters. As a consequence, the members adopted the rules. The subsequent increase in the number of bills reported testifies to the effects of both majority opposition and the creation of rules in diminishing the chairman's powers.

Within the constraints imposed by official goals and charges, committees are relatively free to pursue their own agendas, as long as they do not interfere with the policy demands of the larger body. When the committee fails to fulfill its official duties to the satisfaction of a sufficient number of members, however, the parent body acts to ensure that it mends its ways. The Committee on Education and Labor had a mission of its own, one that changed over the years. Early in his tenure, Chairman Barden regularly thwarted the will of the majority leadership in the House by refusing to call meetings, loading the hearings, limiting the opposing witnesses' time, and employing a variety of other tactics, thereby impeding the fulfillment of the committee's official function. Barden worked to achieve the unofficial goals he had set for the committee. He promoted the agenda of the committee's dominant philosophical faction, a conservative coalition formed in cooperation with the Republicans. As a result, he realized his goals, whereas he and his allies frustrated those of the committee members outside the conservative coalition, as well as those of many House Democrats. Ergo, the committee's de facto function was one of blocking legislation that did not coincide with conservative goals.

Some of the most controversial legislation, clearly favored by the House leadership and by most of the committee Democrats, stood no chance of emerging intact from Education and Labor. If for some reason these bills did survive, the chairman quietly appealed to his conservative friends on the Rules Committee to intervene at the next step in the process (interviews; for an example, see Puryear 1979, 121). For years, this conservative coalition thwarted federal aid to education and proposals favorable to organized labor. With the help of the House leadership, which did not approve of minority rule, the picture began to change. Committee membership from the more liberal, urban Middle Atlantic states, in particular, and the Pacific states grew throughout the decade at the expense of the more conservative South, whose proportion of the committee declined by more than half by the end of the decade. The new composition helped ensure that the official duties of the committee would be performed in accordance with House directives, or at least with the majority agenda. The Democrats retained majority status officially, but the factions in control shifted. As the majority changed, the function changed. The new progressive bill of fare impinged on the dominance of the old conservative menu.

The liberals, aided by the new committee rules, laid the foundation for the new agenda. Accompanied by a more equitable distribution of power in the form of subcommittees and mandatory referral of all legislation, the institution of the rules facilitated the consideration and reporting of bills. It also enabled members to hold hearings without the chairman's approval and, thus, to act on and report more bills. It gave more members an entrée into the legislative process.

When Chairman Barden retired, leaving the committee to a chairman with an entirely different orientation, the committee was in a state of flux. As future chapters will show, this condition was common for Education and Labor.

2

The Chairmanship of Graham Barden

An abundance of institutional prerogatives combined with a personally resourceful chairman who did not mind using them to further his objectives characterized Graham Arthur Barden's chairmanship. His leadership was negative and autocratic. It was negative, not in the sense that he was a bad chairman or that he was ineffective (he was not, in either case), but because he used his authority to keep things from happening, not to make them happen. He used his considerable powers largely to prevent new legislation from being enacted, to restrain organized labor, and to thwart the agenda of the increasingly liberal committee majority. His leadership was autocratic in the sense that he was unresponsive to the majority on his committee, and often the House majority, and actively obstructed their wishes. In his negative actions, Barden apparently effectively represented the viewpoints of the people who elected him rather than those of the majority of his Democratic colleagues. Voters in North Carolina's Third District elected him to thirteen terms.

A Portrait of the Chairman

Knowledge of a chairman's background, constituency, and political ideology helps place his leadership in perspective. It provides some insight into how he exercised his powers. In the case of Barden, it highlights some of the reasons he employed his resources in a negative manner, such as why he blocked "liberal" legislation, particularly federal aid to education and anything viewed favorably by organized labor.[1]

One of six children of James Jefferson Barden and Mary James Barden, Graham Arthur Barden was born near Turkey Township in Sampson

County, North Carolina, on September 25, 1896. He spent his early years on the family farm. Later the family moved to Burgaw so the children could attend high school. After graduating from Burgaw High School, Barden set out for the University of North Carolina at Chapel Hill, intent on a law degree. But World War I interrupted his schooling, and he joined the navy for a brief five months, signing up about a month before the armistice. Barden earned his LL.B. in 1920 and passed the North Carolina bar examination. Instead of setting up practice immediately, he taught and coached at New Bern High School for two years to earn money for a law library. He married Agnes Foy in 1922. After his first year of teaching, Barden established his law practice with a friend. Ten years later, in 1931, he left to practice with Mrs. Barden's brother-in-law.

Barden's public service began in 1921, when he was appointed judge of the Craven County Recorder's Court, a post he held while practicing law. He subsequently was elected to the position twice. In 1926 he entered the Democratic primary race for solicitor of the Fifth Judicial District but came in third. Barden earned considerable recognition during his days as an attorney. He was highly visible and instrumental in bringing down the Great Tiger Klan, a junior version of the Ku Klux Klan (though in later years many considered him a racist because of his opposition to federally forced school integration). Active in several local eleemosynary associations, he also put a great deal of energy into church and civic affairs.

In 1932 Barden ran for the North Carolina House of Representatives on a platform advocating state support of public schools but opposing the ad valorem tax on land that was meant to defray the expenses of the six-month school term. He argued that the state should reimburse counties for a portion of the debts incurred in the construction of school buildings, and he wanted the state instead of the local school districts to spend money for school buses. He also advocated the assessment of property at its real value, a state tax on stocks and bonds of foreign corporations, and disbandment of many state offices, bureaus, and commissions. He opposed corporate lobbying and promised to represent the interests of Craven County. Barden won the nomination and subsequently the election to the state House. He used his assignment on the Appropriations Committee to attract statewide attention, gaining public notice for his activity in behalf of adequate funding for public school, state colleges, and universities, and for his economy-mindedness.

Although the seven-term incumbent U.S. representative Charles L. Abernethy was old and infirm, he insisted on running in the 1934 congressional elections. Abernethy's son, who carried out most of his father's duties, was expected to inherit the seat. Barden and several others decided to challenge the expected inheritance. Barden won a plurality of votes in the Democratic primary and faced Luther Hamilton of Morehead City for a primary runoff. Hamilton questioned Barden's loyalty to the Democratic party, to which Barden replied that he had never voted anything but a straight Democratic ticket and avowed his support for the New Deal and for Franklin Roosevelt. Barden won the second primary by fewer than two thousand votes, but his primary victory was tantamount to election in the heavily Democratic district.

When Barden went to Washington in 1935 for his first term as a U.S. representative of the Third District of North Carolina, he was assigned to both the Committee on Education and the Committee on Rivers and Harbors. His seat on the latter enabled him to provide tangible benefits to his constituents by working for navigational improvements, such as deepening and widening channels, in the coastal counties of his district. His assignment to the Committee on Education allowed him to work for improvements in his area of interest. During his early years in Congress he cooperated with the House leadership and with President Roosevelt while keeping an eye on his obligations to the Third District. Several times, he campaigned for reelection on his record of support for Roosevelt. The American Federation of Labor even lauded him for his prolabor leanings, based on four votes on which Barden voted with the administration (Puryear 1979, 24).

Since Barden was a faithful supporter of the Roosevelt administration, the House leadership named him as one of the three Democratic "official objectors," to keep an eye on all private and consent calendar bills to weed out those without merit in the 75th Congress (1937-38). He studied an enormous number of bills and was recompensed by assignment to the House Labor Committee, which had a vacancy caused by the death of a member. Barden championed Roosevelt's 1937-38 efforts at reducing domestic spending and increasing defense spending. He deplored the "idea that the Federal government is some sort of spiritual Santa Claus having a treasury without bottom and always full of money" (Puryear 1979, 27). Although he voted to cut the president's proposals for relief, Barden also voted to increase funds for vocational education and supported additional spending for military construction and for the administration's farm program. Barden's views conflicted with those of the Roosevelt administration on the wages and hours bill and on antilynching bills, but he represented the views of his district. He held the attitude "that Southerners would take care of themselves if saved from reformers from other parts of the country." Otherwise, he depicted Roosevelt as "the greatest man ever to sit in the White House" (Puryear 1979, 26).

By 1940 the congressman was under attack by his electoral opponents for his antilabor stances. In the previous year he had been in a well-publicized dispute with the administration over the exemption of agricultural workers from the wages and hours bill. When Barden ran for the 1940 nomination, he played down his ties to the administration for the first time. Instead, he focused on his record and experience, his committee assignments, and the projects he had won for the district. He won the nomination and then the election by a three-to-one margin. During the war years Barden concentrated on bringing federal money to his district. In 1941 he was instrumental in getting Camp Davis, a large antiaircraft firing base, built in Onslow County, North Carolina, in his district. The economic benefits accrued to surrounding counties, and Barden reaped the political harvest. The same year the Marine Corps built a large base at New River, also in Onslow County, called Camp Lejeune. Soon thereafter, since the Marines needed an air base, another military installation was built at Cherry Point, in Carteret County, again in Barden's district. The navy also used Morehead City as a sectional base from which to establish coastal and harbor patrols, submarine detection, and mine-sweeping operations.

Besides the sheer financial benefits to his district, one of the many interests Barden cultivated during his early years in the House was vocational rehabilitation. During World War II a need for adequate rehabilitation arose when the wounded returned from the war, work-related injuries grew, and employment increased. One of Barden's pet projects was a bill designed to fund rehabilitation (Puryear 1979, 41). Barden in the House and Robert M. La Follette, Jr. (R-WI) in the Senate introduced identical vocational rehabilitation bills, but after opposition from veterans groups, Congress adjourned without acting on either bill. The failure was attributed to disagreements among veterans groups about which agency should administer the programs. A veterans rehabilitation bill putting control under the Veterans Administration was enacted instead. The next term, in the 78th Congress, Barden deleted the clauses pertaining to veterans in his bill and resubmitted it. This time it survived the legislative process mostly intact and became the Barden-La Follette Vocational Rehabilitation Act (P.L. 78-113).

By the 78th Congress (1943-44), Barden had enough seniority to chair either the Library Committee or the Committee on Education. He opted for the latter, which put him in a more strategic position from which to push both his educational and his vocational rehabilitation interests. Throughout his prechairman stint as a member of Congress, Barden focused his energies in large part on education, labor, and benefits for his district. He faithfully represented the Third District of North Carolina and, in the process, wandered into the policy areas of agriculture and foreign policy.

Orientation of the Chairman

A committee chairman's orientation determines, to a large extent, how he operates his committee and how he treats issues that come before it. His ideological proclivities affect the content and form of legislation reported by the committee and often determine its outcome. Within certain externally imposed parameters, his orientation and his leadership affect committee operations and outputs, thus leaving their mark on public policy. Several sources form the basis for inferences about the chairman's orientation toward his committee and the issues it faced: his constituency and district characteristics, his reputation concerning his philosophy, his voting records, his interest group ratings, and his party-unity scores.

Barden's orientation as chairman of the Committee on Education and Labor reflected, to a large degree, the characteristics of his constituency and district. The people who elected him to represent them in Congress played an important, albeit indirect, role in the operation of this committee.[2] Their characteristics help explain his adamant opposition to federal aid to education, his views toward integration, and his support for labor reform.

He represented the Third District of North Carolina, located on the eastern end of the state and including nine counties: Sampson, Wayne, Duplin, Pender, Onslow, Jones, Craven, Pamlico, and Carteret. The district's economy was based on agriculture. The main crops included tobacco, cotton, corn, peanuts, soybeans, potatoes, strawberries, and blueberries. The lumber industry also provided significant income to the district, with timberland comprising about 70 percent of the total acreage. In the eastern counties of his district, along the Atlantic coast, commercial fishing was a major industry. After Barden had been in Congress for a while, military interests became well entrenched. As Barden's biographer, Elmer Puryear, wrote, "Graham Barden was a product of the region and possessed an understanding of the problems and aspirations of its inhabitants and wanted to represent them in Washington" (1979, 13). Born and raised on a farm, initially he reflected the agricultural concerns of his district. Agriculture took priority over labor (Puryear 1979, 141).

The political characteristics of the chairman's district also provided important elements for his orientation. The South traditionally has been more conservative than many other parts of the country, and Barden's district was no exception. Along with a majority of other southerners, North Carolinians customarily favored states' rights over federal control or centralization. They were also habitually Democratic. Barden was not just from eastern North Carolina; he was of eastern North Carolina. He knew what the people in his district wanted, and he differed from them little in that respect. He was one of them. They long had opposed labor unions. They objected to efforts by the federal government to force them to integrate their schools. They were conservative economically. Barden distrusted bureaucracy, big government, corruption, inflation, and "giveaway" programs and was "suspicious of bigness in any form" (Puryear

1979, 226-27). He followed his own instincts in representing his district, and judging from the absence of serious electoral opposition for most of his career, he was successful.

By both reputation and action, Chairman Barden was a staunch southern conservative.[3] He held fast to the notion of being a Democrat, but in the minds of some, after he became chairman he was a Democrat in name only. Although he was convinced, especially after the 83d Congress, that Republicans "simply don't know how to run the government" (Puryear 1979, 107), he spent a great deal of his legislative time allied with them. He earned the reputation among his Democratic colleagues of being more of a Republican than a Democrat because of his conservative views, especially on federal aid to education and organized labor. He held traditional southern attitudes, regarding labor unions as inherently evil organizations interfering with free enterprise.

The chairman also held traditional southern views on states' rights: the federal government has a job to do, but it must not interfere in the business of state governments. Barden maintained that the responsibility for the operation of the nation's public schools lay in the hands of state governments, not with the federal government, and was suspicious of federal aid to education because it presumed some degree of federal control over state prerogatives. In the early 1950s he was persuaded that since the public schools were having a hard time fulfilling their responsibilities, the federal government should help. He favored aid to federally impacted areas, such as those near large federal installations that provided extra students and no revenues from property taxes. He promoted aid to elementary and secondary schools until the question arose about whether to aid private (i.e., religious) and parochial schools. Federal tax money, he contended, should not be used to support religious education, even if, as his opponents argued, it reduced substantially the burden on the public schools. If his opponents insisted on federal aid to private schools, he would do everything in his power to prevent it, even if it meant putting a stop to all federal aid proposals.

The issue of racial integration was a thorn in his side. He objected to efforts to prohibit federal aid to schools in states that allowed segregation of the races in education, especially since North Carolina was among them. As a consequence, his detractors charged bigotry despite his record of opposition to the Great Tiger Klan. He maintained that he was not bigoted but adamantly opposed federal interference in state functions. To Barden, federal laws dictating that his state could not receive federal funds because it practiced segregation reeked of unwarranted and unwanted federal interference in the state domain. He held the firm conviction that "with federal dollars came federal regulators to interfere in the operation of local schools" (Puryear 1979, 108).

Table 2.1. Barden's Interest Group Ratings Compared with the Average Scores
of Other Members

Group	Year	Barden	E&L Dems	HR Dems	Full E&L	Full HR
AFL	1947-52	3.7	54.5	54.2	34.6	35.0
AFL	1951	20.0	67.1	69.9	55.8	42.5
CIO	1951	0.0	55.0	58.9	40.0	43.7
CIO	1951-52	0.0	57.6	56.1	38.3	40.1
ADA	1951	7.7	60.4	58.9	39.4	40.5
ADA	1952	0.0	58.2	53.4	35.9	37.7
Labor	1953-54	33.3	72.6	66.2	41.5	41.6
AFL-CIO	1947-56	26.3	55.1	52.4	34.0	35.2
ACA	1957-59	52.0	15.9	22.0	39.8	43.6
COPE	1959-60	10.0	88.7	71.8	65.2	54.6
ADA	1960	11.0	88.9	72.2	68.0	56.3

Source: Author's calculations from *Congressional Quarterly Weekly Report* 1951-61.

Barden's conservative and traditionally southern viewpoints aggravated many of the more liberal members of Congress. In their eyes, he used his position as chairman of the Committee on Education and Labor to impede progress on important social problems. He obstructed federal aid to education of all sorts. He also did everything in his power to curtail the activities of labor unions, thus evoking the anger and frustration of friends of organized labor.

In this study, Barden's attitudes are gauged from surrogate measures of ideology—from scores on scales devised by interest groups. Where already-compiled scales were not available, the scores were calculated from the numbers of times Barden supported the positions of the various interest groups based on the number of "right" and "wrong" votes.[4] The chairman's scores are presented in table 2.1, along with those of Education and Labor Democrats, House Democrats, the full Education and Labor Committee, and the full House. The higher the score, the more closely the members conformed to the relevant interest group's position. An examination of the scores shows that Barden voted much more conservatively than did his colleagues on the committee and in the House. There was a difference of more than fifty points between his scores from most liberal interest groups and those of his fellow Democrats on Education and Labor. Barden received substantially higher scores on conservative measures than did his committee Democratic colleagues and most other Democrats in the House. On all the labor union votes and on those of the ADA, he scored substantially lower than did most other Democrats, ranking among the lowest on every scale. Contrary to their reputation in later years, committee Democrats, including the few southerners who brought down the average, did not in the early part of the decade show outstanding

Table 2.2. Barden's Party-Unity Scores Compared with the Average Scores of
          Other Democrats, 1951-1960

Congress	Year	Barden	E & L Democrats	HR Democrats
82d	1951-52	38	77.0	77.0
83d	1953-54	59	76.9	76.6
84th	1955-56	37	75.0	71.0
85th	1957-58	34	72.6	68.3
86th	1959-60	22	76.2	70.7

Source: Compiled from *Congressional Quarterly Almanac* 1951-60.

levels of support for labor issues or other liberal issues outlined by the ADA
in the 1950s. But Barden rated extremely conservative on all union or
liberal scales. On the ACA's ratings, Barden ranked moderately conservative. He scored above the House average and even higher above the committee average. Conservative Republicans often could count on Graham
Barden as a powerful ally in their quests to stop liberal legislation from
reaching the floor.

Also based on votes cast on the floor of the House, party-unity scores
provide additional clues to the chairman's orientation (see table 2.2).
Throughout the 1950s Barden's average party-unity score was 38 percent.
The comparable committee average for Democrats was 75.6 percent, and
that of all House Democrats, 72.7 percent. When the Democrats were in
the minority in the Republican-controlled 83d Congress, Barden voted
more often with his fellow Democrats, scoring only 18 percent lower than
both House and committee Democrats. When majorities of the two parties
were in opposition, it is clear that Barden voted with a Republican majority
much more often than he voted with the Democrats. In all but the 83d
Congress, he supported his party on less than half the occasions that his
committee and House colleagues did. It is understandable that in the 83d
Congress he might vote more often with the Democrats because of their
minority status, and at that time he still thought that the Republicans were
not competent to run the government.

Barden's support for his party diminished as the decade progressed.
His aversion to federal aid to education became more entrenched with the
advent of mandatory school integration and with the increasing probability
of aid going to parochial schools. His suspicion of labor unions increased
with the onslaught of strikes and with the exposure of corruption in union
leadership throughout the 1950s. With increasing frequency, he cast his
vote with the Republicans, who also opposed federal aid to education and
who set out with a vengeance to clean up the labor unions and to restrict
their activities and influence. In short, committee voting behavior aside,
Barden earned his reputation as a conservative.

Table 2.3. Barden's Support for Democrats on Committee Party Votes,
      1951-1960

| | | > 70% Democrats v. > 70% Republicans | | | | |
| | | With Dems | | With Reps | | |
Year	Party votes	N	%	N	%	No vote
1951	0	0	0.0	0	0.0	0
1952	4	0	0.0	4	100.0	0
1955	4	1	25.0	3	75.0	0
1956	4	0	0.0	3	75.0	1
1958	14	7	50.0	3	21.4	4
1959	25	7	28.0	17	68.0	1
1960	14	4	28.6	9	64.3	1
Total	65	19		39		7
Percentage of total			29.2		60.0	

| | | > 50% Democrats v. > 50% Republicans | | | | |
| | | With Dems | | With Reps | | |
Year	Party votes	N	%	N	%	No vote
1951	2	0	0.0	2	100.0	0
1952	11	0	0.0	11	100.0	0
1955	8	2	25.0	6	75.0	0
1956	5	0	0.0	4	80.0	1
1958	18	8	44.4	4	22.2	6
1959	49	8	16.3	39	79.6	2
1960	16	5	31.3	10	62.3	1
Total	109	23		76		10
Percentage of total			21.1		69.7	

Source: Author's calculations from Committee on Education and Labor, *Minutes* 1951-60.
      Votes for 1953, 1954, and 1957 were not available.

The degree of support that the chairman provided to each party is
determined from the party votes taken in committee, as reflected in the
minutes of the committee (see table 2.3). Relying on the 70-percent criterion to define a party vote, Barden's high point of siding with his own party
in committee came in 1958, when he cast half of his votes with the Democrats. With the exception of that year, he sided with the Republicans more
frequently than he did with the Democrats on party votes. His average
support of the Democrats throughout his tenure as chairman was just under
30 percent on party votes. He supported the Republicans, on the other
hand, on an average of 60 percent of those roll calls. In 1956, 1958, 1959,

Table 2.3. Barden's Support for Democrats on Committee Party Votes,
1951-1960, Continued

		> 75% Democrats v. > 75% Republicans				
		With Dems		With Reps		
Year	Party votes	N	%	N	%	No vote
1951	0	0	0.0	0	0.0	0
1952	3	0	0.0	3	100.0	0
1955	2	1	50.0	1	50.0	0
1956	3	0	0.0	2	66.7	1
1958	13	6	46.2	3	23.1	4
1959	23	7	30.4	15	65.2	1
1960	13	3	23.1	9	69.2	1
Total	57	17		33		7
Percentage of total			29.8		57.9	

		> 90% Democrats v. > 90% Republicans				
		With Dems		With Reps		
Year	Party votes	N	%	N	%	No vote
1951	0	0	0.0	0	0.0	0
1952	0	0	0.0	0	0.0	0
1955	1	1	100.0	0	0.0	0
1956	2	0	0.0	1	50.0	1
1958	8	4	50.0	1	12.5	3
1959	11	2	18.1	8	72.7	1
1960	4	0	0.0	3	75.0	1
Total	26	7		13		6
Percentage of total			26.9		50.0	

and 1960, the chairman abstained from some party votes, thus bringing down his average support of both parties.

Using an even stricter measure, an examination of committee roll calls on which at least three-fourths of the Democrats lined up against three-fourths of the Republicans, Barden again predominantly supported the Republicans on party votes. Until 1958 he only voted once with the Democrats on party votes. With the exception of that year, he supported the Republicans on about two-thirds or more of the party votes, averaging 60 percent support of their position and 29.2 percent support of the Democrats throughout the 1950s. As shown in table 2.3, from roll calls

Table 2.4. Barden's Votes on the Winning Side in Committee, 1951-1960

Year	Roll calls	Chair wins		Party votes*	Chair wins	
		N	%		N	%
1951	4	4	100.0	0	0	0.0
1952	23	17	73.9	4	3	75.0
1955	10	5	50.0	4	2	50.0
1956	10	6	60.0	4	1	25.0
1958	30	11	36.7	14	7	50.0
1959	71	50	70.4	25	8	32.0
1960	21	6	28.6	14	4	28.6
Total	169	99		65	25	
Percentage of total			58.6			38.5

Source: Compiled from Committee on Education and Labor, *Minutes* 1951-60. Votes for 1953, 1954, and 1957 were not available.

*Party votes are defined as roll-call votes on which at least 70 percent of the Democrats opposed at least 70 percent of the Republicans.

adjudged to be party votes by several criteria, one can conclude that in the committee Barden voted more like the Republicans than like the Democrats. Even by the most stringent criterion, with 90 percent of the members of one party opposed to 90 percent of the other party, he still voted more frequently with the Republicans.

Another characteristic of Barden's orientation toward the committee and the issues before it can be gleaned from the proportion of times that he voted on the prevailing side on committee roll-call votes. Not only how often his side won but how often his side was victorious on party votes is telling. Party votes are here considered those on which at least 70 percent of the Democrats opposed at least 70 percent of the Republicans (see table 2.4). Although Barden voted with the winning side on a fairly healthy proportion of committee roll calls over the decade, it is interesting to note the generally declining percentages of his victories on party votes. Toward the end of the 1950s, when the House leadership increased the size of the committee and began loading it with liberal Democrats, Barden became less and less effective at creating a majority on roll calls by his alliances with Republicans. Even in 1959, when there was an abundance of roll calls and he cast his ballot on the winning side on over 70 percent of them, his wins on party votes declined. The large proportion of victories on all committee votes that year stems from consideration of labor union financial reporting and disclosure legislation, which consumed most of the committee's efforts. There were enough members who wanted labor reform or who were willing to vote for some provisions to keep harsher restrictions from being adopted to give Barden's side the edge. With the exception of 1956 and 1959, Barden's winning record on all committee votes also declined throughout the decade.

Leadership: Institutional versus Personal Resources

Leadership is important because it affects committee structures, operations, atmospheres, and successes, resulting in different focuses and outputs for the committees and, ultimately, different policy outcomes. Different chairmen exercise different leadership techniques. They use their resources in a variety of ways, depending on a host of factors, including the issues, the composition of their committees, the institutional context, and their personalities. Determined to some extent by institutional context, a chairman's leadership is an interaction between his institutionally derived prerogatives and his personal political skills.[6] His institutional orientation can be inferred from the way he uses the means provided by his position in the organization. His use of personal resources can be gauged by his reputation, expertise, and political skills. Each of the three chairmen of the Committee on Education and Labor examined in this study will be evaluated on his use of institutional and personal resources.

One way to approach leadership is through a framework based on the leader's reliance on the institutionally derived resources at his disposal.[7] An analysis of congressional committee leadership should include discussions of the constraints imposed, of the chairman's reliance on his official prerogatives, written and unwritten, and of his use of rewards and sanctions. A discussion of the use of personal resources should focus on his reputation among his peers, both in the committee and in the House, and on his knowledge of the subject at hand and the rules. When discerned, these elements of leadership should help illuminate the conceptually murky linkage between a chairman and his committee members and the implications this relationship has for public policy.

Knowledge of which resources leaders tend to draw on most heavily provides additional understanding of the interactions between leaders and followers, in this case between a House committee chairman and his fellow committee members. It also helps explain the impact of these relationships on committee outputs. A chairman's manner of running his committee can be approached from various angles, but the framework depicting his use of institutional prerogatives and personal resources is one of the most telling. Moreover, other leaders can be studied in the same manner, and their techniques can be compared readily.

One aspect of a chairman's leadership is how he responds to the expectations of him held by other members of his committee. Much of his influence derives from the prerogatives of the position. All chairmen have at their disposal various tools with which to run their committees. Several are spelled out in the House rules, and others, such as seniority, are unwritten norms of the House. In addition, each committee has some say over the powers of its chairman.

During the first ten years after the establishment of the Committee on Education and Labor in 1947, the chairman had seemingly unlimited power over the committee (MacNeil 1963; Galloway 1953a; Clapp 1963; Goodwin 1970).[8] Few constraints were imposed by the House rules or by the Legislative Reorganization Act of 1946. The chairman controlled the establishment of subcommittees, the referral of legislation within the committee, the calling of meetings, and the scheduling of legislation for consideration by the committee. He determined whether and when the committee was to hold hearings and investigations. He had final approval over the lists of witnesses to testify before the committee. He presided at hearings and at committee meetings and had the authority to choose whether or not to recognize people to speak. He controlled the committee funds, authorized committee-related travel, and oversaw the employment and discharge of staff members and the assignment of staff duties. The chairman recommended to the Speaker appointments to conference committees and also acted as the primary manager in those groups. He had the authority to manage committee bills and to control their debate on the floor, whether he favored or opposed them. One of his most important resources was his power over the timing of legislation. There were so many bills referred to the committee that members could not possibly consider them all. The chairman influenced which bills were chosen and when they were discussed.

One of Barden's most effective weapons in his institutional arsenal was the chairman's control over subcommittees. Until the revolt against him in 1957, when the committee adopted rules concerning the establishment of standing subcommittees, Barden ran a centralized committee and appointed few subcommittees. He referred little legislation to those he did appoint. Most of the work was done in full committee, where the chairman could monitor it closely. When the chairman was particularly interested in pursuing legislation, he chaired the subcommittee himself, as he did on aid to federally impacted areas. North Carolina, and Barden's district in particular, had several large military bases. He could serve his district well by making sure that it got at least its fair share of federal aid money. Moreover, he could wield enough influence in the subcommittee to ensure that his provisions maintaining state control and minimizing federal interference were included.

Unlike members of the Committee on Ways and Means (Manley 1967, 119), Education and Labor members were not universally happy with the lack of reliance on subcommittees. There was no long tradition of not having them, as Ways and Means had. Earlier chairmen had appointed and used them. When Barden named subcommittees, he used them selectively and effectively in accordance with his goals. He refused to establish standing subcommittees, preferring to keep committee matters under his thumb. He appointed a few ad hoc units, though they were usually tools for dispensing with unacceptable but popular legislation, particularly in his later years as chairman. He would appoint a sympathetic subcommittee and refer to it legislation that he preferred never see the light of day. He rewarded his friends and ideological cohorts with subcommittee appointments and chairmanships, and thus not all members were afforded the opportunity to serve. By 1957 the committee members were so dissatisfied with the absence of subcommittees that they threatened a rebellion against the chairman if he did not appoint standing subcommittees with fixed jurisdictions. Even after he complied, subcommittees were not used to the satisfaction of the members, who threatened Barden again in the next session, the 86th Congress.

Barden also prevailed by other means, which included his power to call or not to call committee meetings. Notwithstanding the fact that the Legislative Reorganization Act of 1946 mandated regular meeting days with additional meetings to be called by the chair, Education and Labor members voted in 1952 to meet at the call of the chairman. Several years later they reneged. The lack of meetings was one of the most often-heard complaints by Education and Labor members. In an effort to bury legislation that he found disagreeable, Barden called few meetings, thus frustrating members who wanted to consider bills assigned to the committee. Relying on another institutional prerogative of the chairmanship, Barden decided if, when, and where to hold hearings. If they suited his purpose, fine. If they did not, they were never held. By manipulating the witness lists and the time the witnesses had to speak, he managed to stifle a great deal of dissent.

The chairman also controlled the committee's agenda, which was of primary importance to the committee's output. Everything that came before the committee came first to the chairman, who had the authority to decide whether the committee would consider a particular piece of legislation, if it would be referred to a subcommittee, whether to hold hearings on the subject, and the timing of these steps. His power over these choices was significant. So many bills were referred to Education and Labor that the chairman had to make strategic choices. Barden used this prerogative to his fullest advantage, steering the committee in a conservative direction. He pigeonholed much of the legislation he opposed and referred other bills to ad hoc subcommittees composed of members who were not disposed to report them to the full committee.

Another use of the chairman's institutional prerogatives was his control over the appointment and operations of the committee staff. Unlike the staffs hired by the finance committees and others, Education and Labor staff members did not have to be experts on matters within the committee's jurisdiction. They were to serve at the beck and call of the chairman, a tradition that still holds to a large extent in the 1990s. Staff appointments were strictly under the chairman's patronage. Barden hired the few staff members the committee had, keeping the majority staff small. In name they worked for the committee; in reality they worked for the chairman.

Barden capitalized on the norms and expectations that went along with the role of chairman. Making full use of his prerogatives, he ran a tight ship. Little that he opposed ever emerged from the committee intact. If it did, he relied on his friends in high places, such as the House Committee on Rules, to help him. Committee members voted many of these prerogatives to the chairman during the early and mid-1950s, but they began withdrawing their support for them in later years when they thought Barden was abusing his powers. The committee limited his discretion on the creation of sub-committees and on their size and jurisdictions. The rules adopted in 1957 specified the name, size, and jurisdiction of each subcommittee and mandated that all legislation referred to the full committee be referred to the appropriate subcommittees. The rules granted the subcommittees authorization to hold hearings, receive exhibits, hear witnesses, and report back to the full committee. The rules also specified that regular committee meetings be held at least twice each month and otherwise at the call of the chairman. Later, in 1959, members stipulated that the committee could recall legislation from a subcommittee for immediate consideration in the full committee or for referral to another subcommittee. These provisions diminished the effect of the chairman's pigeonholing power.

After the advent of the new rules, Barden still managed to control his committee more than it wanted to be controlled. He maintained the agenda-setting functions, his prerogatives of recognition in committee meetings and nominations to conference committees, and the ability to construct a winning coalition with the help of the Republicans. Even in later years members continued to grant him the power to employ and discharge committee staff members as he saw fit. He used his powers to full capacity.

The characterization of a chairman's institutional leadership is particularly reflected in his use of rewards. Their distribution implies manipulation of circumstances to benefit the needs of others. It also implies some benefit to the dispenser of the rewards. Committee chairmen have few tangible incentives to induce the desired behavior of other members, since they are limited by the constitutional and democratic need to treat members equally. Moreover, chairmen cannot regulate the pay or the job status of committee members in regard to perceived good or poor performance (Cooper 1977). By virtue of their organizational positions, chairmen in the 1950s did have a number of perquisites available. They could reward members with their names on prominent pieces of legislation, with subcommittee chairmanships, with appointments to subcommittees, with conference committee membership, with management of bills on the floor, and with recognition for contributions. Chairmen also controlled committee office space, travel money, and staff support. Barden, it seems, did not use rewards as frequently as some other chairmen did (see Manley 1967, 128-37). He did not subscribe, at least with the committee majority, to the old axiom that honey catches more flies than vinegar. He rewarded his friends with occasional subcommittee chairmanships and, infrequently, with sponsorship of important legislation.

One example of the latter form of reward came in the Landrum-Griffin Act. The committee had voted sixteen to fourteen to report Carl Elliott's bill, which was similar to a Senate labor reform bill but contained over a hundred amendments mostly designed to make the bill less offensive to unions. Liberals condemned it as too harsh, and conservatives denounced it as too weak. Barden requested that the Rules Committee authorize an open rule, thus allowing other bills to be offered as substitutes for the committee bill. He worked closely with members of a joint subcommittee dealing with labor reform to come up with a more stringent labor bill. As his biographer noted, he "maneuvered a committee shattered by divergent views into accepting a bill he did not want in order to get something before the House" (Puryear 1979, 204). He picked junior members Phil Landrum (D-GA) and Robert Griffin (R-MI) to sponsor the bipartisan alternative, but he managed the bill himself on the floor and won handily. Landrum and Griffin had their names on major legislation because of their support for and alliance with the chairman (Puryear 1979, 196-206).

Barden also appointed his friends to subcommittee chairmanships. During one session, Cleveland Bailey (D-WV) headed three subcommittees, and Carl Elliott (D-AL) chaired two. By and large, Barden's subcommittee chairmen were southerners. There were a few exceptions, such as Augustine Kelley (D-PA), Roy Wier (D-MN), Lee Metcalf (D-MT), and Ludwig Teller (D-NY), though most did not chair subcommittees of major import to the chairman. The chairman, however, liked Teller enough to give him a subcommittee on welfare and pension plans in the 85th Congress. One member recalled that "Barden loved Teller. He was an NYU professor who wrote about the Taft-Hartley Act. Barden appointed him to head a task force to investigate labor corruption. Udall and Metcalf destroyed him" (interview).

A chairman's leadership is also reflected in his use of sanctions. Barden withheld, among other things, subcommittee seats as well as chairmanships from his enemies. The best example of this use of power concerned Adam Clayton Powell, Jr. (D-NY), who, as the second-ranking Democrat on the committee, thought he was entitled to a subcommittee chairmanship. With the backing of most of the full committee members, Barden refused to appoint Powell to a subcommittee chairmanship, even though the seniority norm dictated it, and did not appoint him to a subcommittee until the 85th Congress. Barden did issue travel vouchers to Powell to get him out of the way, although he sometimes denied them to others.

In sum, Barden rarely relied on the use of rewards and then only when it suited his personal goals. He may have been thinking of them more as tools than as rewards. Nevertheless, he favored those who supported him and on whom he could rely with subcommittee chairmanships and sponsorship of major legislation. He dispensed these perquisites for political reasons and not because they were well deserved by the recipients. He was also not averse to withholding seemingly deserved rewards when it suited his purposes.

Personal leadership is the other important aspect of a chairman's overall leadership. Although personal resources may be related to the organization, they do not accrue to anyone as a result of being in a leadership position. On the contrary, they may be instrumental in helping the leader attain or retain his position. They are accentuated or diminished by the institutional context in which they are used. Personal power in Congress is shaped by the use of personal resources in managing institutional prerogatives (and by the institutional context). It depends on what constraints the chairman is under, what prerogatives he has at his disposal, and how he employs them. It also depends on his political skills and leanings. The chairman's personal resources include his mastery of the subject matter and the rules, his reputation, and his political skills and goals.

In Congress, as in other organizations, an important element of influence rests on knowledge of the subject matter in a leader's jurisdiction, whether it is substantive, as in the case of standing committees, or procedural or political, as in the case of the House leadership. A chairman's expertise and experience provide him with resources not readily available to other committee members. Hall (1986, 1989) emphasized that experience and expertise reduce the opportunity costs of participating in committee decision making. They provide the chairman with a solid base from which to try to influence others. Several psychologists studying leadership concluded that "group members tend to defer to the perceived expert. Perceived expertness tends to legitimize the leadership role" (Stogdill 1974, 285). Education and Labor's jurisdiction makes it hard for any member to be the chief expert. Everyone knows something about education and has an opinion on it. The same holds true for labor. The issues under this committee do not inspire compromise on technicalities, as does Ways and Means legislation, for example. Education and Labor issues are more clear-cut. Even so, it helps the chairman if he knows his material.

Barden had a lifelong interest in education and already had some expertise by the time he was elected to Congress in 1935. He had pushed for adequate funding for public schools during his tenure in the North Carolina state legislature. In Congress, he was assigned to the Committee on Education, as well as to the Committee on Rivers and Harbors. While the latter proved to be a solid base for serving his district, the Education Committee also gave him the opportunity to benefit the folks back home and the chance to pursue his interest in education. As the former schoolteacher accrued seniority on the Committee on Education, he gained national recognition for his educational achievements, and later he gained notoriety. He championed the cause of North Carolina public schools and the efforts that the state had made to keep them going. He fought to keep from his state the unfair burden of having to compensate for the lack of fiscal efforts by other states to maintain their public school systems. Throughout his career he maintained close contacts with the education establishment back in North Carolina (Puryear 1979). Barden also worked on legislative programs for vocational rehabilitation, his real area of expertise and interest. In 1943 he wrote and aided the passage of the Barden-La Follette Vocational Rehabilitation Act, which emphasized state roles in rendering services to train disabled persons to support themselves. Barden's biographer noted that "throughout his career Barden kept a jealous eye on the administration of the act, insisting upon necessary appropriations and the retention of state control" (Puryear 1979, 45). Many of the education bills referred to the committee resulted in new bills offered by Barden. He gained considerable expertise by having his fingerprints on most of the education legislation to emerge from the committee. He especially left his mark in maintaining state control over education, an area that he strongly believed to be outside the purview of Congress.

Since by organized labor's standards Barden had a perfect voting record on labor issues in his early years in Congress, he was appointed, without asking for the position, to fill the vacancy on the Labor Committee in 1937. A hard worker throughout his service, Barden made an about-face from prolabor to antilabor stances. He participated in the shaping of the Wagner Act (49 Stat. 449), the Taft-Hartley Act (P.L. 80-101), the Landrum-Griffin Act (P.L. 86-257), the Fair Labor Standards Act (P.L. 75-718), and many others. In his early years in Congress Barden also accumulated expertise and national attention in the arena of labor policy when he switched from being a strong supporter of New Deal legislation to an antilabor stance. He opposed the president on exemptions in the Fair

Labor Standards Act as he tried to secure broader exemptions for agricultural workers (Puryear 1979, 29).

While Barden certainly could be considered an expert on both education and labor legislation, he did not have the reputation as a technical expert enjoyed by Wilbur Mills on Ways and Means. Mills knew the tax code better than just about anyone else and could run rings around most of his fellow committee members, who frequently deferred to his expertise (Manley 1967, 112-15). Barden, though, did have extensive knowledge of the legislation that came under the jurisdiction of his committee. Most of the Education and Labor Committee's legislation was not of the extreme technical nature that Ways and Means bills were, so it was not necessary for Barden to master the details to the same extent that Mills did or for his committee members to defer to his leadership.

Barden also had an impressive mastery of the procedural rules of the House. He knew them backward and forward and was known for being able to use them to attain his goals—generally, thwarting liberal legislation. Because of his adroit manipulation of the rules, he was known as a master of parliamentary maneuver and played the role to the hilt.

A telling element of a chairman's personal leadership is his reputation among his colleagues. Barden was highly respected in the House for his ability to achieve his purposes and for his high principles. He had many friends, especially among the southerners and the leadership. He relied on these allies to support him when he could no longer contain an issue in his committee. Some of his powerful friends in the House, however, disagreed with Barden enough to stack his committee against him.

His colleagues on Education and Labor admired him for his persistence, for his principles, for his ability to manipulate things to his best interest, for his knowledge of procedure, and for his prowess in building coalitions, but many did not much like him (interviews). Not that he was an unlikable person—many people said he was absolutely charming. But he frustrated too many people to be popular among his fellow committee members. In fact, some members downright deplored him. A staff member recalled, "Barden just drove Adam Powell wild" (interview). Another former staff member, on the other hand, characterized Barden as "great, jovial, and a good chairman. He was pretty good to his staff, but he disagreed with Fred Hussey [the staff director] once in a while. Barden was lots of fun" (interview).

Barden's adroit manipulation of rules and circumstances earned him high regard. Even his staunchest opponents recognized great political feats when they saw them. His last committee meeting as chairman provided just one example of why he commanded grudging respect among his fellow committee members. Trying to keep the liberal committee members from offering a Calendar Wednesday resolution to have the House consider common site picketing and minimum wage, he arranged for Carl Elliott to drag on for hours on a seemingly minor bill, much to the frustration and anguish of other members. According to Puryear, "Whenever Elliott showed signs of running down, Barden asked him carefully phrased questions with long pauses for meditation in order to get just the right word. The chairman brushed aside points of order, parliamentary inquiries, demands for votes and motions to adjourn until the next day" (1979, 208). Barden had the timing figured out so that when Elliott finished, the House would be in session. He adjourned the committee without ever getting around to the liberal proposals, thus sealing their fate. One of his harshest critics, Frank Thompson, Jr., (D-NJ), admitted that Barden had carried off a masterful political move. Later Chairman Carl Perkins also confessed to a grudging respect for Barden's abilities and his canniness at running the committee to suit his own needs.

Committee chairmen, in particular, have at their disposal numerous ways to exert negative influence. When chairmen successfully obstruct legislation, they are using their resources in a negative manner, as they are when they fail to use the seemingly appropriate rewards. Some do so more than others. Chairman Mills of Ways and Means, for example, rarely took advantage of his many opportunities to block or adulterate legislation or to oppose his committee outright (Manley 1967, 137). Barden, on the other hand, was a master of negative influence. He relied a great deal on the negative use of resources to achieve his purposes. Manley (1967, 137) cited him as the prime example of a chairman who used his authority to provoke extreme hostility, tempered by grudging respect, from his fellow members.

Failing to call meetings to prevent legislation from being discussed or reported was a frequently employed negative practice. A Capitol Hill observer described the situation: "Graham Barden of North Carolina . . . ruled the House Education and Labor Committee with an arbitrariness that approached tyranny. Barden, a conservative whose committee members often saw the country's legislative needs differently from him, at times simply blocked passage of all legislation under his jurisdiction by refusing to call any sessions of his committee. With the committee unable to act, the legislation referred to the committee died a-borning" (MacNeil 1963, 172-73). When obliged to hold a meeting, Barden rounded up his Republican and southern Democratic allies to speak on matters of little importance or on anything but what the liberals were trying to have the committee consider. In effect, he encouraged filibustering. His treatment of his last committee meeting in 1960 where he effectively buried common site picketing legislation provides just one example of his negative leadership. His adjourning committee meetings for lack of a quorum when he knew that sufficient members were on their way provides another.

Barden's refusal to rely on subcommittees is also an example of his negative use of institutional resources. Had his failure to appoint subcommittees ensured that all members had a say in what went into the legislation or had it promoted unity or played down differential influence among members, his use of this power would have been positive. Barden used his authority, however, to keep legislation he believed undesirable from being considered and reported. He made sure that it was taken up in the full committee if it was considered at all. He declined to use subcommittees so that he could capitalize on the rampant dissent among members on most issues, playing up their differences to prevent them from forming winning coalitions. His actions enhanced centralization and facilitated his dominance of the committee.

Subcommittee assignments were another negative tool available to Barden because of his position. On several occasions he stacked subcommittees with opponents of a particular type of legislation, as when he named a subcommittee with anti–federal aid to education proclivities to consider just such legislation. When he created a subcommittee for some purpose or another, he made sure that he or his allies were present to protect his interests. Ironically, the House leadership used this same strategy against Barden when they assigned a host of liberals and no Democratic southerners to the committee beginning in 1956.

Withholding rewards was another aspect of Chairman Barden's negative leadership. He used almost every available tactic to ensure that his preferences prevailed, including denying what should have been granted, by tradition, to other members. Powell, denied both a subcommittee chairmanship and subcommittee membership, was an object of this negative exercise of power.

Barden also used his committee as a tool for intimidating opponents or for uncovering perceived wrongdoing. He participated actively in investigations of labor unions. In 1951, shortly after assuming the committee's top spot, he created and chaired a subcommittee to investigate allegations of racketeering, waste, and conspiracy to violate the Taft-Hartley Act by the Atomic Energy Commission, E. I. du Pont de Nemours and Company, the U.S. Employment Service, and labor unions affiliated with the American Federation of Labor on the Savannah River Atomic Energy Plant (see Puryear 1979, 175-76). The chairman also served on the 83d Congress's Subcommittee to Investigate Welfare and Pension Plans. For several years he doggedly pursued investigations of abuses by and proposals to abolish the Wage Stabilization Board and took advantage of all opportunities to curtail the powers of organized labor. In the eyes of the liberal, prolabor members, Barden made full use of his prerogatives in curbing legislation favorable to unions and in enforcing as many sanctions on them as he could muster.

Barden's negative leadership was apparent in instances when he walked out of committee meetings in frustration, as he did several times during the consideration of federal aid to education legislation. He left a committee meeting during a discussion on the National Defense Education Act of 1958 (P.L. 85-864), exasperated over the issue of federal scholarships. Although they could not act officially without the chairman, members continued deliberations. On another occasion, the chairman walked off the floor of the House during consideration of a school aid bill that he was managing. The subcommittee chairman had to take up where Barden had left off (Puryear 1979, 127).

Barden's negative use of personal resources often was evident in behind-the-scenes maneuvering. When his committee reported a bill over his opposition, he consulted his friends on other committees to help block it. Friendship with Howard W. Smith (D-VA), chairman of the Committee on Rules, provided Barden with many opportunities to affect the fate of legislation after it had passed his committee and before it went to the floor. On occasion, instead of doing everything he could do or was authorized to do by his committee to ensure passage of reported legislation, Barden asked Judge Smith not to issue a rule for a bill, thus precluding its consideration on the floor (Puryear 1979). This became the fate of several general aid to education bills. At other times, Barden colluded with conservatives on the Rules Committee to get an open rule for an Education and Labor bill, thereby ensuring that it could be amended beyond recognition on the floor or replaced entirely with legislation more to his own liking. This strategy determined the fate of the legislation that eventually became the Landrum-Griffin Act.

Capitalizing on his friendship with Judge Smith, Barden secured both an open rule and, later, no rule on a school construction bill sponsored by Frank Thompson in 1960. When the Education and Labor Committee bypassed the chairman and reported the bill, Barden requested his allies on the Rules Committee not to issue a rule. Two months later, after Education and Labor members threatened to circumvent Rules by use of Calendar Wednesday, Barden asked for an open rule. The bill was amended on the floor and passed, one of the first general aid to education bills ever to make it through the House. After the Senate passed its own education bill, opponents tried another tactic. This time, Smith and his allies refused to allow the bill to go to conference with the Senate, thus sealing its fate (see Puryear 1979, 135-37).

Barden profited from the prerogatives of his position, from his ability to manipulate rewards and inducements, from his expertise on the rules and on the subject matter, and from his political acumen. He combined them, by application, into a negative leadership. Realizing the futility of trying to convince the liberal members of his committee that labor unions were inherently evil and that the federal government should not interfere with the rights of the states to determine their own education policies, Barden made use of the strategies he deemed appropriate. Since his fellow Democrats would not see the light as he thought it should be seen, he set about to do everything to prevent their wattage from being more powerful than his.

Barden's mission was to prevent liberal legislation from being enacted, and his tool was the Committee on Education and Labor. While the chairman had a majority coalition at his disposal, his mission also became the committee's function. Through manipulation of the committee, he successfully obstructed federal aid to education for years and prevented or diluted proposals favorable to organized labor. Moreover, he used his committee as a vehicle for protecting states' rights. His idea of good public policy in education was to leave it to the states, and he used all the accessories that came with the chairmanship to fulfill his mission. Barden subscribed to the principle that "he never knew the Republic to be endangered by a bill that was not passed" (Puryear 1979, viii).

Barden's Leadership in Retrospect

For most of Barden's chairmanship, the institutional context, particularly the laxity of the rules in the 1950s, allowed chairmen to act autocratically and provided the instruments for them to do so. Barden had a wide variety of institutionally derived resources at his disposal. The combination of the wealth of prerogatives and his personal orientation led to a negative approach. Another individual might have used the powerful chairmanship to promote a positive or active agenda. Barden's leadership, in large part, was the result of his personality, orientation, and political beliefs. These traits led him to oppose a positive agenda and instead to focus on preventive measures and to use his resources accordingly. When Barden repeatedly thwarted the will of the House majority and stultified the democratic process, members reacted by putting stringent limits on him, thereby taking away some of his means. As his institutional resources diminished, the chairman drew increasingly on his personal reserves, such as his own political skills and his friendships with members of the Rules Committee, to secure his ends effectively.

Committees lagged their parent chamber in leadership evolution. As two scholars noted of House leadership, "by 1940, the personal, political skills of the leadership, rather than its sources of institutional power, had become the critical determinant of the fate of party programs" (Cooper and Brady 1981a, 420). In the 1950s institutionally derived powers still were more important than were personal resources in committee leadership, although the latter were not inconsequential. Not until the institutional inducements were removed in the late 1950s did personal resources begin to emerge as the primary aspect of leadership among committee chairmen.

3

The Committee during
the Powell Years

Adam Clayton Powell, Jr., Democrat of NY, held an entirely different
hand in the game of leadership than did his predecessor, and he played the
game in an atmosphere entirely different from that surrounding Graham
Barden. The political focus of the nation had largely shifted from international affairs to domestic programs, promoting Education and Labor
proposals to the forefront of the president's agenda. Under the Powell
chairmanship, Education and Labor reformed its committee structure,
enabling it to accommodate the newfound enthusiasm for matters under its
domain and to facilitate the rush to enact the new liberal program. Powell's
cards also included a committee generally more inclined to agree with him
than to block him. The committee environment was conducive to his
leadership—at first.

Setting

Powell assumed the chairmanship of the Committee on Education and
Labor in an era of great social reform.[1] A number of factors converged to
make it possible. The new Democratic administrations under John F.
Kennedy and Lyndon B. Johnson brought new emphasis on social welfare
programs, including education, labor, and manpower. In addition, the
conservative and obstructionist Graham A. Barden departed the committee
and Congress, thereby removing a significant stumbling block to progressive legislation. Furthermore, the liberals who had been assigned to the
committee by the party leadership to outvote Barden were entrenched by
the time that Powell became chairman.

    The newly elected Kennedy administration provided a prominent vehicle for education and labor issues in the early 1960s. Although the sagging economy was a major problem, the president actively promoted federal aid to education and antipoverty initiatives. Other liberal programs, doomed throughout the Eisenhower years, finally had a chance under the Kennedy administration. These included a number of important initiatives: increases in the minimum wage and in vocational education, loans and grants for school construction, broadening of Social Security benefits, major housing legislation, manpower training programs, anti–water pollution measures, subsidies for economically distressed areas of the country, voting rights, and urban renewal.

During Powell's tenure as chairman, other obstacles to the long-delayed liberal social agenda were removed. Several legislative compromises, formulated in the early to mid-1960s, enabled the passage of federal aid to education, which had been stymied for so many years (with the exception of the National Defense Education Act of 1958 [NDEA, P.L. 85-864]). The *Brown* v. *Board of Education* cases and the Little Rock crisis had smoothed the way. The Civil Rights Act of 1964 (P.L. 88-352), which contained guarantees blocked by southern conservatives for decades, finally was enacted. It prohibited the use of federal funds for segregated facilities and gave the federal government the power to sue for school desegregation, effectively removing one of the major obstacles to federal aid to education.

A committee with little or no major legislation to its credit as it began the decade of the 1960s, Education and Labor became one of the more important House committees because of its jurisdiction over issues that not only were prominent on the national agenda but that had a prayer of passing. The committee faced many of the same issues that had divided it for the preceding decade or so, but few of the structural and policy obstacles remained. The adoption and enforcement of legal barriers to segregation as well as institutional changes removed most of the racial hurdles.

The committee's menu included a wealth of education issues in the Powell years. The major impediment to federal aid remaining was the question of whether to fund private and religious schools. Under Powell, carefully formulated compromises involving education associations and church representatives, as well as members of Congress, diluted the religious dispute. After lengthy debate, a compromise aimed at providing aid to students rather than to schools resulted in the Elementary and Secondary Education Act of 1965 (ESEA, P.L. 89-10). By the end of Powell's chairmanship, neither race nor religion was sufficiently controversial to block national education legislation, a marked change from the previous decade.

Other education measures were somewhat less controversial. In addition to the reauthorization of the NDEA, in 1963-64 the committee considered medical school construction and student loan programs that had been in dispute for the previous decade. Moreover, via the committee, Congress authorized grants and loans for the construction of college buildings and for expanded vocational education programs designed to deal with civil rights and unemployment problems. Later, in 1965-66, prominent committee and national issues included elementary and secondary education, higher education, vocational rehabilitation, and library services.

Bridging education and labor, poverty issues rose to the forefront of the political agenda early in Powell's chairmanship. Poverty policies begun during the Kennedy administration had been propelled to national attention primarily as a result of Michael Harrington's book *The Other America* (1962). When Lyndon Johnson assumed the presidency after the assassination of President Kennedy in November 1963, Congress proceeded with his agenda rapidly and successfully. In his first State of the Union address, President Johnson called for an unconditional declaration of "war on poverty" in the United States (Johnson 1964). Large portions of the resulting "poverty program" came under the jurisdiction of Education and Labor.

The civil rights issues that dominated much of the domestic political scene in 1963-64 contributed to the momentum of the War on Poverty. Blacks pushed for equal rights in voting, employment, education, and housing. Thousands demonstrated for equality in Birmingham, Alabama, in Washington, D.C., and in hundreds of other cities across the country. At the same time, both Republicans and liberal Democrats worked for strong civil rights bills to combat racial discrimination in all areas of life. Growing awareness of the problems facing blacks also helped focus attention on the plight of the poor in America.

As had been the case during most of the previous decade, education issues largely eclipsed labor issues during Powell's chairmanship. Since Congress had enacted a strong labor reform bill in 1959, labor-management questions generally were subjugated to other problems in the 1960s. Minimum-wage legislation, however, blocked for so long under Barden, was the first item on Powell's agenda in 1961-62. The new law raised the minimum wage to $1.25 and subsequently, in the 89th Congress (1965-66), to $1.60 an hour. Amendments to the Davis-Bacon Act, which required payment of the prevailing wage in government contracts, also were considered, as were several bills relating to migratory labor. Coal mine safety, the Federal Employees Compensation Act, and manpower development and training also occupied the committee's time.

Congress defeated committee and administration proposals for the repeal of Taft-Hartley Act provisions allowing states to enact laws banning the union shop. President Johnson's troubles over the increasing money and casualty pit in Vietnam affected other legislation. Eventually, the War on Poverty, as well as several other Great Society programs, fell victim to the increased attention to the high cost of involvement in the other war.

Composition of the Committee

The demographic composition of the committee, new members and seniority, and the ideological leanings of the members are all important determinants of committee development and outcomes. They also affect the
success of the leadership in carrying out the committee function. Compared
with what it had been in the Barden era, the committee membership under
Powell was relatively stable. That is not to say, however, that it did not
change at all. Although the major changes had occurred in the mid- and late
1950s, the membership from 1961 to 1966 shifted slightly away from the
Middle Atlantic states and the South and increasingly toward the East
North Central states. The dominant regional factions alternated between
the Middle Atlantic and the East North Central states. Representation
from the West North Central states decreased slightly, and membership
from Pacific and External states grew a bit after the 87th Congress (see
tables 3.1 and 3.2).

Southern membership never reached the proportion it had been in the
Barden era. It increased by one member during Powell's chairmanship after
a decline at the beginning. Even a slight southern increase was surprising
given that few southern congressmen (and few others) wanted to serve on a
committee chaired by a black man, especially one as flamboyant as Powell,
whose actions many considered irresponsible (Hickey and Edwin 1963,
133; Wilson 1960, 367). Although the relatively conservative Phil Landrum
(D-GA) remained on Education and Labor until he transferred to Ways and
Means in 1965, he was the only southerner who also had served on the
committee under Barden. New southern appointees included Ralph Scott
(D-NC), first assigned to the committee in 1961 despite his opposition to
nearly everything appearing liberal, and Sam Gibbons (D-FL), assigned in
1963, who had relatively favorable labor ratings.[2]

The shift in the regional bases of its members had important ramifications for the measures the committee considered. The issues under its
jurisdiction were not amenable to compromise for most members and
especially not for southerners, who would be forced into declaring positions on federal aid to education and on the racial and religious issues that
accompanied it. Several highly conservative Education and Labor southerners had been replaced, largely by more liberal northerners and west-
erners, during the later Barden years, softening the opposition to this
proposal.

Some of the geographic changes in committee membership were reflected in the Democratic representation, which shifted to the North and
East under Powell. As Democrats gained members from the Middle Atlantic, New England, East North Central, and Pacific states, they decreased
their proportion of members from the South and nearly decimated their

Table 3.1. Regional Composition of the Committee in 1960s (percentages)

Region	Congress		
	87th	88th	89th
	Full committee		
New England	6.5	0.0	3.2
Middle Atlantic	32.3	25.8	29.0
East North Central	25.8	29.0	22.6
West North Central	9.7	6.6	6.5
South	6.5	9.7	12.9
Border	6.5	9.7	6.5
Mountain	0.0	0.0	0.0
Pacific	12.9	16.1	16.1
External	0.0	3.2	3.2
	E & L Democrats		
New England	5.3	0.0	4.8
Middle Atlantic	36.8	31.6	33.3
East North Central	15.8	15.8	19.0
West North Central	5.3	0.0	0.0
South	10.5	15.8	9.5
Border	10.5	10.5	9.5
Mountain	0.0	0.0	0.0
Pacific	15.8	21.1	19.0
External	0.0	5.3	4.8
	E & L Republicans		
New England	8.3	0.0	0.0
Middle Atlantic	25.0	16.7	18.2
East North Central	41.7	50.0	36.4
West North Central	16.7	16.7	18.2
South	0.0	0.0	18.2
Border	0.0	8.3	0.0
Mountain	0.0	0.0	0.0
Pacific	8.3	8.3	9.1
External	0.0	0.0	0.0

Source: Author's calculations from data in Inter-University Consortium for Political and Social Research. The sums of some columns are not exactly 100.0 percent because of rounding.

representation from the West North Central states. The proportion of Democrats from Border states also decreased. Republican membership, on the other hand, shifted heavily away from the Middle Atlantic and Pacific states toward the center of the country, to the East North Central states. In the Powell years, the number of Republicans from the East North Central states was double the number of Republicans from the previously prevalent

Table 3.2. Percentage Change in Average Regional Representation from
Barden's Tenure to Powell's, 1950s-1960s

Region	Full E & L	E & L Dems	E & L Reps
East North Central	+ 11.7	+ 10.8	+ 16.2
Pacific	+ 5.9	+ 11.3	− 2.9
New England	+ 1.1	+ 1.0	+ 1.2
Middle Atlantic	− 7.6	+ 2.2	− 22.7
South	− 3.0	− 10.1	+ 5.9
West North Central	− 1.6	− 8.1	+ 9.3
Border	− 0.2	− 2.0	+ 1.2

Source: Compiled from Inter-University Consortium for Political and Social Research.

Middle Atlantic states. Republicans also increased the average proportion of their membership from the South, as well as from the West North Central and Border states.

The proportion of new members fluctuated slightly but remained relatively stable across the Barden and Powell years. Chairman Powell always had to deal with a significant number of new members—between 25.8 percent and 32.3 percent of the membership (see table 3.3). About 30 percent of the committee's members who served under Powell first arrived on the committee during his stewardship, an average of 9.3 members per term. This figure is quite similar to the percentage of new members named during the 1950s, averaging 9 new members per term during the Barden years.

Almost 68 percent of the members first assigned to the committee during the Powell years were freshmen. Freshmen made up 62.5 to 70 percent of each class of new committee members, constituting an average of about a fifth of the committee each session, slightly more than did two-term members. Other members came from committees such as Post Office and Civil Service, Government Operations, Interior and Insular Affairs, and House Administration. Some surrendered their assignments on other committees, while other members held dual assignments. The influx of new members and, particularly, of freshmen meant that the committee had a new chance to consider progressive legislation that had been bottled up by Barden's capitalizing on disagreements for a decade. Furthermore, new blood and, ostensibly, new ideas could be brought to the arena.

The new members filled vacancies created by defeat at the polls, appointment or election to another office, or transfer to another committee. It seems that a substantial portion of the members used this committee in one way or another to get somewhere else—to the Senate, the presidency, the cabinet, or a governorship. In addition to the few who ran for the Senate, some other members considered themselves transients on Education and Labor. They really did not intend to stay. They just filled the need

Table 3.3. Seats, New Members, and Freshmen, 1961-1966

		Number								
		All members			New members			Freshmen		
Congress	Year	Full	Dems	Reps	Full	Dems	Reps	Full	Dems	Reps
87th	1961-62	31	19	12	8	4	4	5	1	4
88th	1963-64	31	19	12	10	6	4	7	5	2
89th	1965-66	31	21	10	10	6	4	7	5	2
	Total	93	59	34	28	16	12	19	11	8
	Mean	31.0	19.7	11.3	9.3	5.3	4.0	6.3	3.7	2.7

		Percentage					
		New members			Freshmen		
		Full	Dems	Reps	Full	Dems	Reps
87th	1961-62	25.8	21.1	33.3	16.1	5.3	33.3
88th	1963-64	32.3	31.6	33.3	22.6	26.3	16.7
89th	1965-66	32.3	28.6	40.0	22.6	23.8	20.0

Sources: Author's calculations from Committee on Education and Labor, *Calendar* 1961-66; *Congressional Directory* 1959-66.

for bodies on the committee until they had gained enough seniority and put in enough time to be rewarded with their first-choice assignments: Appropriations, Ways and Means, Rules, Agriculture, or some other more highly sought committee (interviews).

An average of almost 27 percent of the committee membership left the committee after each Congress (see table 3.4). Since the Republicans seemed to draft more members for service on what was seen to be an unprofitable committee, it is not surprising that they left at higher rates than did the Democrats. At least a third of the Republicans did not return to the committee after each term. Presumably this high rate of departure could be attributed in part to heavy Republican losses in the Democratic landslide in 1964 and the resultant new vacancies on other committees. But interestingly, more Republican committee members suffered defeat in the 1962 elections, when the party picked up two House seats, than in the 1964 elections, when the Republicans lost thirty-eight seats. Only one Education and Labor Republican was beaten in 1964, and one transferred to another committee. Two others ran for the Senate and lost that year.

Nevertheless, committee Republicans suffered a higher rate of defeat than did the Democrats. No committee Democrats were defeated in the 1966 elections, when the Republicans gained forty-seven House seats at Democratic expense. The rate of defeat among those who left the commit-

Table 3.4. Percentage of Members Who Left after Each Congress, 1961-1966

Congress	Year	Full	Dems	Reps
87th	1961-62	32.3	31.6	33.3
88th	1963-64	22.6	15.8	33.3
89th	1965-66	25.8	19.0	40.0

Source: Compiled from Committee on Education and Labor, Calendar 1961-66.

tee during or after the 1961-67 period was slightly lower than the 1950s rate of defeat, 31.1 percent.

During the Powell years, transfers to other committees accounted for the loss of 36 percent of the members. Four Democrats went to Appropriations, one to Ways and Means, and one to Agriculture, and one sacrificed his seat for assignment to two other committees. For the 1961-67 period, only two Republicans transferred: one went to Rules and one gave up his Education and Labor seat to devote full time to his duties on Foreign Affairs.

It is interesting to note that the four members who opted for Appropriations transferred from a committee that had a reputation in the House for having a partisan and contentious membership to one that recruited members who, according to Masters (1961, 239-41) and Fenno (1973, 20), had "a responsible legislative style." House leadership, therefore, seemed to reinforce the tradition of contentiousness and partisanship of Education and Labor, not only by assigning highly partisan and committed members to it but by removing the responsible and ostensibly moderating members by naming them to other committees. Three of these four members had spent only one term on Education and Labor. Perhaps the leadership wanted to get them to Appropriations before they had a chance to be corrupted completely by the partisan ways of Powell's fiefdom, or perhaps Education and Labor was only a holding tank during Powell's chairmanship. Only one committee member (a Republican) had transferred to Appropriations in the preceding decade.

Fenno remarked that "Education and Labor does little to alter the image of a lopsidedly liberal Democratic committee heavily dependent on its liberal Democratic coalition allies" (1973, 78-79). This reputation was earned in the 1950s when Speaker Sam Rayburn, in the hope of one day being able to outvote Chairman Barden, infiltrated the apparent bastion of conservatism with liberals. Organized labor's informal but traditional role in the selection process for Democratic members also contributed to the influx. The liberalization of the committee membership that had begun during the Barden years continued during Powell's tenure, and the magnitude of the ideological differences between House and committee members increased. Committee members were substantially more liberal than the House as a whole. Writing about committees during this period, Fenno noted that "control of the selection process by organized labor and party leaders has produced a markedly unrepresentative committee—a 'stacked' committee as its members call it on the Democratic side" (1973, 74).

The committee's ideological cleavages were aggravated by House Republicans' use of the assignment process in their attempts to deadlock the committee and prevent the reporting of liberal legislation. The two-to-one Democratic majority often made such efforts futile, however. Not one of the Education and Labor bills enacted in the 87th, 88th, and 89th Congresses was sponsored by a Republican. Nevertheless, actions by both parties provided fodder for disputes and made compromises difficult.

Ideological differences are reflected in the liberal-conservative continuum ratings calculated by the liberal Americans for Democratic Action (ADA) and Committee on Political Education (COPE) and the conservative Americans for Constitutional Action (ACA) (see table 3.5).[3] The most telling statistics are the differences between House and committee averages on the interest group scales (see table 3.6). The comparisons indicate how representative the committee members were of their House colleagues. Throughout the early and mid-1960s, committee Democrats, according to these measures, consistently voted the liberal position more than did House Democrats. They topped their House colleagues on both the ADA and COPE scores and lagged on favorable ACA scores. The most notable difference came in 1966, when Democratic committee members averaged 26 points higher on the ADA scores than did House members and about 15 points lower on the conservative-oriented ACA scores.

Committee Republicans, on the other hand, were not quite so unrepresentative of House Republicans, although the interest group scores do not bear out Fenno's assertion that Republicans were "a faithful replica of their party colleagues in the House" (1973, 74). Their scores averaged in the more conservative direction than did those of their House colleagues for the 87th and 88th Congresses, with the largest Powell-era disparity (10.1 on the COPE rating in 1963-64) showing committee members more conservative than House Republicans at the height of the presidential election season. House Republicans scored 23.6 on labor's COPE scale, while committee Republicans mustered only 13.5. Committee Republicans took a slightly more liberal bent in the 89th Congress, scoring higher than their House colleagues in the 1966 ADA and 1965-66 COPE scores and lower in the 1966 ACA ratings. This deviation may have resulted from a backlash against conservative Republicans in the 1964 elections. Or it could have been a function of the issues that finally reached the congressional agenda.

Despite its ideological differences, the committee managed to reach compromises on several pieces of Great Society social legislation in the 89th

Table 3.5. Interest Group Scores, 1961-1966

	ADA Scores			
	1962	1963-64	1966	
HR Dems	68.8	69.0	56.8	Mean
	31.6	29.3	34.8	SD
	261	252	297	N
E & L Dems	88.3	82.7	82.8	Mean
	21.0	20.8	20.8	SD
	18	19	21	N
HR Reps	23.8	15.7	10.5	Mean
	26.1	18.9	17.6	SD
	175	175	134	N
E & L Reps	20.7	12.0	16.5	Mean
	21.7	11.9	28.0	SD
	14	12	10	N
	COPE Scores			
	1961-62	1963-64	1965-66	
HR Dems	74.9	76.5	70.5	Mean
	30.4	30.2	36.6	SD
	264	251	297	N
E & L Dems	90.9	90.0	89.2	Mean
	18.9	19.8	21.9	SD
	19	19	21	N
HR Reps	12.7	23.6	11.6	Mean
	19.1	21.1	22.8	SD
	173	176	134	N
E & L Reps	5.2	13.5	16.1	Mean
	7.1	9.8	30.7	SD
	12	12	10	N
	ACA Scores			
	1961-62	1957-64	1966	
HR Dems	22.5	21.5	28.8	Mean
	27.7	24.6	29.3	SD
	263	252	296	N
E & L Dems	9.4	10.1	13.6	Mean
	16.6	15.4	17.7	SD
	19	19	21	N
HR Reps	75.8	80.1	77.0	Mean
	17.6	17.2	17.2	SD
	172	176	134	N
E & L Reps	81.1	85.3	73.4	Mean
	15.5	12.0	21.5	SD
	12	12	10	N

Source: Author's calculation from *Congressional Quarterly Weekly Report* 1961-66. N is the number of members whose votes were included in the calculations.

Table 3.6. Difference between Mean Interest Group Scores: House Members versus Education and Labor Members, 1950s-1960s

Group	Year	Dems	Reps
AFL	1947-52	+0.2	−6.5
AFL-CIO	1947-56	+2.7	−8.8
CIO	1951-52	+1.5	−10.5
ADA	1951-52	+3.0	−11.7
Labor	1953-54	+6.4	−2.5
COPE	1959-60	+17.0	−4.4
ADA	1960	+16.6	−0.5
ADA	1962	+19.5	−3.1
ADA	1964	+13.7	−3.7
ADA	1966	+26.0	+6.0
COPE	1961-62	+16.0	−7.5
COPE	1963-64	+13.5	−10.1
COPE	1965-66	+18.7	+4.5
ACA	1957-59	−6.2	+4.1
ACA	1961-62	−13.1	+5.3
ACA	1957-64	−11.4	+5.2
ACA	1966	−15.2	−3.6

Source: Compiled from *Congressional Quarterly Weekly Report* 1950-66.

The + signifies that committee members had higher average scores than did their House counterparts. The − signifies that the committee mean was less than the House mean. For AFL, CIO, Labor, ADA, and COPE scores, the + indicates that committee members were more liberal than House members; for ACA scores, the reverse is true.

Congress. Some committee Republicans voted with committee Democrats on long-standing controversial issues, including federal aid to education. The committee as a whole was more liberal than the House in the 89th Congress. This unrepresentativeness boded ill for earning the trust of the House membership and for carrying the committee's bills on the floor.

Given the liberal character of the majority of the committee during Powell's chairmanship, it is not surprising that many other House members looked for ways to sabotage or to dilute the committee bills. The Committee on Rules provided one such tool. It locked up liberal committee bills in the early 1960s, stifling three major education bills in the 87th Congress. In addition, it issued open rules for several other pieces of legislation, enabling them to be amended severely on the floor.

Voting Patterns

Characterized as a committee with zero-sum issues and distinct ideological cleavages (Hinckley 1975), Education and Labor earned its reputation for being one of the most contentious and least unified subunits of the House. Rampant partisanship, exceeding levels of the Barden years, characterized it during the early and mid-1960s. Interparty unity reached all-time lows at the same time that party cohesion was apparent in most aspects of committee operations, particularly in roll-call voting. Party conflict was high, markedly more so than it was in the House.

Although the party-unity measures showed only lukewarm support for partisan alignments, the Rice Index Scores did not. On party-unity measures, the Republicans generally did not seem to fit the image of a committee renowned for its high partisanship. They had lower average scores than did all House Republicans in the 87th and 89th Congresses. According to the Rice Index Scores, however, committee Republicans acted in a highly partisan fashion, even more so than did the Democrats. Issues not under the jurisdiction of Education and Labor, as well as election returns, perhaps inspired a relatively high rate of defections among committee Republicans on the floor, since the same patterns are not apparent in committee voting. Committee Democrats, on the other hand, lived up to their reputation as being more partisan than the average Democratic House member. Their party-unity scores topped those of House Democrats for all three Congresses, as they had for the terms during Barden's tenure. Their Rice Index Scores also exhibited a high degree of party cohesion.

Party-unity scores based on House floor votes provide a gauge of the degree of partisanship in the House environment, as well as a measure of intraparty consensus among committee members. Average scores of committee members are compared with those of all House members in an attempt to show the extent of partisan voting by committee members versus voting on the floor and whether committee members were, in fact, representative of the entire body (see table 3.7). For a committee with a reputation for being so partisan, it is interesting to note that while committee Democrats averaged higher party-unity scores than did their House counterparts for all three terms, committee Republicans had lower average scores than did their House colleagues during the 87th and 89th Congresses and higher scores in the 88th. The differences, however, were small. Committee Democrats did surpass the minimum threshold (70 percent) for party voting as gauged by their average party-unity scores in all three terms. The Republicans only did so in the 88th Congress.

Large proportions of roll calls in the Committee on Education and Labor did not meet the 70-percent criterion for minimum intracommittee cohesion, as gauged by Rice Index Scores (see table 3.8). Only 19.6 to 30.6 percent of the votes qualified in the three Congresses. The least conflictual term was the second session of the 87th, in 1962, when half of the votes met the minimum standards. That year, at least 70 percent of the members voted together on five measures: the elimination of federal funding for

Table 3.7. Party-Unity Scores, 1961-1966

	Congress			
	87th	88th	89th	
Chairman Powell	61.0	44.0	63.0	
HR Dems	70.0	69.1	62.5	Mean
	20.1	21.9	25.1	SD
	59.4	59.2	48.0	% > 70
E & L Dems	79.7	74.5	76.0	Mean
	13.6	17.0	21.5	SD
	83.3	68.5	71.4	% > 70
HR Reps	70.3	71.2	67.8	Mean
	17.5	17.2	16.9	SD
	57.7	62.8	52.2	% > 70
E & L Reps	66.6	75.1	63.2	Mean
	25.1	12.2	17.1	SD
	50.0	75.0	50.0	% > 70

Source: Compiled from Congressional Quarterly Almanac 1961-67.

segregated institutions of higher education, amendments to the prevailing wage sections of the Davis-Bacon Act, extension of the child labor provisions of the Fair Labor Standards Act of 1938, the manpower training act, and the production and distribution of educational films for the deaf.

On the other hand, in 1964, when the poverty program was under consideration, only about 11 percent of the committee roll calls showed even a remote degree of cross-party unity. The preponderance of members agreed on only three amendments out of the twenty-four roll calls on the Economic Opportunity Act. On at least one of these votes, however, the large number of Democrats voting obscured the fact that all nineteen Democrats opposed all eight Republicans present. Only one roll call illustrated a substantial amount of agreement, with all the Democrats voting with the majority of Republicans present and voting. Otherwise, the roll calls in 1964 showed high party unity and low overall unity. Only eleven of the fifty-six votes taken in the 88th Congress exhibited minimal cohesion.

The roll-call statistics corroborate what other scholars have said about the low level of political harmony on this committee. Calculating how often each committee member voted on the House floor with every other committee member on roll calls on committee proposals, Dyson and Soule (1970) determined that Education and Labor was one of the least cohesive committees in the House during the late 1950s and the early 1960s, although fragmentation was the norm in the House. The Rice Index of Cohesion measure applied to all Education and Labor roll calls supports their findings of low agreement. The average scores, ranging from 27.4 to

Table 3.8. Committee Roll Calls Meeting Minimum Cohesion and Mean Rice
          Index Scores, 1961-1966

Congress	Year	N	Full E & L	Dems	Reps	%	N
			Rice Index			Full E & L RI > 40	
87th	1961-62	74	27.4	84.0	88.7	21.6	16
88th	1963-64	56	31.0	87.1	87.8	19.6	11
89th	1965-66	36	38.2	70.2	81.4	30.6	11
	Total	166					38
	Mean		31.0	82.0	85.8	22.9	

Source: Compiled from Committee on Education and Labor, *Minutes* 1961-66.

38.2 during the Powell years, do not reach the standard of a score of 40 for a minimally cohesive committee (70 percent of the committee voting together on the majority of votes).

Despite the relatively low full committee cohesion scores, the Rice Index applied to committee votes by members of each party shows a high degree of party alignment on Education and Labor (see table 3.8). With the exception of Democrats in the 89th Congress (1965-66), all the averages exceed 80, which means that few members defected from either party on all votes taken in the committee. On average, over 90 percent of the members of each party cast their ballots with their party colleagues. For both parties, but especially for the Republicans, all members of each party voted together on a large number of roll calls, resulting in a score of 100 for each roll call. As shown by the average scores, the Republicans seemed to show more unanimity than did the Democrats, although the latter, too, displayed their fair share.

The Rice Index Scores project a markedly different picture of the degree of partisanship apparent on Education and Labor than do the House party-unity scores. Judging by the Rice Index Scores, it would seem that members preferred to vote with the majority of their own party more frequently in committee than in the House. Whereas the unity scores illustrate moderate levels of partisanship on House votes, both Republicans and Democrats showed less reluctance to support their own parties in committee. Each party's scores were high throughout all three terms Powell was chairman.

The party vote statistics confirm a marked party cleavage on Education and Labor. The low rate of full committee cohesion and the high rate of partisanship illustrated by the Rice Index Scores for each party are borne out in high degrees of party conflict. About three-quarters of the roll calls pitted the parties against each other. The primary measure of committee interparty differences in this study is the percentage of party votes: committee roll calls on which at least 70 percent voting Democrats cast their

Table 3.9. Percentage of Party Votes in Committee by 50-, 70-, 75-, and 90-
          Percent Criteria, 1961-1966

Congress	Year	N	(number of qualifying roll calls in parentheses)			
			> 50%	> 70%	> 75%	> 90%
87th	1961-62	74	87.8 (65)	82.4 (61)	79.7 (59)	47.3 (35)
88th	1963-64	56	82.1 (46)	75.0 (42)	73.2 (41)	62.5 (35)
89th	1965-66	36	80.6 (29)	61.1 (22)	52.8 (19)	25.0 (9)
	Total	166	(140)	(125)	(119)	(79)
	Percentage of total		84.3	75.3	71.7	47.6

Source: Compiled from Committee on Education and Labor, *Minutes* 1961-66.

ballots against at least 70 percent of voting Republicans. For easy comparison with other studies, table 3.9 also presents statistics on other commonly used levels of party voting. By the 70-percent opposition criterion,
the committee divided into partisan factions on 75.3 percent of the votes
taken while Powell was chairman, a rather high rate of party conflict. The
statistics at the 75-percent level are strikingly similar. More remarkably, on
nearly half of the committee's roll calls, over 90 percent of the voting
members of each party opposed over 90 percent of those of the other party.

If there was some basis for integration on Education and Labor, it was
party. As they had in the previous decade, the issues under the committee's
jurisdiction promoted partisanship instead of full committee agreement.
The committee's subject matter frequently was morally based and thus not
amenable to compromise. For the most part, the topics were the fundamental issues underlying the party differences, which were reflected in committee voting patterns. During the 1960s, when issues under the committee's
jurisdiction were at the top of the legislative agenda, members warred
bitterly for their beliefs. Most of the time the antagonists divided along
party lines. Republicans fought to maintain the status quo of limited federal
involvement in the social arena. Liberal Democrats, on the other hand,
having endured years of frustration at the hands of conservatives, battled to
have their social programs enacted and expanded. Party provided the basis
for whatever degree of committee integration existed.

For the first time in years, the issues of interest to the Democrats were
at the height of public interest. They had a chance to push through federal
aid to education, antipoverty measures, and manpower development and
training legislation that either had been languishing in committee for years
or had yet to reach the fore. Democrats had to band together to protect their
newfound progress and their potential programs. The Republicans, on the
other hand, bound together to prevent the irresponsible expenditure of
public funds and the interference in state prerogatives. They united in their

opposition to federal aid to education and to the poverty program. Many of the divisive roll calls concerned minority-sponsored amendments that would have diluted, restrained, or failed to extend federal aid bills or provisions of the Economic Opportunity Act.

Even if Dodd's (1972) conception of integration as value agreement across a broad range of issues had been used, Education and Labor still would show little unanimity. The issues under the committee's jurisdiction were among those underlying the basic differences between the two parties, and they inspired party voting to the detriment of full committee cohesion. When such underlying issues are discussed, members and their parties are not likely to give in gracefully. Even with a large margin of Democrats over Republicans, the levels of full committee unity remained low. On the whole, the average full committee cohesion Rice Index Scores for Powell's tenure were slightly greater than those for Barden's.

During the 87th Congress, several major issues contributed to the lack of full committee accord, dividing members mostly along party lines. A large number of roll calls, an indicator of divisiveness itself, centered on federal aid to education. All but two such roll calls showed low degrees of cohesion. Bills related to school construction, to the National Defense Education Act of 1958, and to impacted areas caused a great deal of controversy in the committee, necessitating at least 60 percent of the roll calls. Other divisive issues included youth unemployment remedies, the Davis-Bacon Act, migrant agricultural laborers, and various provisions of the Fair Labor Standards Act of 1938.

Antipoverty legislation spawned the major controversies of the 88th Congress. Nine roll calls during the first session pertained to the creation of a Youth Conservation Corps, a predecessor of the major antipoverty program. Almost all of the second session votes concerned items in the Economic Opportunity Act of 1964 itself. Out of twenty-four roll calls, only three inspired any inkling of unanimity between the parties. During the first session, bills related to manpower development and training generated controversy as well.

Much of the lack of full committee agreement in the 89th Congress stemmed from legislation related to elementary and secondary education, either the main bill or amendments to the 1965 act. There were fewer roll calls in the 89th Congress than there were in the 88th, but the votes in the 1965 and 1966 sessions were predominantly related to education. Members seemed to be more unified in their outlooks on higher education legislation. Perhaps the barriers had been overcome by the previous education programs. In addition to education, the poverty program was still a hot issue, as were amendments to the Fair Labor Standards Act of 1938.

The fact that the committee's jurisdiction covered such important parts of the administration's domestic legislative agenda also contributed to the divisiveness. The president's advancement of these issues increased their visibility and public interest, thus stimulating partisan conflict, since the minority hardly wanted the Democrats to have the credit. The really important issues that the committee considered during the Powell years were the ones that most contributed to the image of controversy and detracted from a potentially unified committee. Although committee members were unified on some roll calls, either the stakes were lower or dissenters wanted to get the bill out of committee so the House could defeat it. Usually, the issues on which the committee was more cohesive were not those exemplifying the fundamental bases of party division. Members had little trouble voting together on providing training films for the deaf or on creating a teaching hospital at Howard University. On the other hand, they had difficulty coming to terms on whether there should be antipoverty legislation and federal aid to education and, if there should, how to go about it. The issues just did not inspire agreement.

Committee Structure

In part because of Adam Clayton Powell's personality and behavior, the committee structure changed significantly from what it had been under his predecessor. It became markedly more decentralized, universalistic, democratic, and complex. The committee was also more capable of acting. Unlike most other House committees, the Committee on Education and Labor, by the time Powell came to power, had a well-defined set of rules enacted as a result of the abuses of the former chairman, Graham Barden. Despite these provisions, Barden had managed to obstruct legislation and frustrate the committee. As a result, compared with other committee chairmen, Powell confronted a rather formidable set of rules. He still maintained control over the referral of legislation, but his discretion was restricted.

Before Powell had a chance to take advantage of his position, the committee members in the 87th Congress (1961-62) approved several new rules governing committee operations (Committee on Education and Labor *Rules*, 89th Cong.). According to at least one member, however, the provisions adopted at this time contained only minor changes from those enacted in the previous session (interview). The 1961 rules remained in effect until well into the 89th Congress. Some were a direct reaction to the abuses of former chairman Barden. Others were precautionary measures designed to enforce majority rule instead of tyranny. A few others were directives about record keeping. Some of the rules and traditional practices adopted under Barden were clarified in the 87th Congress.

Several committee rules changes were drawn directly or indirectly from the rules of the House: keeping a journal, setting party ratios, stating the committee's jurisdiction, and recording votes on demand of one-fifth of those present. In addition, the new committee provisions applied House rules to the operation of the committee, including setting time limitations on the questioning of witnesses. Other changes instituted in 1961 concerned subcommittees. When standing subcommittees were specified in the rules, their jurisdictions were left undefined. Their inclusion in the rules had not yet been institutionalized. Moreover, other House committee chairmen had reasonably strong control over their subcommittees at that time. The omission of specific subcommittee jurisdictions left Chairman Powell with a great deal of discretion over bill referral. He could assign bills to whatever subcommittee he wanted.

According to staff, Education and Labor members took the measure of their new chairman and presently decided that if they wanted travel money and subcommittee funds, they would be better advised not to threaten him with hobbled authority. One staff member said, "Their willingness to cooperate was because they wouldn't get to go far and do much because he held the purse strings" (interview). In addition, they finally had a chairman who wanted to get things done. Another staff member said, "They were willing to give Powell a free hand. Barden had been prone to bottle up education legislation, so they curtailed him. Thinking Powell would be liberal, there was a willingness to let him go" (interview).

The new rules authorized the six standing subcommittees to act as agents of the full committee, and they were given the power to do so. As a result, their status was upgraded. Barden had not authorized subcommittees to act on behalf of the committee in the previous decade. The rules also set subcommittee membership ratios at 60 percent from the majority to 40 percent from the minority. Except for the subcommittee chairmen, members retained their seniority on their original subcommittees. The ranking members of the majority party were to be the chairmen of the standing subcommittees. The rules also included a provision for a subcommittee chairman to be replaced if he missed more than three successive subcommittee meetings, except for reason of illness or of official congressional duties.

The other two rules changes concerned the use of committee staff by members and limitations on proxy voting. One provision allowed the members of the committee to use the committee staff for assistance not regularly rendered in the course of normal duties, but only after authorization from the chairman. There had been no such privilege under Barden. The other limited the use of blanket proxy votes. Whereas proxies were recognized in the previous sessions, the new rules required that they had to be in writing and in the hands of the clerk before or during each roll call in which they were to be voted. Proxies also were approved for use in subcommittees.

The Committee on Education and Labor was far ahead of other committees in instituting more democratic rules and procedures in 1966. Unfortunately, this leadership was not the result of remarkable foresight or
sincere desire that everyone share in the wealth of power. These changes
were too often the reaction to abuses of power by the chairmen of this
committee. Chairman Barden had abused his powers of referral and his
authority to call and preside over committee meetings. In different ways,
Chairman Powell also abused power: for example, he was absent at strategic times when members needed him to request a rule, or he refused to
report a bill to the House that the committee had ordered reported. Both
Barden and Powell frequently found it convenient to be elsewhere when
the majority of members wanted to act. Barden used truancy as a tool to
prevent liberal legislation from being considered or reported by the committee. Most of the time, Powell did not necessarily want to prevent
legislation from being considered, though ostensibly that was the reason for
some of his absences (interviews). He seemed to have better things to do,
such as traveling to Bimini or going on junkets to other places around the
world. His nonattendance seemed to be a gesture of contempt for other
members and for the institution, and committee members responded by
adopting rules to control him (interview; Committee *Rules*).Prerogatives
formerly reserved for the chairman now were shared with the majority
membership of the committee. As Powell put it, "The net effect of the
reorganization would be an enormous reduction of the powers of the
committee chairman and a vast increase in the authority of the subcommittee chairmen. It also began to look like an outright battle over the overall
seniority system that governs all House conduct" (1971, 207).

Given the chairman's chronic absences, committee members had to
provide some way to operate when he could not or would not be found or
controlled. As a result, they deprived him of some responsibilities formerly
vested solely in the chairman. They voted to impose time limits on bill
referral to subcommittees, to allow majority members to vote to call
meetings, to appoint the ranking member to preside in the chairman's
absence, and to designate another committee member to report bills to the
House. According to a former staff member, "the committee put the situs
picketing bill out. . . . He [Powell] didn't do anything about it for two
Congresses. From this came the rule that the chairman had to take the bill to
the floor when it was reported" (interview). This action and Powell's failure
to report the poverty bill in 1966 precipitated changes in reporting authority. Additional rule changes provided that each member had to receive
written notice of any full committee meetings other than those regularly
scheduled. For at least forty-eight hours prior to a mark-up session, each
member was entitled to a copy of each bill reported by a subcommittee and
a section-by-section analysis of proposed changes in existing law.

The committee also reacted to the chairman's practices of slighting some of his subcommittee chairmen. In one instance, Carl Dewey Perkins (D-KY) headed a subcommittee, but it was a long time before Powell referred any legislation to it (interview, staff). Apparently he did the same to some of the other subcommittee chairmen. Powell had violated an understanding about who was to get which bills and, on occasion, had removed a bill from a certain subcommittee to punish the chairman and referred it to another; hence subcommittee jurisdictions and prompt, mandatory referrals were specified. The chairman no longer had full control over the referrals; the majority members of the committee also could direct that a bill be referred to a particular subcommittee. Otherwise, the chairman had to refer bills to the appropriate subcommittee within one week of receipt by the full committee. He was required to provide written notification of every referral to the subcommittee chairman, who had three days to file objections. Bills reported by subcommittees had to be taken up in full committee in the order in which they were reported unless the committee voted to the contrary.

Committee members also rewrote the subcommittee jurisdictions into the rules and mandated that the party ratio on each subcommittee reflect that of the House. Moreover, the majority members delegated to themselves the power to establish subcommittees in addition to those set out in the rules and to authorize subcommittee hearings outside of Washington, D.C. The standing subcommittee chairmen could approve travel within the limits of their budgets and had the authority to appoint, discharge, and direct the activities of subcommittee staff members. Another change diminished the chairman's discretion concerning conference committees. It required him to appoint as conferees, in order of seniority, the members of the subcommittee that reported the legislation.

The budgetary and staffing provisions resulted from unauthorized expenditures of committee funds. Some staff members traveled with the chairman, and others were said to have traveled with the chairman but in fact did not.[4] Nevertheless, the money was spent. Family members were kept on the payroll, even though they did not perform official duties in Washington, D.C., or in the state of New York.[5] The manager of the House Stationery Store told later committee employees that a few staff members charged office supplies to the committee through the House Stationery Store and then returned them for cash (interviews).[6] Other supplies were bought for the committee and used elsewhere: some were found in the Abyssinian Baptist Church in Harlem (interview).

Newly instituted budgetary procedures required the chairman to prepare a preliminary budget and subcommittee chairmen to draw up supplemental budgets. These plans were to include the necessary amounts for staff, travel, investigations, and operations. The budgets would be consolidated by the clerk, approved by the committee, and submitted to the House for approval. Thereafter, the budget could not be changed without the approval of the full committee. In addition, the chairman was directed to supply an accounting of the amount and purpose of all expenditures to the full committee once a month.

Perhaps the size of the majority or the degree of outrage allowed committee members to impose these rules on Powell but not on Barden, who also was renowned for being unavailable. Or perhaps their confidence in their authority to control a chairman expanded after they changed the rules on Barden. Both chairmen stretched the patience of their colleagues to the limit, albeit in different ways. Each thwarted rules or traditions, much to the exasperation of his colleagues. Members had to keep the committee functioning, even if the chairman was not. The rules might have been more effective had they been enacted sooner. As it was, they were not enacted until the last months of Powell's leadership.

The facts that Education and Labor itself imposed constraints on its chairman and that these rules were not applied by the House to all committee chairmen are telling. Because of obstructionist and dilatory tactics, the committee members had to restrain the chairman to preserve or to facilitate democratic decision making. They capitalized on Powell's low status in the House to take the advantage. Both he and Barden had crossed the line of tolerance.

The 1966 rules might have had more immediate impact had not other elements intervened shortly after their enactment. They were in effect just four months before the House Democratic Caucus effectively deposed Powell for funding irregularities and installed the ranking member, Carl Perkins (D-KY), as the new chairman. In the face of well-publicized legal problems, shortly thereafter the House denied Powell his seat (see Jacobs 1973), an action subsequently overruled by the Supreme Court.

The size of the Committee on Education and Labor increased slightly at the outset of Powell's chairmanship from what it had been under Barden. The leadership added another seat in the 87th Congress, leaving the committee at thirty-one members for the duration of Powell's tenure. The heavily Democratic partisan split on the committee throughout his chairmanship reflected as accurately as possible the party division in the House, given the uneven number of members and the inclusion of the ratio in the committee rules. The party ratio ranged from a nineteen-to-twelve Democratic majority in Powell's first two terms as chairman to a subsequent twenty-one-to-ten Democratic advantage.

The overwhelming Democratic majority in both Congress and the committee in the 89th Congress, a consequence of President Lyndon Johnson's landslide victory over ultraconservative challenger Senator Barry Goldwater in 1964, gave the Democrats the votes to override the Republicans at will. Although the Democrats had had the votes in the 87th and 88th Congresses, there were still enough conservative southerners left to team up with the Republicans and at least give liberals a run for their money. In the 89th, however, conservative opposition could be defeated easily because of the abundance of Democrats and other liberals. The committee ratio permitted Democrats to overcome much of the opposition that had deadlocked the committee for years. On occasion during the 1960s the liberal Democrats even received some help from Republicans, almost unheard of under Barden.

Under the new Democratic administration, much of the subject matter under the jurisdiction of Education and Labor moved to the forefront of the congressional agenda. About 40 percent of the president's domestic legislative agenda related to education and labor laws (Committee, *Activities and Accomplishments*, 87th Cong., 1961, p. viii). The committee set up six standing subcommittees, one more than in the previous term, to meet the challenge of an expected increase in the amount and salience of referred legislation. The new 1961 standing subcommittees were the general, special, and select subcommittees on education and on labor. The General Education and Special Education subcommittees were holdovers from the previous term. Although "select" committees generally were established by the House to study a certain subject, the select subcommittees on education and labor had the same status as the other standing subcommittees. *General, special,* and *select* were simply the names chosen; the titles connoted nothing about jurisdiction or function, which was undefined.

Additional ad hoc subcommittees were created as needed, with their jurisdictions determined by the chairman. Certain issues either crossed jurisdictional boundaries or were salient enough to warrant the creation of special units for their treatment. Normally bills on such matters might have gone to one of the standing subcommittees, but they generated enough interest among other members to make it advisable to establish additional subcommittees. For example, in the 88th Congress, the poverty issue inspired sufficient public attention and member interest that the chairman appointed a subcommittee solely for that subject. The narrow scope of an issue constituted another reason for the establishment of an ad hoc subcommittee. Special investigative committees, such as the task force investigating a labor dispute on the nuclear ship *Savannah* and the subcommittee investigating activities of the National Labor Relations Board, are examples of these units.

Ad hoc subcommittees also provided rewards or incentives. Often their chairmen did not have enough seniority to have standing subcommittees of their own. Since the rules required that the standing subcommittees had to be chaired by the senior members of the majority party, the creation of new units offered ways for the chairman to involve other members. The chairman could reward desirable behavior with a subcommittee chairmanship or with the investigation of an issue that might have been of special concern to a member. Being able to hold hearings in one's own district was one benefit of chairing an ad hoc subcommittee.

The chairman also used ad hoc subcommittees to work on legislation or to investigate activities in which he took a particular interest or over which he wanted to maintain control. The War on Poverty Subcommittee is an example of the latter. In the 88th Congress, Powell chaired three ad hoc subcommittees himself. In the 89th, he ran the Subcommittee on De Facto School Segregation, an issue of particular interest to him. Surprisingly, he left the Subcommittee on Integration in Federally Assisted Education to Dominick Daniels (D-NJ).

Seniority dominated the new structure. As the rules mandated, standing subcommittee chairmanships were reserved for the most senior members of the majority party, who chose, in order of seniority, which subcommittees they wanted to head. As members gained seniority, some were likely to trade education subcommittees for labor subcommittees, or vice versa, when chairmanships became open. The seniority rule was followed except in one case, that of Phil Landrum (D-GA), who not only did not have a chairmanship but did not sit on any subcommittee during the 87th Congress. He was assigned to the ad hoc Subcommittee on the War on Poverty in the 88th, probably at the suggestion of the administration, which wanted him to manage the bill on the floor, but he was not assigned to a standing subcommittee. Although the rules stated that standing subcommittee chairmen were to be the ranking members of the majority party, Landrum is reputed to have turned down a chairmanship because he believed that Powell would not give him jurisdiction over any important legislation (Lewis 1963, 95-96). Landrum was a conservative, and the liberal chairman was not likely to give a conservative the reins over liberal bills important to the administration. Also, there was some speculation that Landrum may have been paying for the earlier refusal of his friend and southern ally, Barden, to appoint Powell to a subcommittee chairmanship during the 1950s (interview), even though his ranking-member status warranted a chairmanship by tradition. Powell had fought hard, but unsuccessfully, to establish this as a requirement under Barden.

Frequently the chairmanships of the ad hoc subcommittees went to the next most senior members in line after the standing subcommittee chairmen. On other occasions, such as in the case of Sam Gibbons (D-FL), they reached further down the seniority list. As seventeenth out of nineteen in seniority among the Democrats, Gibbons chaired a subcommittee to study education and serious crime.

With the exception of Landrum, all committee members were assigned to at least one standing subcommittee each term, and frequently more. The

Table 3.10. Education and Labor Subcommittee Assignments, 1961-1966

| Congress | Average Number of Assignments to Subcommittee, per Member | |
	Democrats	Republicans
87th	2.4	2.5
88th	3.1	3.1
89th	2.9	3.4

| | Average Number of Subcommittee Seats per Member, by Type | | | |
| | Democrats | | Republicans | |
	Standing	Ad Hoc/Other	Standing	Ad Hoc/Other
87th	1.3	1.0	1.4	1.1
88th	1.8	1.3	1.7	1.5
89th	2.1	1.1	2.2	1.2

Source: Author's calculations from Committee on Education and Labor, *Calendar* 1961-66.

rules required, insofar as practical, that the appointments be made with regard to the preferences of the members. Table 3.10 shows the average number of assignments per member and the average number of committee seats per member, by type of subcommittee. Because the rules stated that the full committee chairman and the ranking minority leader were ex officio members of all subcommittees, the numbers do not reflect their assignments. These statistics show that Democrats allocated seats in nearly the same proportions as did the Republicans throughout the Powell years. Fenno quoted one member as saying that "you can get practically any subcommittee you want so everybody is happy with his assignments" (1973, 101).

Despite being the committee workhorses, Education and Labor subcommittees lacked clearly marked jurisdictions during all three Powell Congresses. The fuzzy boundaries were used by the chairman as a political tool to reward his friends and punish his enemies. For example, although one reasonably might have expected that legislation relating to youth unemployment would be referred to a labor subcommittee, it was referred instead to the General Subcommittee on Education, chaired by Perkins, who had a particular interest in the work training programs. A bill to provide for an additional assistant secretary of labor was assigned to Edith Green's (D-OR) Special Education Subcommittee. The subcommittee chairmen took full advantage of the maneuvering room. Ordinary members, too, sometimes could arrange for seemingly incongruous referrals for their pet bills.

Members of the Committee on Education and Labor had a reputation among their colleagues for lacking the degree of specialization apparent on other committees, a specialization ordinarily fostered by subcommittee membership. A member of Education and Labor, on the whole, may have been more interested in education than in labor, or vice versa, but it was hard to develop a speciality, particularly given the subject matter. It was also more difficult for members to be perceived as specialists by other members of Congress, particularly when every representative seemed to consider himself an expert on this committee's issues. Committee members may have had specialties, but few House members deferred to them. Despite the well-defined structure of the standing subcommittee system in Education and Labor, it was actually quite permeable. Unlike members of many other committees, Education and Labor members were (and still are in the 1990s) free to participate in subcommittee deliberations in subcommittees other than the one they were assigned to initially. They could not vote, however. Although this practice was allowed, it was not prevalent.

Powell took advantage of the existing standing subcommittees and also established others to work on special projects. Most of the ad hoc subcommittees he created were chaired by members who were not already chairmen of standing subcommittees, thus placing these new chairs in his debt. In this way, the power resources in the committee were broadened. A larger number of members were able to share in the power distribution than would have if there had been no ad hoc subcommittees or, as was the case in the early Barden years, if there had been little or no reliance on standing subcommittees. There did not seem to be any systematic prejudice in favor of or against particular subcommittees, although allegedly there was.[7] All the subcommittees were able to participate fully in committee decision making.

One major drawback to Education and Labor subcommittees was the lack of deference afforded their decisions. Fenno asserted that "subcommittee decisions carry very little weight in the full committee. . . . On major bills, the subcommittee has no standing with the full committee" (1973, 102). Vogler supported this argument, stating that "Education and Labor subcommittees do not make decisions for the whole committee. There is no expertise mystique preventing other subcommittees and the full committee from questioning decisions made in Education and Labor subcommittees" (1974, 133). Frequently, if a subcommittee member could not get his amendment approved in subcommittee, he would offer it again when the bill was marked up in the full committee. Other members also frequently proposed amendments. Often, the Republicans tried to kill or dilute Democratic-sponsored legislation with a "death by amendment" strategy. More often than not, they failed.

Although not all of the bills reported by subcommittee were amended before being reported to the House, many were. Instead of sending the subcommittee version with all its attached amendments to the floor, clean bills (renumbered versions of the legislation with all the committee amendments incorporated) were introduced frequently as a result of full committee amendments to bills reported by subcommittees. When the clean bill was referred to the committee, it would be reported to the floor immediately. About 39 percent of Education and Labor bills reported to the House in the 87th Congress (1961-62) had been reintroduced as clean bills (Committee *Calendar*, 1962). The committee also used another practice, that of striking everything after the enacting clause and replacing it with the language of a new bill incorporating all the amendments. The relatively common occurrence of the introduction of clean bills and of the replacement of the original text with new language substantiates Fenno's allegation that the full committee did not place wholehearted trust in the work of the subcommittees, at least not for the final versions of bills.

Committee and subcommittee staffs are another important element of committee structure. After the relative paucity of committee employees during the Barden years, the Powell staff seemed bountiful. The rules delegated to the chairman the authority to employ and discharge staff members. As a result, when Powell became chairman, he nearly doubled the number of committee employees. He increased both the professional and support staffs for the committee majority and, to a lesser degree, the number of staff members for the minority. Powell, in effect, institutionalized subcommittee staffs. Before his chairmanship there were few, if any, subcommittee staff, professional or support. That lack is understandable, since there were few subcommittees under Barden until 1957. Even then there were only two professional subcommittee staff members and four clerical employees. In 1960 the total was even smaller. When the committee began to rely more on the established standing subcommittees, the staff had to be increased. At one point, after 1964, Powell had 143 persons on the committee payroll. A subcommittee investigating Powell's activities contracted with a private firm to determine whether, in fact, all these staff members were real people (*New York Times*, Dec. 20, 1966, p. 34, col. 3).

Fenno (1973) repeatedly cited the lack of reliance on committee staff members for policy advice. He gave the impression that staff members were so unhappy that the turnover was high, especially on subcommittee staffs. It should be noted, however, that because Powell delegated the authority and funds to hire staff to his subcommittee chairmen, when a chairman switched to head another subcommittee, as was the case on several occasions, he generally took his staff with him. Many of the examples Fenno cited could have been subcommittee staff members changing subcommittees with their chairmen. Fenno and several of the committee members he interviewed gave the impression that the committee staff members generally were incompetent, although Powell claimed that he hired "the highest caliber men and women available" (Powell 1971, 202). A holdover from Barden's committee staff said, "The new people from New York Powell brought in didn't know anything. One asked, 'What's a calendar?'" (interview). Many of the so-called professional staff members were not professionals in the sense of being experts on matters under the committee's jurisdiction, or even knowing anything about it. Some appointments were political favors. The chairman may have been just "salting them around," in the words of one former staff member (interview). Others, however, were hired by the subcommittee chairmen precisely because they had experience dealing with the issues under the committee's jurisdiction and were exceedingly competent. Although sometimes he did hire experts, the chairman had little incentive to import only staff members who were experts on the issues under consideration. The benefits of hiring political allies or aides outweighed the benefits of having a knowledgeable, professional, committee-oriented staff. Normally, the latter would be helpful in formulating policy, but in a committee with a jurisdiction so controversial and so nontechnical, it was hard to maintain an aura of specialized competence.

Another factor worth noting about the Education and Labor staff was its partisanship (Morrow 1969, 56). The chairman hired the majority staff, and the ranking minority member was responsible for the minority committee personnel. The two had little official interaction. One scholar accused Education and Labor, along with one or two other committees, of having an "aggressive, ideologically scrappy" staff (Goodwin 1970, 152).

Jurisdiction, Work Load, and Function

A look at the committee's jurisdiction, work load, and function provides insight into what mission the Congress assigned the committee, what the committee did, and whether its mission changed under Powell. During his chairmanship, jurisdiction expanded, work load increased dramatically, and function shifted from blocking to activist. External factors, such as the Great Society, and internal dynamics, such as the chairman's personality and behavior and the composition of the committee, were catalysts for these developments.

In the Powell years the jurisdiction of Education and Labor topped the domestic legislative agenda of two presidents. Both Kennedy and Johnson emphasized aid to education and programs to help the disadvantaged. The committee's work was enhanced by calls for action in presidential speeches and messages and by the concomitant media attention. Charged with writing, handling, and safe passage of much of the domestic political agenda as set out by the presidents, Education and Labor reached a prominence previously unknown. Whereas Education and Labor's jurisdiction is set out in relatively general terms in the Legislative Reorganization Act of 1946, the 1961 version and subsequent editions of the committee rules include a detailed list of the issue areas, legislation, and programs under the committee's purview. The rules list specific pieces of legislation (e.g., the Fair Labor Standards Act of 1938, the Federal Employees Compensation Act, the Federal Coal Mine Safety Act) in addition to more general matters such as welfare of miners, youth programs, and intercultural activities. The jurisdiction expanded insofar as new issues, not anticipated when earlier versions of the rules had been adopted, came onto the agenda. For example, the War on Poverty legislation was referred to this committee, although nothing in the committee's official jurisdiction specifically refers to antipoverty programs. One could argue, however, that the War on Poverty came under "manpower" or "measures relating to education and labor generally." As more issues came to public attention, the committee could make a case for expanding its jurisdiction.

By most measures, the committee work load, activity, and productivity during the Powell years increased dramatically from what it had been during Barden's reign (see tables 3.11 and 3.12). The number of bills referred to the committee grew, albeit not steadily, from the beginning of the Barden years through the Powell years. Moreover, as measured by the number of hearing days, committee activity soared. Productivity, in bills reported, increased dramatically when Powell took over. In his first term as chairman, the number of bills reported exceeded the total number reported in the previous two terms. Productivity stayed high throughout Powell's tenure, peaking in his last term. The average number of bills per term that became public law doubled during his chairmanship. The number is lower in the 88th Congress because ten committee bills were incorporated into other acts and thus are not reflected in the total number enacted.

Several factors contributed to the higher work load and activity of the committee during the Powell years. For the first time, the issues under the committee's purview were high priorities on the administration's agenda. President Kennedy proposed a new national antipoverty program about the time Powell took the chair, and a large portion of it came under the committee's jurisdiction. A second factor was the growth in the number of bills the committee considered and reported. In part, the increased activity was a result of Powell's desire to process legislation. He could have ignored the mounting demands made on the committee by the House. But Powell, along with most others on the committee, had been frustrated under Barden and wanted to get things done. In addition to letting committee members do what they wanted, he also was willing to promote the inves-

Table 3.11. Full Committee and Subcommittee Hearings, 1961-1966

Congress	Year	Days of full committee hearings	Days of subcommittee hearings	Total days of hearings	Percentage of subcommittee hearings
87th	1961-62	1	254	255	99.6
88th	1963-64	4	284	288	98.6
89th	1965-66	2	289	291	99.3
	Total	7	827	834	
	Mean	2.3	275.7	278.0	99.2

Sources: Compiled from Committee on Education and Labor, *Calendar* 1961-66; Committee on Education and Labor, *Activities and Accomplishments* 1961-66.

Table 3.12. Bills Referred to Education and Labor, 1951-1966

Congress	Year	Number referred	Number reported	Number passed HR	Number public laws
82d	1951-52	232	8	7	4
83d	1953-54	268	15	14	12
84th	1955-56	468	12	11	10
85th	1957-58	601	18	14	14
86th	1959-60	720	17	10	8
87th	1961-62	741	44	14[a]	18
88th	1963-64	713	25	14	14
89th	1965-66	959	51	32	28

Source: Compiled from Committee on Education and Labor, *Calendar* 1951-66.
[a] Plus six Senate bills.

tigation and passage of committee legislation. He freely gave his permission for members to hold hearings and conduct investigations, which augmented the activity and productivity of the committee. In addition, he moved things along in committee meetings instead of stalling. A third factor relates to the second. The long-thwarted, newly liberated committee majority also contributed to the rise in activity and productivity. Having been stifled by Barden for so many years, majority members seemed to rush to handle and report legislation that had been pent up for years by the chairman.

During the 87th, 88th, and 89th Congresses, members had the chance to accomplish many of the goals that had escaped them for years. The predominant emphasis was on education and on the poverty program, although the committee considered a healthy sampling of labor issues. Powell's first term as chairman commenced with a flurry of subcommittee activity. Hearings were held on a variety of education topics, including

adult basic education, problems of the aged and aging, educational materials for the deaf, and various aspects of federal aid to education. The major
labor legislation included amendments to the minimum-wage law, the
longshoremen's act, the coal mine safety act, compensation for federal
employees, and migratory labor. The chairman directed that the committee
take up minimum wage first because it had been blocked so successfully in
previous Congresses. Ultimately, the committee saw nine education bills
and nine labor bills enacted in the 87th Congress (1961-62) (Committee
Activities and Accomplishments, 87th Cong., 1963).

The main thrust of the committee in the 88th Congress (1963-64) was
the antipoverty legislation (Committee *Activities and Accomplishments,* 88th
Cong., 1965). This committee was at the forefront in considering bills to aid
Lyndon Johnson's War on Poverty. Not only was the issue with Education
and Labor's jurisdiction, but the close correlation between poverty and race
made poverty an appealing issue for Chairman Powell. Months of deliberations culminated in the Economic Opportunity Act of 1964 (P.L. 88-452).
The committee handled 111 bills related to this topic. Forty-eight of these,
establishing a national peace corps, were reflected in the VISTA Corps
portions of the program, which also incorporated another forty-eight bills
relating to a Youth Conservation Corps and work training programs. The
work-study sections derived from a 1963 bill entitled the National Education Improvement Act.

As a result of the fruition of the civil rights movement during the early
to mid-1960s, the committee worked on seventy-nine bills concerned with
discrimination in schools and in employment, segregated schools, and the
use of federal monies to aid institutions that discriminated on the basis of
race (Committee *Activities and Accomplishments,* 88th Cong., 1965). The
Civil Rights Act of 1964 (P.L. 88-352), handled by the Judiciary Committee, incorporated these efforts.

The committee also succeeded in getting enacted several important
education laws in the 88th Congress. These included the Higher Education
Facilities Act of 1963 (P.L. 88-204), the expansion of provisions of the
NDEA (P.L. 88-665), the Vocational Education Act of 1963 (P.L. 88-210),
and the approval of a National Council on the Arts (P.L. 88-579). The
fourteen committee bills enacted in the 88th Congress do not reflect the ten
bills that were incorporated into other legislation, such as the Economic
Opportunity Act of 1964 or the Civil Rights Act of 1964.

Education bills took the spotlight in the 89th Congress, which became
known as the "Education Congress" because of the scope and magnitude of
the education legislation enacted (Committee *Activities and Accomplishments,*
89th Cong., 1967). The Elementary and Secondary Education Act of 1965
(ESEA P.L. 89-10), a hallmark in the committee's history, was designed to
provide comprehensive assistance to improving education in elementary

and secondary schools throughout the country. Its major focus was on the educationally deprived and disadvantaged, a holdover emphasis from the antipoverty program, although it was designed to help all sectors of society. Committee members had been trying for years to get some sort of elementary and secondary school aid through Congress and had been thwarted at nearly all stages until the Civil Rights Act of 1964 removed the segregationist obstacles from the path of federal aid to education, and a liberal black New Yorker replaced a conservative white southerner as chairman. Other proposals compromised by focusing on pupils rather than on institutions, enabling members to get over the stumbling blocks provided by the issue of aid to church schools. In addition to the ESEA of 1965 and its 1966 amendments (P.L. 89-750), Congress enacted the Higher Education Act of 1965 (P.L. 89-329) and amendments to the aforementioned Higher Education Facilities Act (P.L. 89-752).

The function of the committee in the 1960s was markedly different from what it had been during most of the previous decade. Whereas under Barden the committee's mission had been to block progressive legislation and to maintain the status quo, the committee under Powell had an activist mentality. And by virtue of the Speaker's interference in the assignment process throughout the 1950s, it had a liberal majority. The Democrats, including the chairman, set out to better the human condition and to change the status quo to something more humanitarian. The emphasis was on helping people become better educated, have better job opportunities, and thereby experience a better quality of life.

The predominantly liberal committee was ready to go. Members wanted to pass legislation that had been bottled up by conservatives in previous Congresses. They were successful largely because the chairman did not interfere in subcommittee operations. He gave the subcommittee chairmen free rein. Many of the accomplishments were possible because the chairman generally was on the same side as his majority members, unlike his predecessor, who had sided with the Republicans for the most part. The fact that the administration backed the committee majority in its desire to enact federal aid to education, increase the minimum wage, and find a solution for the poverty problems also facilitated the committee's mission.

The committee did not have smooth sailing. In addition to the substantial controversies generated by the subject matter under consideration, after a while the chairman did an about-face and stopped cooperating. Members faced a situation not so different from what they had had to contend with under Barden: Powell began wielding his powers as chairman as a weapon. He used bill referral to subcommittees to punish his enemies and reward his friends. He pocketed bills instead of reporting them to the House. In the midst of its great legislative strides, the committee had to restrain its chairman and enhance its ability to act without him. Despite well-publicized difficulties with the chairman, the committee accomplished a great deal during the last term of Powell's chairmanship. The committee reported fifty-one bills that term, three times the number reported in the 86th Congress (1959-60), Barden's last. Members were able to push through a large number of bills, some of them with major ramifications.

Although the official jurisdiction was largely the same under Powell as it had been under Barden, it expanded with different types of programs. In addition, the committee's function changed to reflect the mission of the chairman and his committee and in concurrence with an activist Democratic administration. The liberal bent of the committee became institutionalized under Powell. Begun in the Barden years, the committee under Powell generally was considered a place for the most liberal of liberal Democrats and the most conservative Republicans. This is illustrated by more partisan voting patterns under Powell than had been evident under Barden.

The chairman's personality and behavior, along with changes in committee rules, committee size and party ratios, subcommittees, and committee staff, made the committee more decentralized, democratic, universalistic, and complex at the same time that it remained highly partisan and conflictual. Powell, in effect, was no shrinking violet and took advantage of whatever opportunities the chairmanship afforded him to leave his imprint on the committee. His ideological leanings and activist stance helped alter committee jurisdictions and functions, transforming the committee from a legislative barrier to a battering ram for social legislation. At the same time, some of his indiscretions led to a restructuring of power.

The decentralization process began with the inclusion of mandatory referrals to subcommittees with specified jurisdictions in the committee rules during the later Barden years. Although the fixed jurisdictions were removed from the 1961 rules to give an activist chairman some discretion, they were restored in 1966 after Powell abused the privilege. Consequently, the decentralization made the committee more universalistic in that it made favoritism less prevalent, distributing advantages in a less particularistic manner.

Under Powell, committee decentralization was institutionalized. It was attributable, in part, to provisions in the committee rules mandating the use of subcommittees and, in part, to Powell's laissez-faire attitude toward the committee. His disposition may have stemmed partly from his need to depend on his subcommittee chairmen to take committee bills to the floor, since Powell's sponsorship and endorsement were tantamount to a death warrant for a bill. For the most part, unless the matter was of particular interest to Powell, the subcommittee chairmen conducted the show. Since all bills were referred to subcommittees, each subcommittee was free to take up anything that its chairman or members wanted to consider and to hold whatever hearings were desired. The rules allowed legislation to flow through the process as smoothly as its content would allow, without being held up because the full committee chairman did not support it. As a result, most legislation referred to the committee in the 1960s had a better chance of being discussed than did bills referred in the previous decade.

All the provisions giving the majority party members more voice in committee actions democratized as well as decentralized the committee. Members could call meetings, establish subcommittees, report legislation, authorize the hiring of staff, approve travel, and hold hearings. In effect, they could act without their chairman. When they had tried to do that under Barden, the parliamentarian had ruled them out of order.

Subcommittee staffs became institutionalized under Powell. While he controlled the full committee staff, he permitted subcommittee chairmen to hire and manage their own personnel. For the first time, the chairmen had at least some support staff to help in their work. In addition, they had the money to operate.

Prior to Powell's chairmanship, the committee budget was left entirely up to the chairman. The rules enacted in 1966 ostensibly gave the members some control over where the money was being spent; however, Powell's stewardship of committee funds raised questions about the committee's financial management. Subsequently, the House launched an investigation into the financial practices of this committee.

In sum, by the time Powell left office, the democratic, decentralized committee with an expanded membership and staff was here to stay. After the establishment of the structure in the rules, future chairmen would have found it difficult to regain the prerogatives that Barden and Powell had lost. The Powell years represented the heyday of the Committee on Education and Labor. Never had it played such an integral role in enacting the administration's agenda or attracted so much public attention. Never had its legislation earned such widespread support. Never had it had the help of both the majority in the committee and the majority on the floor to accomplish its mission. As Powell said of the committee in the 88th Congress: "The door to the Great Society has now been opened. The threshold has been crossed. These achievements have been made possible by the splendid cooperation of the members of the committee in studying and formulating sound legislative proposals" (Committee *Activities and Accomplishments*, 88th Cong., 1965, p. viii).

By the end of Powell's last term, Education and Labor had nearly reached its pinnacle as a vital, salient committee. Not only had the quantity of work referred to it increased sharply, but the demand for quality became more critical. Members had their chance to make a mark on history, to be remembered for contributing to some of the most innovative ideas and programs that the nation had seen since Franklin D. Roosevelt was in office. In addition to the landmark proposals, the committee considered and saw enacted numerous programs with limited impact, such as the provision of reading materials for the deaf. The committee worked to protect migrant agricultural workers and child laborers. Members tried to alleviate some of the unemployment problems and the problems caused by extreme poverty. Many people would benefit from the work these members did during the 87th, 88th, and 89th Congresses. On the other hand, acceptance of these programs was not universal. Some people regarded them as poorly designed or ill advised. Moreover, they cost taxpayers a great deal, and in the 1990s members are hard-pressed to hang on to the gains they made in social welfare in the early to mid-1960s.

4

The Chairmanship of Adam Clayton Powell, Jr.

One of the Committee on Education and Labor's most productive but evolutionary periods occurred during the chairmanship of Adam Clayton Powell, Jr. (D-NY). Perhaps as much as that of any chairman before or since, his leadership shaped the future of the committee.

Portrait of the Chairman

Adam Clayton Powell, Jr., was an important man. He was an inspirational leader among blacks and chairman of the powerful Committee on Education and Labor during the 1960s. He attracted attention everywhere he went. Part of the appeal was his flamboyant personal style, in addition to his charm and physical attractiveness. Another part derived from his oratorical skills, which he fine-tuned as pastor of the Abyssinian Baptist Church in Harlem. He spoke eloquently on a broad array of topics and could move people with his words. People listened when he preached, on political as well as religious issues.

Powell was born on November 29, 1908, in New Haven, Connecticut, the son of a Baptist preacher. In his autobiography, Powell claimed that his paternal grandmother, Sally, was part Cherokee Indian and part black and bore a son by a white slaveholder of German descent. The slaveholder died, leaving Sally to fend for herself and her unborn child. A former slave named Dunn took them in and raised Adam Clayton Powell, Sr. Powell Jr. claimed that Adam, Sr. married a young woman sired by Colonel Jacob Shaefer of the brewing family. The daughter of the brewer and his mistress was the mother of Adam Clayton Powell, Jr. Charles V. Hamilton, a noted political scientist and one of Powell, Jr.'s biographers, could find no evidence of these claims, however (see Hamilton 1991, 41-43). Evidently Powell's ancestry was mixed, and although he went through most of his life as black, he did not seem to be quite sure how black he really was (Hickey and Edwin 1965; Powell 1971).[1]

Powell's father took a job as minister of the large Abyssinian Baptist Church in Harlem and moved the family there weeks after young Adam was born. Adam, Jr. grew up there and attended New York City public schools. In 1925, at sixteen, he entered the City College of New York. He failed out of school his first semester but was allowed to return because of a family friendship with the president of the college. He failed five courses in his second semester and was expelled (Powell 1971, 27). After months of education that only the streets of Harlem could provide, Powell enrolled in Colgate University.

Powell apparently passed as white for a brief period while at Colgate (Hickey and Edwin 1965, 34-35; Lyons 1972). He and a white roommate pledged a white fraternity. Apparently the fraternity background check was responsible for raising a question about his racial background. One of his friends recalled his discovery that Powell was not white: "'When the fall term started, the track coach told me to hunt up a Negro boy named Powell who was supposed to be a good 440-yard-dash prospect.' Vaughn was unable to find him. Then, a few weeks later, Vaughn's German professor was reseating his students in alphabetical order, and in so doing, called out the name 'Powell.' Vaughn looked at the freshman student, and thought 'That can't be my 440 man. He's white.' But then he looked harder and decided that Powell was, in fact, a Negro" (Hickey and Edwin 1965, 34-35) When the news leaked, Powell was shunned all over campus. He thereupon joined a black fraternity instead of the white one and stilled the disruption. In 1930 he graduated from Colgate.

After Colgate, Powell attended Union Theological Seminary. He left the seminary after several disagreements with its president, Dr. Henry Sloane Coffin, who told him that no minister could marry anyone in show business or anyone who was divorced (Powell 1971, 37). Powell then enrolled in Columbia Teachers College and earned a master's degree in religious education (Powell 1971, 37).

When his father retired in 1937, Adam, Jr., took over the ministry of the Abyssinian Baptist Church and began cultivating a large part of what soon would be his congressional constituency. In 1930, at the request of several prominent New York citizens, he agreed to organize the local populace for the fight to admit blacks to city hospitals. Later, he wrote: "And so for the first time I heeded the call of the masses and became part of the struggles of the people of Harlem—not through any wish of my own, not through any divine call, but simply because I had been born to begin my work in the Great Depression" (Powell 1971, 57). He became a gadfly and an activist in New York politics. In 1941 he was elected to the New York City Council. In addition to his religious and political activities, Powell also edited and published a city newspaper from 1941 to 1945 and claimed to have taught religious education at the extension school of Columbia University from 1932 to 1940. Hamilton noted, "The last item must have been quite a revelation to officials at Columbia University" (1991, 59).

Powell was elected to Congress for the first time in 1944. He referred to himself as the "first bad nigger in Congress" (Powell 1971, 70). Speaker Sam Rayburn called Powell into his office and told him:

"Freshmen members of Congress are supposed not to be heard and not even to be seen too much. There are a lot of good men around here. Listen to what they have to say, drink it all in, get reelected a few more times, and then start moving. But for God's sake, Adam, don't throw those bombs."

I said, "Mr. Speaker, I've got a bomb in each hand, and I'm going to throw them right away." . . . After that first exchange Mr. Sam and I became close friends. [Powell 1971, 72]

Powell went into Congress with his mouth at full throttle, advertising his presence from the first day to the very last. For him to have done otherwise would have been as difficult as hiding a bull in a bean hamper.

Orientation of the Chairman

Adam Powell's orientation differed dramatically from Graham Barden's. He appropriated for himself a broad national, liberal constituency interested in advancing civil rights and progressive positions. He could not confine himself to a relatively narrow, conservative district. He promoted an activist federal government instead of minimal federal interference. Philosophically, he was much more representative of his party and his committee majority than was Barden. On a personal level, Powell's demeanor was as flamboyant as Barden's was courtly and reserved. All of these factors contributed to a different type of management of the committee and to different committee outputs.

Although his electoral constituency lived within the geographic boundaries of the Fourth District of New York, Powell cultivated assiduously his larger national constituency. He viewed all blacks and civil rights supporters as his people. As one pair of his biographers said to him concerning his early years in the House, "That he spoke for Negroes everywhere—not just those in Harlem—became increasingly apparent" (Hickey and Edwin 1965, 95). Of course, by improving the lot of his national following, he also made advances on behalf of his reelection. Part of the reason for this phenomenon was the tremendous overlap between the people in his district and those in his national following. And many of the national black leaders had Harlem connections. Powell seemed to have a black mandate, especially when he was first elected. The more whites criticized him, the surer black America was that it had a true black representative in Adam Powell (Hickey and Edwin 1965, 91-92).

Powell's district in the 1960 census was about 86 percent black and Puerto Rican and was centered in Harlem. There were more than 107,000 people per square mile in his district, with a total population in 1960 of 431,330 (U.S. Department of Commerce, 1963). He first was elected on the tickets of three parties, a fact that seemed to give him license to do and say anything in Congress and risk little wrath at home. Although his geographic and reelection constituencies were in Harlem, Powell's most supportive constituency was even closer to home. Powell took advantage of his pulpit at the Abyssinian Baptist Church to cultivate his primary constituency among church members, of which there were thousands. The church was both battery and power train of his political organization. Hickey and Edwin described the situation as follows: "Adam [has] practically unlimited appeal to the females. Some overstater has said, in fact, that the Reverend Powell slithered into the House on the kisses he has implanted on Abyssinian's glassy-eyed sisters every Sunday morning" (1965, 105).

In many ways, Adam Clayton Powell was a polar opposite of Graham Barden. The committee could hardly have had such a different chairman, particularly one of the same party. Whereas Barden was known for his conservative tendencies, Powell was renowned as an extreme liberal, particularly regarding civil rights issues. He long had been known as a defender and promoter of minority rights and was famous—and notorious in some quarters—for his "Powell Amendment," denying federal funds to states that discriminated on the basis of race. He tried to attach it to dozens of appropriations bills before the House. Powell was for federal interference and anything else necessary to make gains for nonwhites. Powell used his chairmanship of the Committee on Education and Labor to advance civil rights. His congressional district was in Harlem, but he made few efforts to make gains for Harlem in particular, crusading instead for equality for all blacks. He preached to a national constituency of blacks, working for black causes nationwide and sometimes on the international scene. He was a prominent figure in the civil rights movement, although frequently he disagreed with other black leaders.

Powell was a hard pill to swallow for many House members, including some on Education and Labor. He had flouted the traditions of the House, angering many people along the way. For instance, he ate in the members' dining room—a whites-only bastion since opening its doors—and was the first black to do so (Powell 1971, 82-83). He incited Democratic contempt for his public support for the reelection of Eisenhower in 1956 against Democratic challenger Adlai Stevenson.

Powell's legal problems also disgruntled the House. He was indicted for tax evasion after the Internal Revenue Service and a federal grand jury had investigated him intermittently for several years. Shortly after he assumed the chairmanship, his case was dismissed in federal court (Powell 1971, 182). Powell also was involved in a libel suit that lasted until 1968 and included at least four civil or criminal charges of contempt of court against him (see *Congressional Quarterly Almanac* 1966, 520-21). And in 1959 the FBI investigated possible bribery charges against him. Charges were never filed, however, because agents could not prove that Powell received money in exchange for introducing a bill that would have guaranteed a particular immigrant permanent residency status in the United States (Hamilton 1991, 421).

A great many House members resented this particular black man's having the chairmanship of an important committee (interviews, members), although William Dawson of Illinois, chairman of the Committee on Government Operations, did not stimulate any noticeable flow of bile. Powell certainly would not stay "in his place." Southerners, in particular, feared the legislation that might come out of his committee and, in their eyes, have adverse effects on their constituencies. Other members resented his flamboyance (Powell 1971), his irresponsibility (Hickey and Edwin 1965; Wilson 1960), his eloquence, and his legal difficulties. They did not think that anyone, particularly a black, as flamboyant and as irresponsible as Powell, much less anyone who was under indictment for tax evasion, should be rewarded with a committee chairmanship (interview). Barden even had delayed his retirement in the hope that Powell would not be around to succeed him. He finally gave up because Powell was a much younger man than he and signaled no intention to quit Congress anytime soon (Puryear 1979, 219). So many members despised Powell that, in order to promote its passage, no legislation reported by his committee bore his sponsorship, although he took credit for a great deal of the progress.

On the other hand, liberal members of Education and Labor were delighted finally to be rid of the previous chairman. With Barden gone, their legislation had a substantially better chance of reaching the floor and of passing. With Powell at the helm, the legislation not only would not be blocked by the chairman, but it might even be facilitated as long as it treated blacks well. Members knew, for example, that Powell favored federal aid to education, given that it did not discriminate against his constituency.

Powell also looked out for himself and his personal gain (Powell 1971; Hickey and Edwin 1965). He used his chairmanship as he used his pulpit. He fought hard for his people and enjoyed the perquisites of the chairmanship as he had those of the pastorate. He could live in high style, and the chairmanship of a salient committee provided him high visibility. He put his friends and his wife on the payroll. He signed approval of his own travel and took whomever he wanted with him. In effect, he no longer had to have everything approved by someone else before he could do it. He was finally the one who did the approving.

The chairmanship offered Powell additional access to the media, and he loved the attention. He was an accomplished, stage-wise performer. According to his colleagues, he was charming and had mastered the knack of sounding articulate without really knowing much about a subject. He drove fancy cars and usually had beautiful women within arm's reach. He used his chairmanship to help his celebrity status, frequently taking credit for work that was done by others (interviews, members and staff).

The chairman's ideological leanings can be inferred from surrogate measures of liberalism and conservatism, namely from interest group scores (see table 4.1). Ratings by Americans for Democratic Action (ADA), Americans for Constitutional Action (ACA), and the Committee on Political Education (COPE) are considered. Throughout Powell's tenure as chairman, his ratings by the liberal interest groups were high. They were always above 80 percent, and several times he rated 100 percent support. His scores on the conservative ACA scale were low. During his first term as chairman, Powell scored the extremes on all three scales. He had 100 percent approval by the ADA and by COPE and voted "wrong" on every issue counted by the ACA. He voted more liberally than already liberal Democratic committee member averages.

A comparison of Powell's and Barden's interest group scores for the 1950s illustrates how much more liberal Powell was than Barden (see table 4.2). The data show Powell far outscoring his southern colleague on the surrogate measures for liberalism. Using 1950s ADA and labor support scores, the average difference between Barden's scores and the mean scores of his committee colleagues was almost fifty-five points. For the same period, the difference between Powell's scores and those of the committee Democrats averaged just over seventeen points. His ratings would have been higher had he been present for all of the votes included. Powell voted "wrong" only occasionally, according to the interest group records, but his absences lowered his scores. The conservatives rarely could count on Powell, as they could on Barden, to side with them. During the 1960s the differences between Powell's ADA and COPE scores and the average scores of Democratic committee members were even smaller, averaging nine points. In contrast to Barden, he was fairly representative of his majority committee members.

House party-unity scores, measuring how frequently a member votes with other members of his party on party votes, indirectly shed light on the

Table 4.1. Powell's Interest Group Ratings Compared with the Average Scores
of Other Committee Members, 1961-1966

Group	Year	Powell	Dems	Reps
ADA	1962	100.0	88.3	20.7
COPE	1961-62	100.0	90.9	5.2
ACA	1961-62	0.0	9.4	81.1
ADA	1964	92.0	82.7	12.0
COPE	1963-64	82.0	90.0	13.5
ACA	1957-64	13.0	10.1	85.3
ADA	1966	88.0	82.8	16.5
COPE	1965-66	100.0	89.2	16.1
ACA	1966	10.0	13.6	73.4

Source: Compiled from *Congressional Quarterly Weekly Report* 1961-66.

Table 4.2. Interest Group Ratings of Barden and Powell in 1950s

Group	Year	Barden	E & L Dems	Difference	Powell	Difference
AFL	1947-52	3.7	54.5	− 50.8	70.2	+ 15.7
AFL	1951	20.0	67.1	− 47.1	90.0	+ 22.9
CIO	1951	0.0	55.0	− 55.0	90.0	+ 35.0
CIO	1951-52	0.0	57.6	− 57.6	62.5	+ 4.9
ADA	1951	7.7	60.4	− 52.7	77.0	+ 16.6
ADA	1952	0.0	58.2	− 58.2	61.5	+ 3.3
Labor	1953-54	33.3	72.6	− 39.3	90.4	+ 17.8
AFL-CIO	1947-56	26.3	55.1	− 28.8	89.4	+ 34.3
COPE	1959-60	10.0	88.7	− 78.7	100.0	+ 11.3
ADA	1960	11.0	88.8	− 77.8	100.0	+ 11.2

Source: Compiled from *Congressional Quarterly Weekly Report* 1951-61.

The − signifies that the chariman was more conservative than the average committee
Democrat. The + indicates that the chairman was more liberal.

chairman's orientation. Their informational value is limited to measuring a
member's support for his party on party votes and, given the lack of unity
among Democrats on certain issues, they cannot be used as measures of
liberalism or conservatism. Powell's House party-unity scores were low, in
sharp contrast to his high degree of party support when voting in committee.

Powell, it seems, did not rush to demonstrate particularly high degrees
of partisanship on the floor during the 87th, 88th, and 89th Congresses. He
showed only moderate support for his party, averaging over twenty points
lower than did his committee Democratic colleagues (see table 3.7). His
88th Congress score was particularly low. The relatively low unity scores
added to the resentment that his colleagues felt for him, but they took no

Table 4.3. Powell's Rate of Attendance at Committee Meetings, 1951-1966[a]

Year	Total number of meetings	Powell present		Powell absent	
		N	%	N	%
1951	11	1	9.1	10	90.9
1952	14	2	14.3	12	85.7
1955	14[b]	4	28.6	8	57.1
1956	15	4	26.7	11	73.3
1958	33	11	33.3	22	66.7
1959	37	11	29.7	26	70.3
1960	28	11	39.3	17	60.7
1961	41	36	87.8	5	12.2
1962	32[b]	21	65.6	11	34.4
1963	29	21	72.4	8	27.6
1964	22	8	36.4	14	63.6
1965	29	25	86.2	4	13.8
1966	21	18	85.7	3	14.3

Source: Compiled from Committee on Education and Labor, *Minutes* 1951-1966.

N is the number of meetings held each year.

[a]Data do not include hearings. Data for 1953, 1954, and 1957 are missing.

[b]Attendance data not available for two meetings.

action to chastise him at this time. Later, in the 1980s, low scores reportedly prevented other members from being awarded chairmanships or other party roles (interviews).

At least two factors may have affected Powell's scores. First, he had a well-deserved reputation for poor attendance, and his absences detracted from the degree of party support measured by the unity scores.[2] For example, according to one of his committee colleagues, Sam Gibbons (D-FL), Powell missed 164 of 218 floor roll calls in 1966 because of vacations in Bimini or elsewhere (Robertson 1966; *Congressional Quarterly Almanac* 1966, 520).[3] Hamilton stated, "Actually the question about Powell was not *how* he would vote, but, on important roll call votes on the floor, *if* he would be around to cast a vote" (1991, 356-57). (See table 4.3.) Second, Powell may have thought that some of the issues on which party votes occurred were biased against blacks. He withheld his support on numerous programs because he thought either that they were discriminatory or that blacks could be treated better.

A rather ironic note is that Powell's party-unity scores for the 87th, 88th, and 89th Congresses are reminiscent of Barden's low party-unity scores in the 1950s. Nor were Powell's 1950s scores high. Over the years that Barden was chairman, Powell averaged 64.2 percent support for the Democratic party on House party-unity votes, and Barden averaged 38

Table 4.4. Powell's Support for Each Party on Committee Party Votes,
1961-1966

| | | With Dems | | With Reps | |
Year	Party votes	N	%	N	%
1961	50	46	92.0	3	6.0
1962	11	11	100.0	0	0.0
1963	17	14	82.4	1	5.9
1964	25	25	100.0	0	0.0
1965	17	17	100.0	0	0.0
1966	5	5	100.0	0	0.0
Total	125	118		4	
Percentage of total			94.4		3.2

Source: Compiled from Committee on Education and Labor, *Minutes* 1961-66.

Party votes are defined here as roll-call votes on which at least 70 percent of the Democrats opposed at least 70 percent of the Republicans.

percent support. After Powell became chairman, he supported his party on just over half of the unity votes.

An examination of Powell's voting record on committee votes shows that his low degree of partisanship on the floor did not carry over to the committee. His committee votes show how frequently he voted with his fellow Democrats, on all votes and on party votes, and how often his side prevailed (see table 4.4). Contrary to his predecessor, Powell rarely defected to the Republican side on party votes. What is more, he sided with his fellow committee Democrats much more frequently than he did with a majority of House Democrats. His support for the Democrats on those roll calls was exceedingly high: 100 percent in four of the six years he was chairman, 94.4 percent for his entire tenure. He abstained or was absent on several other votes. He voted with the majority of the Republicans on 15.7 percent of all committee votes, although many of these votes had a large portion of the Democrats aligned with a large portion of Republicans (see table 4.5).

In all but the last year of his chairmanship, Powell had an impressive record for voting on the winning side. The large Democratic majority helped his chances. Aside from his frequent introduction of the Powell Amendment in the 1950s, majority members had little problem with Powell's voting behavior. Over the period 1961-65, he averaged victories on more than 82 percent of committee votes, winning on over 90 percent in 1964, when the poverty bill was considered. During his last year as chairman, however, he was on the prevailing side on only 41.6 percent of the tallies (see table 4.6).

Table 4.5. Powell's Support for Each Party on Committee Roll Calls, 1961-1966

Congress	Years	Roll calls	With Dems		With Reps	
			N	%	N	%
87th	1961-62	74	67	90.5	10	13.5
88th	1963-64	56	51	91.1	9	16.1
89th	1965-66	36	29	80.6	7	19.4
Total		166	147		26	
Percentage of total				88.6		15.7

Source: Compiled from Committee on Education and Labor, Minutes 1961-66.
This table includes all committee roll calls, not just those on which the parties were opposed.

Table 4.6. Powell's Votes on the Winning Side in Committee, 1961-1966

Congress	Roll calls	Chair wins		Party votes*	Chair wins	
		N	%		N	%
87th	74	63	85.1	61	53	86.9
88th	56	48	85.7	42	38	90.5
89th	36	26	72.2	22	20	90.9
Total	166	137		125	111	
Percentage of total			82.5	75.3		88.8
Mean per term	55.3	45.7		41.7	37.0	
Mean per session	27.7	22.8		20.8	18.5	

Source: Compiled from Committee on Education and Labor, Minutes 1961-66.
*Party votes are defined as roll-call votes on which at least 70% of the Democrats opposed at least 70 percent of the Republicans.

Powell's 82-percent overall winning record does not mean that he lost on 18 percent of those votes. On about 45 percent of the votes that he did not win, he was absent, passed, or voted present for the record (see table 4.3). In fact, he lost on only 16 of the 166 total roll-call votes taken during his chairmanship. That means that of the 150 votes on which he cast either a yea or nay ballot (either in person or by proxy), he was successful on about 90 percent. On the losing roll calls, he generally voted with most of the Democrats against a few Democrats aligned with virtually all of the Republicans. Divisions among the Democrats accounted for most of his losses.

In his first term as chairman, Powell voted on the losing side on several amendments to the College Academic Facilities and Scholarship Act, which was never enacted. In addition, he failed in his bid to keep National Defense Education Act (NDEA) funds from being slashed. In 1963-64, Powell's side lost on an antidiscrimination amendment to the extension of impacted areas legislation, on an exemption in the Federal Coal Mine Safety Act for mines with fewer than fourteen people, and on two amendments to the poverty program. In 1965 he lost on minimum wage, the higher education bill, and a procedural motion.

That there were only twelve committee roll calls during the 1966 session and that Powell was absent or voted "present" on five of them may have lowered his overall success record. Two of those votes related to some serious problems he had in his committee. He had provoked his colleagues into proposing restrictions on the chairman's powers. Naturally, he voted against the motion to consider such rules changes and then cast a "present" vote on their adoption. The other issue he lost on was an amendment to the Economic Opportunity Act of 1964 concerning education payments relating to Indian children under the poverty program.

Comparatively, Powell was much more successful in voting with the winning side in committee than was Barden as chairman during the 1950s. Barden never won on more than 75 percent of the party votes, and generally, the more party votes there were, the worse his record was. Barden won on 58.6 percent of all votes and on only 38.5 percent of the party votes. Powell, on the other hand, voted on the winning side on over 82 percent of all committee roll calls and on 88.8 percent of the party votes during his tenure as chairman. While it is a rare chairman who can win on every vote, Powell was substantially more representative of his party and of his committee than was Barden.

Leadership: Institutional versus Personal Resources

The manner in which a chairman combines the use of his official prerogatives and personal resources is a manifestation of how he exercises leadership. Powell's reliance on the written and unwritten prerogatives of the chairmanship, his use of rewards and sanctions, his reputation among his peers, and his knowledge of the rules and of the subject at hand distinguished him from Graham Barden. The committee, though composed of many of the same members, was a different organization under the leadership of each chairman. It worked differently, had a different reputation, and produced different outputs. The chairmen of Education and Labor provide evidence that leaders perceive and respond to environmental constraints and expectations in myriad ways. These variations, plus dissimilarities in personality and personal resources, yield diverse leadership patterns and impacts.

The 1960s committee had a new agenda, this time led by the administration and carried out by a liberal majority that was created largely as a result of the House leadership's skewing of assignments. This agenda was important to a variety of people, and it received a great deal of media attention. By and large, Powell, unlike his predecessor, let the committee run itself. Powell increased the staff, the number of meetings, and the number of hearings. He delegated much of the authority and took credit for the accomplishments. An active subcommittee system did most of the work.

Since his power base derives in large part from the position's prerogatives, a primary aspect of a chairman's leadership behavior is his response to expectations held by other members of his committee. If his actions coincide with their expectations and those of the House, he will be successful, and the committee will run smoothly. If not, he will be restrained. Whatever personal influence a chairman has augments the wealth of resources at his disposal.

Despite the addition of some amendments to the committee rules when Powell took the helm, he had more discretion than Barden had had in the previous term. Although the subcommittees had been established by the 1961 rules and were given the authority to act as agents of the committee, the major difference was the lack of firmly defined jurisdictions. This lack left Powell a great deal of discretion over the referral of bills. He also had the authority to establish additional subcommittees as he wished. In other, generally less-consequential ways, the new chairman had less discretion. He was required to assign all members to one or more subcommittees. The rules designated the ranking majority members as subcommittee chairmen and directed the chairman to recommend as conferees with the Senate the members of the subcommittee that reported the bill in question. Without an outright confrontation, however, there was little way to enforce these provisions. The chairman could disregard the rules until a majority was willing to call him on it. Few members relished challenging the chairman.

Powell relied heavily on subcommittees. Virtually all the legislation referred to the Committee on Education and Labor subsequently was sent to a subcommittee. Powell was good at delegating the details to others. He gave the subcommittee chairmen free rein to run their subunits. He let them do the work and was adroit at taking much of the credit for programs that survived the process. Members voiced few complaints about Powell's referring legislation to the wrong subcommittees, at least for the first two terms. According to staff, Powell and the members had a "gentleman's agreement" that if somebody had worked on a particular subject for a long time, related legislation would be referred to whichever subcommittee he happened to chair or sit on, regardless of the subcommittee's jurisdiction. For example, during the 87th Congress, bills relating to aid for the fine arts came under the jurisdiction of the Select Subcommittee on Education, chaired by Frank Thompson, Jr., (D-NJ). In the 88th, Thompson chaired the Special Subcommittee on Labor, which then considered bills to aid the growth and development of the fine arts. Also in the 88th, bills on "quality education," either relating to the NDEA or to cooperative research, were sent to the Special Subcommittee on Labor, where Representatives Hugh Carey (D-NY) and James G. O'Hara (D-MI) served. Powell generally referred bills to the subcommittees where their sponsors and promoters served.

Powell did establish special subcommittees for his personal interest, as well as for the interests of other members. He chaired a subcommittee on the International Labor Organization because of a personal interest—in the travel benefits, it is said (interview). He also chaired the Subcommittee on the War on Poverty Program, comprising the most senior Democrats and assorted Republicans, and another on the study of shared time education. In the 89th Congress, he sat as chairman of the ad hoc Subcommittee on De Facto School Segregation, which handled an issue of long-standing interest to him. It gave him another platform from which to decry racism and to take credit for efforts to abolish it. Powell also let other members chair subcommittees concerning issues of personal interest. He established a subcommittee to study the impact of automation on employment and appointed as chairman Elmer Holland (D-PA), who had a particular interest in labor and unemployment. Powell initially favored John Dent (D-PA) with the chairmanship of the ad hoc Subcommittee on the National Labor Relations Board, but its ranking member, Roman Pucinski (D-IL), took it over when Dent was appointed chairman of the Subcommittee on the Impact of Imports and Exports on American Employment. Both subcommittee chairmen had strong labor constituencies that were adversely affected by automation and by imports. Powell, too, had a strong interest in the effects of automation on black labor and used the issue to needle labor unions about their discriminatory practices.

The creation of these ad hoc committees may have led one scholar to accuse Powell of circumventing the established subcommittee system by creating a new subcommittee structure, assigning the new subcommittees jurisdictions similar to the old ones, and appointing to them members who shared his views. Morrow (1969, 40) argued that Powell then referred most of the major bills to the newly created subcommittees. An examination of the committee's activities and accomplishments and the ad hoc subcommittees that Powell established, however, provides little support for this argument.[4] The Subcommittee on the War on Poverty Program was the only ad hoc unit created to deal with major legislation. For the most part, the chairman assigned bills to the standing subcommittees. On occasion, he set up a task force or a subcommittee to investigate complaints or to study a subject in which he or another member was interested, but the standing subcommittees did most of the work.

The gavel provides one of the chairman's most valued resources. With gavel in hand, he controls, among other things, the conduct of meetings and hearings, the recognition of members to speak, the power to make parliamentary rulings, the authority to call votes, the scheduling of legislation, the time allotted to consider a proposal, and conferences with the Senate. Moreover, he can do whatever he can get away with until someone challenges him.

Powell had no qualms about calling meetings during his first two terms as chairman. If Powell was indisposed, Carl Perkins (D-KY) presided with his blessing. During the 89th Congress, however, the members were angered by Powell's increasingly frequent absences. Powell was indisposed so often that the members were frustrated in several attempts to push through their legislation. In the session before, in 1964, Powell had attended only 36.4 percent of the committee's meetings. As a consequence of his absences, his committee colleagues instituted rules legitimating their actions when he was not present. Verifying current practice, the new rules allowed the ranking majority member present to preside in the absence of the chairman. A former staff member, however, disagreed with the need to change the rules, commenting that "Powell's absences never stopped a thing. Perkins could do it. He followed Adam's instructions to the letter" (interview).

Powell let his committee members hold hearings on just about anything. The 1961 committee rules authorized subcommittees to hold hearings, receive exhibits, take testimony, and report the results or findings to the full committee. The chairman had to authorize any hearings held outside Washington or during a recess or adjournment. As a result of these rules and of a cooperative chairman, the number of hearings increased under Powell.

By all accounts, Powell was effective in his use of the gavel and its associated prerogatives, although he was not always fair to his opponents. He ran the meetings efficiently, but the Republicans claimed, on occasion, that he "stampeded" them. In response to one such accusation during the poverty hearings, Powell replied, "I am the chairman. I will run this committee as I desire" (Committee on Education and Labor, *Hearings on the Economic Opportunity Act of 1964*, 88th Cong., 2d sess., 1964, p. 1150; cited in Bibby and Davidson 1972, 239; Zarefsky 1986, 54; and Jones 1984, 99). On another occasion, he retorted, "It's my game, baby" (Green, Fallows, and Zwick 1972, 135).

The chairman also has the power to control the committee's agenda. He can decide which legislation merits the most attention and which should be ignored. For the most part, Powell did not attempt to exercise strict control over what the committee considered. The committee had a full menu, and he allowed his subcommittee chairmen to take advantage of the opportunities afforded by the new salience of poverty and education. In the process, he exploited the racial aspects of every issue, holding up some long-awaited labor legislation because unions were unfair to blacks.

By virtue of the rules of the House, as chairman Powell controlled the appointment and duties of committee and subcommittee majority staff members. The ranking minority member had the same authority over minority party staff. By the committee rules, Powell could delegate staff members, after consultation with subcommittee chairmen, to subcommittees wherever he saw fit. Other committee members desiring staff assistance were required to petition the chairman for his permission.

Although the previous chairman had appointed what little staff there was in his last Congress, Powell allowed subcommittee chairs effective control over their own employees. One member recalled: "Under Powell, for the first time, the committee budgets were raised, and there was adequate staff. Barden had kept all the committee staff to himself. The subcommittees also had staffs for the first time. The committee now had the capability to get things done" (interview). One member, who claimed a large part of the responsibility for separate subcommittee staffs, commented: "Committee members wanted Education and Labor to be immunized from Powell. He was uneven. I knew I could take advantage of Powell's status in the House and establish a precedent to have separate guaranteed funding for subcommittees. Banking and Currency—the housing subcommittee headed by [Albert] Rains—was next. Now several subcommittees have it. It was easy to diminish Powell's power" (interview). Powell kept control of the full committee majority staff, keeping only two who had been with Barden. He hired almost all new people. Although some of his committee employees were professionally qualified, Powell also staffed the committee with friends and relatives, much to the chagrin of the rest of the committee and, ultimately, of Congress.

Powell started his staffing abuses early in his congressional career. An Abyssinian Baptist Church aide, his secretary in the days before he became chairman, was convicted of, among other things, being on a congressional payroll long after she had returned to New York (Hickey and Edwin 1965, 118-21). Powell was accused of taking kickbacks from her congressional salary, although no one ever could prove it. Powell also abused his chairmanship privileges by hiring his wife at a salary of nearly thirteen thousand dollars per annum, his girlfriend, a clerk who served as a maid in his Bimini home (Hamilton 1991, 411-14, 447), and other people deemed unacceptable by the committee majority. Everybody knew it by 1966, when his then-estranged wife, Yvette, who lived in Puerto Rico and was on the committee payroll at a salary of more than twenty thousand dollars, complained that she had not been receiving her checks. Powell allegedly had endorsed her checks and kept the money (Udall 1972, 254). In addition, he frequently was accompanied by staff members, usually beautiful women, on his travels about the world (see Jacobs 1973, 251).

Powell brought a torrent of criticism and attention to himself by flaunting his congressional privileges. In the process, he drew unfavorable attention to Congress itself. Many questions were raised about the propriety of taking his secretary, a former beauty queen, and another attractive female staff member on a trip throughout Europe at government expense, ostensibly to study equal employment opportunities for women in the member countries of the Common Market. The trip caused such a clamor back in the United States that Powell's career never recovered. His House colleagues even laughed at him when he returned to the floor (Hickey and Edwin 1965, 222-23).

The chairman of the Committee on House Administration, Omar Burleson of Texas, threatened to reduce Powell's staff funding. Powell responded and further embarrassed the House by saying that he had done nothing that white Congressmen had not been doing for years. His supporters accused the Congress of scrutinizing Powell because he was black. The chairman exploited this argument to its fullest potential, saying, "I wish to state emphatically that I will always do what every other Congressman and committee chairmen do in the House" (*Congressional Quarterly Almanac* 1966, 520).

Some of the minority committee members seemed to have a generally favorable view of how Powell ran the committee, but such an opinion was far from universal. It is notable that a Republican cast the only dissenting ballot when the rules changes were instituted in 1966 and that a longtime Republican committee staff member stated that Powell was a good chairman. Nevertheless, Powell did not cater to the Republicans. On Powell's treatment of the minority, one majority member recalled: "Powell treated the minority shabbily. He didn't give them a lot of attention. He wouldn't kowtow to them. When there was big stuff, he courted Republican support. He was solicitous of them. When the battle lines were clear, he ran right over them" (interview). Powell did have his disagreements with the Republicans and was well known for his partisanship on the committee. In one instance in 1961, he took control of the minority's office space, sparking nearly an all-out war with ranking minority member Carroll Kearns (R-PA). Kearns refused to move, and Powell blocked the door (interview, member; Saloma 1969, 120; Fenno 1973, 87).

In 1966 the minority complained that hearings were scheduled at irregular hours, that members were not given proper notice, and that Powell was using the gavel to stifle dissent (Bibby and Davidson 1972, 239). In House debate on Title I of the Elementary and Secondary Education Act of 1965, Powell requested that the debate and amendments be cut off by 6:15 P.M., thus precluding discussion of nine amendments to be offered by Republican committee members (Saloma 1969, 123; Eidenberg and Morey 1969, 135). As the partisan wrangling continued, one of the Republicans complained that the product aptly could be entitled the "Railroad Act of 1965" (Saloma 1969, 124).

In the hearings on the War on Poverty, the Republicans charged Powell with promoting unfair partisanship. According to one account, "Chairman Powell selectively enforced a five-minute time limit on the cross-examination of witnesses, becoming especially strict when Republicans were questioning. The minority party was not allowed to question a witness until six Democrats had done so, although the committee's custom was to alternate between majority and minority members. Republicans further complained that they were not given sufficient advance notice of the committee's meetings" (Zarefsky 1986, 53-54). Nor were Republicans happy when the administration supplied a parade of witnesses in favor of the program and outnumbered opponents. Fifty-six people testified as primary witnesses in favor of the bill, whereas only nine testified against it (Bibby and Davidson 1972, 239).

On occasion, the chairman also employed other techniques to irritate Republicans. When the antipoverty bill was marked up, Powell locked out the Republicans, and the final amending and revisions were done by committee Democrats (Zarefsky 1986, 54). During the mark-up session, the Republicans picketed the locked meeting room carrying a sign saying, "Open the door, Adam" (Fenno 1973, 87). Powell's actions were ironic. Eighteen years earlier he had complained bitterly that the Taft-Hartley Act had been marked up by the Republians in secrecy (Hardeman and Bacon 1987, 329). Everything the minority proposed was rejected, usually by straight party vote, and members alleged that the chairman did not allot them sufficient time to explain or justify their proposals (Zarefsky 1986, 54).

In sum, Powell did not always act favorably toward the Republicans. He exploited and exacerbated party rifts and sometimes intentionally annoyed Republicans. While the minority, for the most part, agreed that Powell was an effective chairman, when the time came, they too voted to curb his behavior and adopted new committee rules. He had no reliable allies among the Republicans.

As defined by Stogdill, "reward power implies the ability of one individual to facilitate the attainment of desired outcomes by others" (1974, 287). Powell had to take advantage of his reward power to attain his own outcomes. In effect, he had an implicit arrangement with the subcommittee chairman. Because his name on a bill or his association with a particular position on an issue generated so much automatic opposition he needed allies to achieve his policy goals. Carl Perkins (D-KY) told the author that "it was poison for Adam Clayton Powell to have a bill with his name on it. Pure, blatant racism" (interview). A frequently repeated comment reinforces this point: "Powell loses twenty votes every time he stands up on one side or another on an issue" (quoted in Eidenberg and Morey 1969, 53).

Powell used bill sponsorship as a basis for and a reward for support. On several occasions, while avoiding sponsorship himself, Powell managed to look magnanimous by stepping aside and allowing someone else to sponsor and manage an important piece of legislation. For instance, about sponsorship of the poverty bill, two scholars wrote: "Powell took an active interest in the bill, though he agreed to the administration's tactical suggestion that a respected southern moderate, Representative Phil M. Landrum (D-GA), serve as the bill's principal sponsor" (Bibby and Davidson 1972, 238). By having a conservative introduce the bill and by keeping Powell's name off of it, southerners and other conservatives ostensibly might be more likely to support it.

Powell rewarded members with bill sponsorship on lesser measures as well. For example, in 1965 the committee responded to a large earthquake in California by passing unanimously a disaster relief bill in the form of amendments to the impacted areas legislation. In those days, only one sponsor's name could appear on a bill. The chairman selected the most senior of the five freshmen assigned to the committee in 1965, William D. Ford (D-MI), to sponsor the clean bill, a major piece of legislation with good chances of passing the House. Powell earned Ford's support because the latter had been in the House for only two months and already had a law with his name on it. Next the chairman went to Patsy Mink (D-HI), Lloyd Meeds (D-WA), William Hathaway (D-ME), and James Scheuer (D-NY). He gave each a bill with his or her name on it that would probably pass (interview, member) or another vehicle to allow him or her to excel. Hamilton quoted John Brademas (D-IN) as remembering an incident that happened early in his tenure in Congress: "'John, I want you to be chairman of a task force to take a look at what the federal government should be doing in the way of higher education.' Well, for a fresh second-term congressman to be given that kind of opportunity was a marvelous thing. And he said, 'Here is some staff money. You pick out the other members of your task force'" (1991, 346).

Powell's main use of his reward power was to let the other committee members do as they pleased. Then he claimed the credit for their accomplishments. He could do so using the rationale that he let them do it; he did not stand in the way of progress, but he could have. One member said, "Powell took credit for everything like it came from his tutelage. There was no such thing as a Powell tutelage. This was just to feed his ego. He acted like he was behind the scenes" (interview). Powell even had the audacity to take credit for the ideas in and for drafting one of President Kennedy's speeches. When confronted by a Kennedy aide about his claims, Powell said, "Well, you know those tape recorders. They have all those knobs that you turn on and off. . . . they put other things in other places . . . that's what happened" (Hickey and Edwin 1965, 248).

One pair of scholars suggested that Powell let "the committee have its head" because he did not want to have his authority challenged (Eidenberg and Morey 1969, 52). Evidence also suggests that he let the committee do as it pleased largely because he was not interested in doing the nitty-gritty work necessary to produce good legislation. He much preferred to act as the "committee mouth" and let others act as the hands. By all accounts he also had a short attention span. Bolling said it "has been variously estimated as ranging between forty seconds to two minutes" (1966, 98). Dr. Deborah Wolfe, the committee education chief, recalled that the chairman often got "a little wiggly" at hearings (Hamilton 1991, 349). Powell could relax in Bimini or on the government's cruise ship and let the more diligent members write the legislation and haggle over the small print (interviews, members and staff).

Powell's taking credit for all committee accomplishments was one of two themes dominating the literature and the author's conversations with committee members and staff. The other was Powell's hands-off mode of committee operations, resulting in a rather smoothly functioning organization. Although members generally were pleased that the chairman had followed this practice, they were less enthusiastic over his claiming credit for other members' work, thus depriving them of possible national acclaim.

Another way Powell employed rewards and sanctions was by the referral of bills. According to several staff members, although the chairman usually referred bills to the designated subcommittees, he sometimes used his referral powers to "punish his enemies and reward his friends," particularly in his last term (interviews, staff). He ran afoul of his committee when he violated the "gentleman's agreement" on bill referral. He assigned bills without regard to tradition, a practice that annoyed committee members. On several occasions, he sent a subcommittee chairman's coveted bill to another subcommittee. For instance, Edith Green (D-OR), who chaired the Special Education Subcommittee, had had jurisdiction over the Juvenile Delinquency and Youth Offenses Control Act of 1961 (P.L. 87-274) since the 87th Congress. In the 89th, Powell took it away from her and referred it to the General Education Subcommittee. Staff members said that he "swapped situs picketing around, too" (interview). According to Hamilton (1991, 388), Powell was ready with the stick. When Edith Green reneged on a promise to support a bill if her wishes to keep religion out of the elementary and secondary education bill and other matters were accommodated, Powell threatened to remove vocational rehabilitation from her subcommittee, to fire her sister from the committee staff, and to give her pet bill, the higher education legislation, to John Brademas.

Another of Powell's actions that could be considered a sanction concerned the speed, or lack thereof, with which he referred bills to subcommittees. Since there was no routinized procedure concerning referrals, bills were sent to subcommittees when the chairman got around to directing that they be sent. Members became irritated when Powell's absences and poor office procedures delayed the transmittal. A former staff member said, "I don't know if the delays were deliberate or if they were a result of sloppiness. The clerk would not act without specific directions, and frequently Powell was not available" (interview).

Several people connected with the committee during the 1960s said that Judge Howard W. Smith (D-VA), chairman of the Rules Committee, had a rumored and unpublicized practice of letting Education and Labor have only one rule a year. "No rules for schools was a known Smith policy" (Johnson 1971, 209). According to staff, "Powell played games with this. He created a jam in the committee over whose bill it would be. The last in line wouldn't make it" (interview).

Powell also used sanctions for bargaining purposes with the House, not just the committee. On several occasions Powell held up actions on major bills until promises made to him were fulfilled. He delayed action on elementary and secondary education legislation in 1965 until he was granted the $440,000 he had requested for operating expenses for the committee. Although the House balked because members were "edgy about his conspicuous junketeering" (Goldman 1969, 302), President Johnson persuaded the House to give him his money so the committee could act (Johnson 1971, 211).[5]

Another example of his bargaining tactics occurred with 1966 amendments to the Economic Opportunity Act of 1964. He held the bill hostage for four months after the committee reported it on June 1 while he negotiated for what he wanted in the program. He also withheld a task force report that he had received in March showing the antipoverty policy to be a good program until one week before the bill was to be reported on the floor in September 1966 (*Congressional Quarterly Almanac* 1966, 257, 520). His absences, as well as an unusual Rules Committee action, contributed to the delays. The Committee on Rules had issued a rule giving the Speaker the option to bypass the committee chairman in calling up the poverty bill. Powell was insulted and refused to cooperate with efforts to secure a floor vote. He finally relented and allowed it to be scheduled for September 26. His actions on this bill led to the committee revolt against him four days before the bill came to the floor (see Loftus 1966b; *Congressional Quarterly Almanac* 1966, 520).

Chairman Powell also balked on two labor bills considered important by the liberal Democrats on the committee and in the administration. AFL-CIO leader George Meany was not pleased when Powell delayed action on the repeal of section 14B of the Taft-Hartley Act that gave states the right to enact "right-to-work" laws outlawing the union shop. Powell refused to report the bill to the House until legislation, which had yet to be introduced, strengthening federal laws against prohibition of discrimination by labor unions had been enacted. He later moderated his position and reported the bill, along with a twenty-one-day resolution to speed its trip to the floor (*Congressional Quarterly Almanac* 1965, 827; 1966, 520).

Powell also held up the situs picketing bill of 1966 because the construction unions discriminated against blacks. After it had been approved by the committee, he delayed reporting the bill pending Senate action on it and on an anti–discrimination in employment bill and until the House had passed the minimum-wage bill. By May 1966 these conditions had not been met. Powell arranged with the Speaker to have the situs picketing bill removed from the House calendar, an action that, in effect, was a pocket veto (*Congressional Quarterly Almanac* 1965, 832-43; 1966, 85, 520, 820; and Loftus 1966a, 1966b, 1966c).

A chairman's personal power is shaped by his use of institutional prerogatives, by the institutional context, and by his personal attributes. These include his expertise on the committee's subject matter and the rules and his reputation as a leader, both among his constituents and in Congress. His personal resources also shape his use of institutional tools. Powell was an expert on neither the subject matter nor the rules. While other members spent hours poring over the details of major legislation, Powell either could not or would not. He claimed to have the expertise but, in fact, did not. A fellow committee member described him as "pretty irresponsible. Other committee members were afraid that he'd get up on the floor and make some terrible blunder because he didn't know what was going on. He took a lot of credit but really didn't know" (interview). According to people who knew him, Powell became bored easily. He was undependable. He could not be counted on to be there when he was needed, much less to say what he was supposed to say or to support what he was supposed to support. Moreover, many thought that he could undermine progress with one fell swoop of his "Powell Amendment" (interview).

On the other hand, Powell was an expert at thinking on his feet and at articulating those thoughts. He could make a sound and eloquent case for a proposal while knowing little about it. His expertise lay in his oratorical skills. He left the details to be worked out by others. One of his committee members said, "Powell was there to open debates on the floor, but then he turned it over to those who worked on it" (interview). In one episode, he had been before the Committee on Rules presenting the case for an Education and Labor bill. When Rules members asked him about another Education and Labor bill, about to be pleaded by Representative Green, Powell had no inkling of what they were talking about but extricated himself gracefully by presenting a persuasive and articulate case for why Mrs. Green would be the best one to talk to about the bill (interview, member).

Powell also was expert at exploiting the racial aspect of every issue. He could find a racial argument in just about every issue or position that he opposed, saying that it was detrimental to blacks or accusing the people supporting it of being bigots or "Uncle Toms." He used race as a tool for achieving his goals, almost as blackmail. One House member and author referred to this practice as the "racial bugaboo," saying that "for years Mr. Powell successfully answered all criticisms with cries of 'bigotry' and 'racism'" (Udall 1972, 255). On the floor of the House he intervened with a point of order to question the propriety of Congressman John Rankin's use of the term *nigger* in his speeches before the House. Although Speaker Joseph W. Martin, Jr., ruled that he had heard *Negro* rather than its more offensive variation, by raising the issue, Powell had forced it to be printed in the *Congressional Record*, thereby bringing it to public attention (Hickey and Edwin 1965, 111). He put some of his fire to paper in his book, *Marching Blacks* (1945), a controversial history of the black struggle that drew attention to many of the problems of blacks. He particularly attacked the South and urged blacks to move to the North, where the schools were not segregated, there was no poll tax, and even the worst conditions were better than those in the South.

Although not a widely renowned parliamentarian, Powell had sufficient expertise to manipulate the rules of the House and of parliamentary procedure to his advantage. His closure of the debate on the Elementary and Secondary Education Act was an example of such skill. But he was not known particularly for his ability to run rings around the Congress or to tie it in procedural knots by tactical maneuvers. Instead, he raised sticky questions that involved it in debate or stalemate for hours. Nevertheless, in his last term, by thwarting the rules altogether, he delayed or prevented legislation from coming to the floor.

Few people could deny that Powell was one of the great orators of his day. He was a Baptist preacher by training. He could manipulate a crowd on the street or a group in the House. One House member said, "He had crowds eating out of his hand. He moved people. That was his talent and what he enjoyed doing. He was a preacher—not much as a legislator" (interview, member). Hickey and Edwin described a campaign speech in 1958: "For thirty minutes, Powell held them rapt. It was a strange and highly-charged scene. . . . His words, gestures, intonations, and appearance were almost calculatedly sensual. At one instant, he roared his pain so that it rumbled across the black faces; at the next he was silent, unbreathing, and tentative, until the next rush of passion tumesced in him. He worked over them with the attention and fastidiousness of an amorist" (1965, 151-52).

Powell had the reputation of being one of the most influential and powerful black politicians of his day and "one of the Congress's most warmly disliked members" (Eidenberg and Morey 1969, 52). One member said, "He could have eclipsed Martin Luther King" if he had played by the rules of the game (interview). Another wrote: "Adam Clayton Powell equals Martin Luther King in magnetism, in intellect. But King has something Powell has not: exemplary character and moral force. But more important, Powell had something King could never hope to have: cold political power beyond that ever held by a Negro. His lack of King's character threw this magnificent potential away" (Udall 1972, 254). Powell's reputation as one of the most influential black leaders often put him in competition with other blacks prominent in the civil rights movement. He frequently played hard ball in efforts to prove his importance and to maintain his reputation as a preeminent leader of black causes. Taylor Branch brought to light an incident in which Powell resorted to blackmail to prevent Martin Luther King, Jr., from picketing the 1960 Democratic National Convention in Los Angeles over the civil rights plank in the platform. Reportedly Powell threatened to tell the press that King was having a homosexual affair with Bayard Rustin, who was known among black leaders to have a homosexual "problem" (Branch 1988, 314-15; Garrow 1986, 140).

Powell's reputation as a leader among blacks also made him a much sought after prize in the endorsement competition accompanying the 1960 presidential campaign. He had supported Lyndon B. Johnson prior to the Democratic National Convention but was persuaded to make ten speeches—purportedly for a payment of fifty thousand dollars—in support of John F. Kennedy after the latter received the nomination (Branch 1988, 343).

Adam Clayton Powell also had a well-deserved notorious reputation. There was nothing even remotely inconspicuous about him. Everything he did attracted attention—his speeches, his cars, his female companions, his travels, and his absences. He earned renown for being a philanderer. Wherever he went, he was in the company of beautiful women. This attracted a great deal of attention, some of it flattering and some of it not, among his constituents and among his colleagues in Congress. Defending himself from accusations of hedonism, Powell said: "I have been criticized during my life for admitting that I enjoy the company of women. And there have been times when I have been told that it would be better not to let photographers shoot me with a glass in my hand. I have also been accused of almost everything—of being a black racist, an Uncle Tom, a rabble-rouser, a pleasure-seeker, a slanderer, and much more. But I have never been accused of being a hypocrite, of saying anything I did not believe in, or doing anything I did not enjoy" (1971, 235).

Powell's reputation among his constituents differed from his reputation among his congressional peers. Many of his constituents seemed proud, whereas most members of Congress were annoyed or embarrassed. In his district, the chairman was known as the Reverend Powell of the Abyssinian Baptist Church. Although he referred to himself as a "poor parish priest," his constituents' admiration for him grew from his role as pastor, his physical attractiveness, and his efforts to advance minority rights (Valenti 1975, 187; Udall 1972, 252).

He had a fiery style in the pulpit. He could move crowds with his words like few others and could manipulate them to do just about anything. He had a flair for making people believe in the image he put forth. Hickey and Edwin cited several examples of the loyalty of his constituents as he was being tried for tax evasion.

I'm standing here praying for him. I know God will answer my prayers. He champions the underprivileged and is a leader of people in all walks of life.

I love Reverend Powell. He began helping us workers years ago. I know this day he's being prosecuted for helping us. I intend to stand for him until the end of this unfair trial.

Reverend Powell is the greatest living Negro we have. It's a downright shame he has to suffer for this.

I feel that because he has been so outspoken in representing us is the very reason he's in there.

I'm for Adam because he can't be bought. He fights hard out there for me and I know it. [1965, 167-68]

In addition to his appearances of uprightness, Powell also was dashing and had a great appeal among the Harlemites, especially the women. His reputation as a womanizer was not hurt by his escorting women who were among the most beautiful in the world. He frequently was seen in the company of Corinne Huff, a former Miss Ohio who also had been a runner-up in the Miss Universe pageant and was on the committee staff.

More important to his career, Powell had a reputation for fighting for the rights of "colored" people and of irritating a great many whites in the process. He frequently was in the forefront of public attention in the civil rights movement, although he had his differences with other black leaders, such as Martin Luther King, Jr., and A. Philip Randolph. Powell advanced his reputation and broadened his public appeal via his editorial column, "Soapbox," in the *Amsterdam News*, a weekly New York newspaper of the time. Later the column appeared in the *People's Voice*, established to enable Powell to reach a larger constituency than only the Abyssinian Baptist Church and the New York City Council. He used it to make anti–right wing declarations, attacking fascism at home as well as abroad and pronouncing against racial inequities (Hickey and Edwin 1965).

Powell's colleagues in the House had an entirely different impression of the fiery speaker and angry young man from New York than did his flock. In Congress, many considered him a troublemaker, especially the southerners. They thought him "the very opposite of the model 'good Negro' as typified by Representative Dawson of Chicago," chairman of the House Committee on Government Operations (Hickey and Edwin 1965, 135). Powell frequently referred to Chairman Dawson as an "Uncle Tom" or a "house Negro." Powell was convinced that Dawson had undermined a strong civil rights plank on the 1952 Democratic party platform (Powell 1971, 90-91). Powell also irritated other Democrats in Congress because he would not toe the party line. When he bolted the Democratic party publicly to support Eisenhower's reelection in 1956, his image as a troublemaker grew. The party, in effect, had its hands tied, because every suggestion that Powell be disciplined was greeted with accusations of racism on the part of House Democrats because (until years later) they had failed to discipline other members who also had deserted the party.[6] Many members of Congress thought that Powell himself was a racist. He agreed: "The white man just doesn't understand what the Negro is thinking. Everything they call me downtown—demagogue, racist—strengthens me uptown. My people want me to be a racist—we're all racists" (Hickey and Edwin 1965, 153-54).

Members of Education and Labor accused Powell of playing to his constituency and of insincerity in his use of the "Powell Amendment." Many perceived his frequent use of his amendment as a ploy to annoy those trying to win aid for education. Once during the Barden years, the use of this amendment allegedly led to blows when Powell offered the anti-discrimination rider and Representative Cleveland Bailey (D-WV), accusing Powell of trying to destroy the public school system, landed a punch on his jaw, knocking him to the floor. Both gentlemen denied the incident.[7]

In his favor, Powell had the reputation among many of being one of the brightest members of Congress. *Brilliant* was a word frequently used to describe him. He certainly was one of the most articulate. One of Speaker Rayburn's lieutenants said that Powell was one of the twelve smartest men in the House, one that "you don't tangle with until you've done your homework" (Hickey and Edwin 1965, 211). Another party wheel said, "He was brilliant, amoral, and an excellent chairman" (interview, member). One member said that columnist Murray Kempton called Powell "brilliant, beautiful, and treacherous. Like a pet ocelot in the House." The member continued, "Powell had catlike movements, too. If you turned your back, you were likely to get clawed" (interview). Another wrote that he was "a study in contrasts: brilliant, but erratic" (Udall 1972, 252).

In addition to his brilliance, Powell seemed to cultivate the reputation of being irresponsible. Several committee and staff members alluded to this trait in interviews with the author, as did Hamilton (1991, 365) in his biography of Powell. The chairman's many absences were a contributing factor to this facet of his ill repute. His limited attention span was another. One member commented, "When Adam Clayton Powell was interested, he showed up. If he wasn't, he didn't" (interview). Columnist Murray Kempton predicted that Powell would be a terrible chairman because he was "lazy, careless, and selfish" (1960).

Powell was reputed to be a debonair, articulate, verbose, and irresponsible troublemaker who did not know his place. This combination was a formula for ill will in the House. His reputation affected his acceptance by other members and, ultimately, his career. Bills lost support rapidly if Powell's name was attached. Two scholars noted that Powell always was able to provoke a "high level of personal antagonism" (Eidenberg and Morey 1969, 53).

Powell's Legal Difficulties

Powell's troubles with the law did little to aid his reputation in Congress.[8] He flouted authority left and right throughout all his legal troubles, ignoring court orders and claiming ignorance or poverty. First, two of his aides and a congressional secretary were indicted for tax evasion. When Powell was called to bring his financial records and to testify at the trials of the two aides, he claimed that all the records had been destroyed in a fire at the Abyssinian Baptist Church and that he knew nothing of any improprieties that might have occurred. Subsequently, the indictments against one of the aides were dropped. The other was convicted and sentenced to a year in prison and payment of a one-thousand-dollar fine in 1956. His secretary, who had worked at the church for years, stood accused of receiving a congressional salary after she had returned to Harlem. She was charged with kicking back her salary to Powell between 1948 and 1952 and was convicted and sentenced to prison for seven months. The investigation focused on Powell, but no concrete evidence against him could be found.

The government's investigation of Powell was now public knowledge. He finally was indicted for tax evasion in 1958. He allegedly prepared false returns for his wife, Hazel Scott, who was not charged, and underreported both their earnings. But in January 1960 the indictments against Powell were dismissed. Hamilton (1991, 340) noted the seeming coincidence that on the same day that the administration announced its decision to drop its tax case against him, Powell uncharacteristically announced his decision not to pursue his antisegregation amendment on school aid legislation, thus removing a major stumbling block to the president's agenda.

The third legal difficulty adding to his image problems stemmed from a 1963 judgment in a libel suit brought by Mrs. Esther James, a black domestic, whom Powell had referred to in a televised interview as a "bag woman" (i.e., graft collector) for the police department in Washington Heights, New York. Powell claimed that he was only providing information to his constituents and claimed congressional immunity from prosecution. He was convicted of libeling Mrs. James, and the jury set damages at more than two hundred thousand dollars, of which the bulk was for damaging the plaintiff's reputation and earning power. Powell refused to pay and was cited for contempt of court. He could not be arrested because of congressional immunity while the Congress was in session. In New York, it was illegal to serve a civil summons on Sunday. Hence, he returned to his district only on Sundays to deliver his sermon at the Abyssinian Baptist Church. Mrs. James had great difficulty in getting her money, because Powell no longer received a salary from the church or had property in his own name in the state. His house in Puerto Rico was in his wife's name and his congressional salary could not be garnished.

Again he was held in contempt of court for nonpayment and nonappearance. He was served with a criminal summons one Sunday outside of his Harlem church. His lawyers negotiated an agreement that enabled him to return to New York with immunity. Mrs. James agreed not to pursue court action until after the court ruled on his appeal. The judges refused to dismiss the judgment but considered it excessive and reduced it to $46,500: $11,500 compensatory damages and $35,000 punitive damages. They agreed to drop the contempt charges. The legal troubles dragged on for years. Powell still refused to pay Mrs. James. He took the case all the way to the U.S. Supreme Court, which refused to review it. He held that the point was moot since he did not have $46,500.

In a second case, Mrs. James alleged that Powell and his wife had transferred property in Puerto Rico to his wife's relatives to avoid its attachment to satisfy the original judgment. Powell failed to file an answer. In February 1965 a jury awarded Mrs. James $350,000. The trial judge reduced the award to $210,000. After Powell repeatedly failed to appear in this case and failed to pay the court-ordered damages, the court ordered him to pay even more damages. The court issued several arrest warrants for Powell on contempt of court charges. As a result of the James suits, for several years Powell could not go back to his district without being arrested, except on Sundays or on election day.

Powell's blatant disregard for the authority of the law further undermined his standing in the House of Representatives. "For a Member of this House to behave in such fashion as to cause the courts to describe his course of conduct as 'flagrantly contemptuous,' as promoting 'the tragic disrespect for the judicial process as a whole,' as displaying 'blatant cynical disregard for the law on the part of a United States Congressman (which) is detrimental to the law, the ministry and to democracy,' and as 'a very bad example for the youth of this city and this country,' clearly brings great disrespect for the House of Representatives" (*In re Adam Clayton Powell* 1967, 13). In addition, a New Jersey House member asked him if he would not mind slowing down a bit because the state police were complaining that Powell roared through the state in his flashy sports car at 110 miles an hour on his way to and from his district. The troopers could not keep up with him. Powell promised that in the future he would not go over 90 (interview, member). Members of the House eventually came to realize that they could no longer tolerate his irresponsible, illegal, immoral, and flaunting behavior (interviews) and refused to seat him in 1967.[9]

Powell's Leadership in Retrospect

When Powell assumed the chairmanship in 1961, the new Kennedy administration was emphasizing social issues. He was able to capitalize on the Kennedy proposals and parlay his position into one of great influence. The administration frequently sought Powell's assistance and support for its policies. In return, Powell put up few obstacles to the president's programs. He spoke articulately for the causes and moved the legislation through his committee, tolerating little opposition from Republican dissenters. According to Fenno: "He wanted his chairmanship to be judged by the large number of bills passed. And he wanted the kind of credit that coalition members—from House to White House—showered upon him. For he traded heavily on that credit to furbish his image as a powerful leader of a nationwide black constituency. An implicit bargain—autonomy for the subcommittees, credit for the chairman, and good public policy for the liberal-Democratic policy coalition—was the basis for normal decision making during the Powell chairmanship" (1973, 130).

In many respects, Powell was a "good" chairman, in the words of his committee members, who largely approved of his committee leadership. He presided competently and ran meetings well. He facilitated the consideration and approval of legislation that members and the administration deemed important. He was an eloquent spokesman for the committee. During his first few years as chairman, Powell used his institutional resources to the benefit of the majority—for the committee rather than against it. For the first time members were allowed to do what they wanted to do and to accomplish what they wanted to accomplish. One of his committee colleagues, John Brademas, said of Powell: "He was a tragic figure. He had intelligence, charm and power, but he lacked the character to put it all together. He was an effective chairman in the early years, but then he ran out of gas" (quoted in Lyons 1972).

Committee members have said that Powell let the committee run itself. He took advantage of his institutional prerogatives and personal resources to exercise permissive, facilitative, and flashy leadership, at least until his last year. His permissiveness resulted in compromises that could not have been worked out and in legislation that never would have been reported under Barden. Expressing a sentiment echoed frequently by former members and staff, one pair of scholars wrote: "He was content to let the subcommittees do their work with latitude and freedom. The smaller work groups handled much of the detail and tedium of guiding legislation through the floor. Powell was satisfied to act as chairman and to receive the perquisites of office (symbolic and material), and generally let others run the legislative show" (Eidenberg and Morey 1969, 54-55). Throughout his chairmanship, Powell exercised his authority largely at the expense of the Republicans and went along with or facilitated the will of the majority. Nevertheless, toward the end of his tenure, he pushed the limits by his high-handed use of his institutional prerogatives concerning bill reporting.

For the most part, Powell relied on institutional prerogatives more than on personal factors to operate the committee. With a wealth of resources at his disposal by virtue of his position, particularly his broad discretion over the referral of bills, the chairman could act as he wished, within bounds, without having to rely heavily on personal resources. As he departed from the policy goals of the majority, he took advantage of the chairman's discretionary powers and betrayed the committee's trust. As happened with Barden, members rebelled and voted to curtail the chairman's institutional prerogatives near the end of his tenure. His use of personal resources, on the other hand, resulted in difficulties with the entire House.

Institutional context, in addition to personal factors, dictated that he could not be authoritarian toward the Democrats and get away with it for several reasons. For one, his predecessor had run the committee entirely according to his own wishes and contrary to the policy goals of the majority party. Powell knew that he would not succeed with similar practices for long or committee members would revolt against him, too. Congress was never meant to be a hierarchical institution. Second, the chairman did not have the backing of the House leadership and membership to support an authoritarian leadership. He was disliked by many members, and he knew that they were looking for ways to get rid of him. Third, the composition of the committee was such that he agreed with his majority most of the time on policy issues; thus he did not have to exercise his options in an authoritarian manner. The 1961 rules allowed him enough discretion so that he could have if he had wanted to, although in the earlier years of his chairmanship he did not need to exercise his authority in a negative manner.

Although a Protestant minister, Powell did not subscribe to the Protestant work ethic. His personality dictated that he talk a good game, rely on others to get the work done, and then take the credit for the success and avoid as much of the blame for defeats as possible. He delegated many of his institutional privileges to his subcommittee chairmen and let them carry out the agenda of the committee.

Powell presided over a committee that had the opportunity to leave its mark on the country by formulating, considering, and approving many of the social welfare programs of the Great Society. When he was chairman, Education and Labor was in its heyday. The issues under its jurisdiction could no longer be ignored. They were ripe for consideration. The chairman's facilitative and permissive use of institutional prerogatives allowed him to make great contributions to the enactment of progressive legislation, to efforts aimed at improving the quality of life for blacks, and to carrying out the committee's agenda. Although he had little to do with the details, he did not stand in the way of, and often facilitated, passage of important legislation. Except when Powell was fighting for his favorite causes, his leadership enabled legislation that had been bottled up for years to be placed on the public agenda, to be considered, and eventually to be enacted.

The chairman's facilitative leadership decentralized power in the committee to a somewhat greater degree than it had been under Barden. More members had a stake in getting the committee's legislation approved. They were willing to work harder because there was a better chance that they would get results. Powell took advantage of their willingness to work and let them.

Until he used his institutional prerogatives to commit the fatal act of thwarting the majority, he was respected by his committee members as an effective chairman. But he crossed the bounds of acceptability by holding important legislation until his demands were met. Once he stalled bills dear to the hearts of his allies, his support diminished, and members acted to curb his ability to delay by creating an institutionally powerless chairmanship (Fenno 1973, 130). They approved rules changes to enable the committee to act when the chairman was indisposed or uncooperative.

Not only was Powell's use of institutional prerogatives of concern to the committee, it also got him in trouble with the House. By delaying several critical bills, he thwarted the will of the House majority. In addition, he hired several unscrupulous staff people who stole money from the committee or who had no business being on the payroll at all. And he abused the travel privileges.

It was largely his reliance on personal resources, however, that led to his downfall. His biggest sin was that he had committed his offenses publicly and then embarrassed the House repeatedly by arguing that he only did what everyone else was doing. In effect, he held his colleagues up to ridicule and would never be forgiven. His personal excesses had offended his colleagues, as had his violations of House rules by his financial practices. Moreover, as a prominent lawmaker he had shown flagrant disregard for the law by repeatedly failing to answer court orders to appear in New York.

Powell had exceeded the limits of acceptability imposed by the institutional context, in the committee and in the House, in his use of both institutional and personal resources. As a result, the committee revolted against Powell just at it had against Barden. The House ultimately took action against Powell, stripping him of his chairmanship and subsequently refusing to seat him in 1967.

5

The Committee during the Perkins Years

The cards Carl Dewey Perkins (D-KY) drew when he became chairman of the Committee on Education and Labor in 1967 did not afford him the opportunities that had challenged his predecessor. Many of the major education controversies had been settled under Adam Clayton Powell, at least temporarily. Perkins faced another, less exciting, but equally critical challenge—that of expanding or maintaining the gains the committee had made in the preceding six years. Moreover, the chairman's institutional resources had been curtailed because of his predecessors' behavior.

From 1967 to 1984 the committee was quite unlike the committee under its predecessors. Its major legislative areas—education and labor—were no longer at the top of the political agenda. It differed in the demographic and ideological composition of its membership, in its voting patterns, in its structure, and in its operations. Not only had the composition changed, but the voting behaviors of the members were slightly less extreme under Perkins than they had been under Powell, the structure of the committee was more complex, and the jurisdiction, function, and orientation of Education and Labor had changed.

Setting

Although the years that Perkins chaired the committee may not have been as turbulent as the early 1960s, it was by no means an era of tranquillity. *Congressional Quarterly* termed 1967 and 1968, Perkins's first two years as chairman, as "two of the most trying years in [U.S.] history" (*Politics in America* 1969, 68). The traumatic political events of the 1960s included the Vietnam War, the assassination of political leaders, inner-city riots, student protests, a deadly fire aboard a spacecraft, a moon walk, riots at the Democratic National Convention, the withdrawal of President Johnson from the political arena, and a host of other occurrences that unsettled the United States. Some of these developments were particularly important to the considerations of the Committee on Education and Labor. The earlier emphasis on large social welfare programs and federal funding for education faded somewhat by 1967, as attention focused on the Vietnam War and war protests. Funds were diverted from social programs and funneled into the war effort (Peters 1982, 241), the cost of which exceeded two billion dollars a month in 1967 (*Politics in America* 1969, 70).

Several large-scale efforts, such as the Poor People's March on Washington and the establishment of Resurrection City, a tent encampment for the impoverished amid Washington's monuments, kept the nation's (and the committee's) attention focused on the plight of the poor. Nevertheless, widespread rioting in the inner cities fostered resentment among many whites. The assassinations of two prominent national leaders, the Reverend Martin Luther King, Jr., and Senator Robert F. Kennedy, rekindled concern over the causes and remedies for the waves of violence buffeting the country.

The war emerged as a major campaign issue in the 1968 elections. Low popularity because of failures in Vietnam led President Johnson to announce that he would not seek reelection. In a campaign aimed at "forgotten Americans"—those not demonstrating or shouting, not racist or sick, and not guilty of crimes—former vice president Richard M. Nixon defeated the Democratic nominee, Vice President Hubert Humphrey, and the American Independent party candidate, Alabama governor George Wallace. By the end of the decade both parties were in upheaval. Nixon was reelected in 1972 in a landslide. He rekindled relations with China and then managed to extricate the United States from the quagmire of Vietnam. The economy, however, was in shambles, and the country faced an energy shortage because of an Arab oil embargo in 1973-74. Vice President Spiro Agnew resigned in October 1973, and Nixon's second term was cut short as a break-in at the Democratic National Committee headquarters precipitated the downfall of the president himself in the infamous Watergate affair. Vice President Gerald Ford succeeded to the presidency in August 1974.

The 1972 and 1974 elections changed the distribution of power in Congress. A tide of young liberal Democrats swept in at the expense of some hard-line conservative Republicans. In the 1974 elections, Democrats picked up forty-nine seats that had been held in the 92d Congress by Republicans. The influx of new faces in the 1970s enabled Democrats to enact a series of major reforms, beginning with the Legislative Reorganization Act of 1970 (P.L. 91-510; 84 Stat. 1140) and proceeding to the 1973 and 1974 House Democratic Caucus reforms strengthening subcommittees.

Democrat Jimmy Carter was elected president in 1976 to preside over a few years of relative calm without wars or major scandals. The economy was the primary concern until the Islamic revolution in Iran became a problem of immense proportions in the United States. Militant Shiite Muslims seized the U.S. embassy in Teheran in 1979 and held fifty-two occupants hostage for 444 days—until the day President Carter left office. As Vietnam had plagued President Johnson, so the hostage crisis plagued President Carter. In addition, a sagging economy, an out-of-control federal budget, and high unemployment and interest rates all added to Carter's image as "weak and ineffective" and led to the election of Republican Ronald Reagan as president in 1980 and to Republican control of the Senate (*Congress and the Nation* 5:3). Reagan's election heralded the rise of the "New Right," the "Religious Right," and political action committees (PACs), which were primarily conservative at first.

Throughout the 1970s and 1980s new issues surfaced on the public agenda, displacing old ones, including many of the staples of Education and Labor. Consumer protection, environmental, energy, and health questions moved to the forefront of American attention and increased in salience throughout the 1980s. These new issues and their high-cost programs impinged on the social welfare programs that had been so prominent in the past. Education and Labor was compelled to defend its turf. In large part, the committee focused on amending and extending previously authorized programs. Members concentrated on education rather than labor legislation, with the exception of programs aimed at the creation of jobs for the unemployed and underemployed.

Composition of the Committee

Committees have been called microcosms of the House—a comparison that presumes a geographic and ideological representation on committees similar to that of the House. This condition does not hold true for the Committee on Education and Labor. In the regions represented and members' seniority, ideological bent, and reasons for leaving, Education and Labor was not a microcosm of the House during this period, although it moved closer to being one before the end of the Perkins chairmanship.

Education and Labor, from the 90th to the 98th Congress (1967-84), attracted its membership predominantly from the Middle Atlantic and the East North Central regions (see table 5.1). Moreover, at least half of committee Democrats and a large portion of the Republicans came from these two regions during every Congress under consideration. Compared

Table 5.1. Regional Composition of the Committee, 1967-1984 (percentages)

Region	Congress								
	90th	91st	92d	93d	94th	95th	96th	97th	98th
Full Committee									
New England	3.1	2.9	5.3	5.6	7.7	8.3	8.3	8.6	2.9
Middle Atlantic	21.9	25.7	31.6	30.6	25.6	30.6	25.0	22.9	22.9
East North Central	28.1	31.4	26.3	25.0	25.6	25.0	22.2	25.7	22.9
West North Central	6.3	8.6	5.3	5.6	12.8	11.1	11.1	11.4	11.4
South	12.5	5.7	2.6	5.6	7.7	5.6	11.1	5.7	8.6
Border	6.3	2.9	5.3	5.6	5.1	5.6	5.6	2.9	2.9
Mountain	0.0	2.9	2.6	5.6	0.0	0.0	8.3	11.4	11.4
Pacific	18.8	17.1	18.4	13.9	12.8	11.1	8.3	11.4	17.1
External	3.1	2.9	2.6	2.8	2.6	2.8	0.0	0.0	0.0
E & L Democrats									
New England	5.6	5.0	9.1	5.0	3.8	4.2	8.7	5.0	0.0
Middle Atlantic	27.8	35.0	36.4	35.0	26.9	37.5	34.8	25.0	27.3
East North Central	22.2	25.0	18.2	15.0	26.9	25.0	17.4	25.0	22.7
West North Central	0.0	5.0	4.5	5.0	7.7	8.3	4.3	5.0	9.1
South	5.6	0.0	0.0	10.0	7.7	4.2	8.7	5.0	9.1
Border	11.1	5.0	9.1	10.0	7.7	4.2	4.3	5.0	4.5
Mountain	0.0	0.0	0.0	0.0	0.0	0.0	8.7	10.0	9.1
Pacific	22.2	20.0	18.2	15.0	15.4	12.5	13.0	20.0	18.2
External	5.6	5.0	4.5	5.0	4.2	4.2	0.0	0.0	0.0
E & L Republicans									
New England	0.0	0.0	0.0	6.3	15.4	16.7	7.7	13.3	7.7
Middle Atlantic	14.3	13.3	25.0	25.0	23.1	16.7	7.7	20.0	15.4
East North Central	35.7	40.0	37.5	37.5	23.1	25.0	30.8	26.7	23.1
West North Central	14.3	13.3	6.3	6.3	23.1	16.7	23.1	20.0	15.4
South	21.4	13.3	6.3	0.0	7.7	8.3	15.4	6.7	7.7
Border	0.0	0.0	0.0	0.0	0.0	8.3	7.7	0.0	0.0
Mountain	0.0	6.7	6.3	12.5	0.0	0.0	7.7	13.3	15.4
Pacific	14.3	13.3	18.8	12.5	7.7	8.3	0.0	0.0	15.4
External	0.0	0.0	0.0	0.0	0.0	0.0	0.0	0.0	0.0

Source: Author's calculations from data in Inter-University Consortium for Political and Social Research. The sums of some columns are not exactly 100.0 percent because of rounding. Territorial representatives are not included in the calculations.

with the proportion of Democratic members in the House, these parts of the country consistently had more than their share of majority committee seats, sometimes even twice the percentage of Democrats in the House. In addition, in seven of the nine Congresses, Republicans from the East North Central states were overrepresented, too.

On the whole, the proportion of committee seats from the West North Central states did not deviate greatly from the proportion in the House. Unless members from these states had a strong interest in education, they found little to attract them to this committee. Most of the programs targeted federal aid to urban areas in various forms or concerned labor union issues, which were not as salient in this region as in others.[1]

Few members represented the Deep South on the committee during the Perkins years, a trend dating from the Barden era when the Speaker stacked the committee with northern, urban liberals and refused to assign southerners. Assignments on other committees would seem more profitable for conservative southerners; Education and Labor offered few inducements to members from rural or conservative, antiunion districts. Border states also were underrepresented consistently from 1967 to 1984.

The proportion of members from the western regions reasonably reflected the proportion of the full House representing those regions, although the percentages fluctuated. With a few exceptions, such as Edith Green (D) and John Dellenback (R) of Oregon, the several members from California's urban areas formed the basis of the relatively large proportion of committee members from the western states. Although still holding a relatively small proportion of the House and committee membership, the mountain states (including the Southwest) gained representation in both throughout the period, particularly among the Republicans.

These statistics on regional representation support the contention that members from northern, urban districts, aided by a large contingent of members from the West Coast, controlled the Committee on Education and Labor. With representation ranging from 65 to 80 percent of the majority membership, members from the Middle Atlantic, East North Central, and Pacific states exerted a great deal of influence over the committee's operations and output. With the exception of the 96th and 97th Congresses, over half of the minority opposition also represented these three regions.

An average of over 40 percent of the members of Education and Labor were freshmen or sophomore members during the period 1967-84. Democrats tended to stay longer on the committee than did Republicans. Democrats had a much higher proportion of members who had served five or more terms and a smaller percentage of new members. With the exception of a few senior members, generally those in control of minority subcommittee staff funds, Republicans tended to stay on the committee for one or two terms and then move on to better assignments. Part of this phenomenon can be explained by the fact that Education and Labor had little to offer most Republicans. Their constituencies and their reputations could be enhanced by service on other committees. According to several former members and staff, most Republicans and many Democrats viewed Education and Labor as a hardship post.[2] With marginal perquisites, oftentimes Republicans served on this committee for a few terms in return for promises of choice assignments on other committees.

Beginning in the late 1970s, a few members of both parties were assigned to the committee temporarily. When there were vacancies, members with major assignments on other committees, such as Energy and Commerce or Foreign Affairs, could sit on Education and Labor. They were committee members in every respect but seniority, ranking behind other members who had permanent assignments. This accounts for a seemingly curious situation where one member who joined the committee in the 96th Congress was outranked by seven new members in the 97th because of his temporary status. One benefit of this practice is that it gives the party the chance to remove members who do not live up to the expectations of other party member.[3]

Republicans far outpaced Democrats in the race to assign new members to Education and Labor. As can be seen in table 5.2, on average, less than a fourth of the Democrats were new each term, whereas nearly 34 percent of the Republicans were first-term committee members. In the 98th Congress (1983-84), over 46 percent of Education and Labor Republicans were recent additions to the committee. New members predominantly were House freshmen from both parties, although occasionally a veteran member would join, especially when bodies were needed to fill vacancies. In the 90th Congress (1967-68), Majority Leader Carl Albert (D-OK) "took a troubleshooter assignment on the Education and Labor Committee because its combative Democratic members were badly divided" (Bolling 1968, 94).[4] He was the only new committee Democrat named in the 90th Congress, for Democrats had lost two seats. The GOP, on the other hand, assigned seven new freshmen.

For a variety of reasons, including death, defeat, retirement, and running for other office, forty-eight members of the committee left Congress from 1968 to 1984, while four were elected or appointed to the Senate and forty-one transferred to other committees. On average, more than one-fourth of the members left after each term: 24.75 percent of the Democrats and 35.8 percent of the Republicans (see table 5.3). The 93d Congress in 1973-74 saw a significant increase in the number of members who did not return to Congress. Half the Republicans did not return to the committee. Several Nixon loyalists on Education and Labor were defeated in the Watergate aftermath, including Earl Landgrebe (R-IN), who was called "Nixon's most extreme and ludicrous defender in the House" (Rapoport 1975, 5). Another committee Republican, Robert Huber, from Michigan, also fell victim to Watergate. Barone, Ujifusa, and Matthews described him as "a solid right winger in the House—with a reputation for zaniness that got him stuck on the hopelessly liberal Education and Labor Committee—

Table 5.2. Seats, New Members, and Freshmen, 1967-1984

| | | Number | | | | | | | | |
| | | All members | | | New members | | | Freshmen | | |
Congress	Year	Full	Dems	Reps	Full	Dems	Reps	Full	Dems	Reps
90th	1967-68	34	19	15	8	1	7	7	0	7
91st	1969-70	35	20	15	6	3	3	5	2	3
92d	1971-72[a]	38	22	16	10	6	4	7	4	3
93d	1973-74	37	21	16	6	3	3	6	3	3
94th	1975-76	40	27	13	14	9	5	13	9	4
95th	1977-78	37	25	12	11	7	4	8	6	2
96th	1979-80[b]	36	24	12	13	6	7	10	5	5
97th	1981-82	36	21	15	10	3	4	9	3	6
98th	1983-84[c]	38	23	13	14	8	6	12	7	5
	Total	331	202	127	92	46	43	77	39	38
	Mean	36.8	22.4	14.1	10.2	5.1	4.8	8.6	4.3	4.2

| | | Percentage | | | | | |
| | | New members | | | Freshmen | | |
		Full	Dems	Reps	Full	Dems	Reps
90th	1967-68	23.5	5.3	46.7	20.6	0.0	46.7
91st	1969-70	17.1	15.0	20.0	14.3	10.0	20.0
92d	1971-72	26.3	27.3	25.0	18.4	18.2	18.8
93d	1973-74	16.2	14.3	18.8	16.2	14.3	18.8
94th	1975-76	35.0	33.3	38.5	32.5	33.3	30.8
95th	1977-78	29.7	28.0	33.3	21.6	24.0	16.7
96th	1979-80	36.1	25.0	58.3	27.8	20.8	41.7
97th	1981-82	27.8	14.3	26.7	25.0	14.3	40.0
98th	1983-84	36.8	34.8	46.2	31.6	30.4	38.5

Source: Compiled from Committee on Education and Labor, *Calendar* 1967-84. The counts include the delegates from Puerto Rico, who can vote in committee but not on the floor of the House.

[a] In the 92d Congress, Adam Powell is not counted as a new member. He was added to the bottom of the seniority list in the 91st after having been omitted from the committee roster in the 90th. Although he never showed up for meetings, he is included in the full committee count.

[b] In the 96th Congress, Peter Peyser switched from the Republican to the Democratic party. Full committee numbers to not show him as a new member, although he is counted as a new Democrat. Raphael Musto (D-PA) replaced Don Bailey (D-PA). Only one is counted as a new member because only one seat was affected.

[c] In the 98th Congress, Thomas J. Tauke is counted as a new member because he was reassigned to Education and Labor after serving in the 96th Congress and sitting out the 97th. He did not retain his seniority because he had a temporary assignment in the 96th.

Table 5.3. Percentage of Members Who Left after Each Congress, 1967-1984

Congress	Year	Full	Dems	Reps
90th	1967-68	17.6	15.8	20.0
91st	1969-70	20.0	20.0	20.0
92d	1971-72	18.4	18.2	18.7
93d	1973-74	29.7	14.3	50.0
94th	1975-76	35.0	33.3	38.5
95th	1977-78	32.4	24.0	50.0
96th	1979-80	32.4	28.0	41.6
97th	1981-82	33.3	19.0	53.3
98th	1983-84	40.0	45.4	30.1

Source: Compiled from Committee on Education and Labor, Calendar 1967-84.

and he was a constant and enthusiastic supporter of Richard Nixon" (1977, 434). David G. Towell (R-NV), who came to Congress on Nixon's coattails, went out on them, too. Generally known as a moderate, John Dellenback (R-OR) was another victim of Watergate and the strong Democratic tide.

While seven or eight committee members left Congress after each term between the 94th and the 98th Congresses, another four to seven members transferred to other committees each term. Eleven members went to Appropriations, four to Rules, and three to Ways and Means. According to Education and Labor staff members, many Democrats particularly wanted an assignment on Appropriations, more so than on any other committee, to protect the funding for Education and Labor programs that were enacted in the 1960s. Republicans, on the other hand, in addition to wanting off of Education and Labor, coveted assignments on Appropriations so they could help cut the large amounts of money appropriated for liberal social welfare programs of the type considered by Education and Labor. Other committees that attracted Education and Labor members during this period included Budget (four members), Judiciary (three), Foreign Affairs (four), Commerce (three), Government Operations (two), Public Works (two), Banking (one), and Small Business (one).

Several institutional changes may have contributed to the increased transfer rate from Education and Labor to other committees. First, at the beginning of the 94th Congress, the seniority system was dealt a severe blow with the institution of a caucus vote on all chairmen and the resultant unseating of three committee chairmen. Members no longer were guaranteed a chairmanship if they outlasted their colleagues on a committees. Length of service was not a sufficient condition for a leadership position as it had been for many years (Abram and Cooper 1968; Copeland 1987). Second, in 1971 Democrats limited members to one subcommittee chairmanship each, extending the availability of power positions to more members. As a result, members do not have to wait as long before acquiring a subcommittee. In addition, the number of subcommittees has increased (Copeland 1987; Smith and Deering 1984). Third, some members may have surrendered seats on Education and Labor to maintain seats on other committees. The transfer statistics mask the fact that many members held dual assignments. After the Democratic Caucus limitation on more than one seat on a "major" or "semiexclusive" committee was instituted in 1973, some members dropped Education and Labor seats in favor of their other assignments.[5] Some members may have had better chances for subcommittee chairmanships, while others may have had better opportunities for constituency service. Still others may have sought any excuse to get off of the controversial committee.

Another explanation for the increased departures from the committee lies in the decreased salience of its jurisdiction. Most of the committee's major work to date was done in the early to mid-1960s when the administration designated the issues under its jurisdiction as top priorities. In the mid-1970s much of the committee's work focused on reauthorizations of existing programs and on maintenance of the gains made during the Great Society days. Other committees, such as the Judiciary Committee, had the headlines in the 1970s. And in addition to the magnetic appeal of Appropriations, Ways and Means, and Rules to many members, other committees increased their drawing power at the expense of Education and Labor, whose limelight seemed to have faded. According to Unekis and Rieselbach (1984, 10), Education and Labor declined from tenth to fifteenth in the attractiveness of House committees to members from the 88th-92d to the 93d-97th Congresses.

The philosophical predispositions of committee members influence committee decisions and operations. The larger the disparity of ideological leanings between the two parties, the higher the degree of partisanship in the committee. The more differences among party members, the greater the likelihood that operations will be on a bipartisan or consensus-building basis. Moreover, if the committee majority is divided, the harder it will be to build a consensus sufficiently large to report and pass a bill. The ideological makeup of the Committee on Education and Labor again is inferred from an examination of ratings by several interest groups with rather well-known tendencies: the liberal Americans for Democratic Action (ADA), the prolabor, liberal Committee on Political Education (COPE), and the conservative Americans for Constitutional Action (ACA). As in past chapters, scores for Education and Labor members are compared with scores for House members in each term in an attempt to show how well the positions of these committee members reflect a cross section of all House members (see table 5.4).

Judging by the magnitude of the ADA and labor union support scores,

Table 5.4. Interest Group Scores, 1967-1984

	Congress									
	90th	91st	92d	93d	94th	95th	96th	97th	98th	
	ADA Scores									
Full HR	38.7	38.3	37.7	39.8	45.1	39.7	42.9	43.9	49.3	Mean
	33.8	31.7	32.3	30.8	33.1	27.9	31.4	53.6	33.6	SD
Full E & L	55.4	54.3	53.2	54.4	55.6	49.2	53.6	56.8	57.6	Mean
	35.0	34.7	29.5	27.5	30.4	27.1	30.0	31.0	32.3	SD
HR Dems	56.3	51.7	51.5	55.1	58.5	50.3	57.3	64.1	70.4	Mean
	32.5	32.7	32.3	28.9	29.9	26.6	28.6	62.9	23.0	SD
E & L Dems	80.9	78.0	73.0	73.2	71.7	61.6	70.7	76.0	79.7	Mean
	12.2	20.3	17.0	16.8	20.6	22.7	19.8	19.0	12.6	SD
HR Reps	15.5	20.5	17.9	20.1	18.2	18.8	18.0	18.1	15.8	Mean
	17.1	19.4	19.8	20.1	20.3	16.5	17.6	17.8	16.0	SD
E & L Reps	20.1	22.9	24.1	30.9	23.5	24.4	24.5	30.9	21.9	Mean
	22.6	22.6	17.0	18.7	19.1	16.2	19.2	24.5	19.1	SD
	COPE/AFL-CIO Scores									
Full HR	48.9	54.6	53.4	53.6	58.1	54.2	49.8	53.3	54.4	Mean
	39.4	33.9	33.0	37.6	31.9	30.3	29.7	54.1	33.6	SD
Full E & L	67.2	68.9	63.4	66.9	69.5	65.4	58.7	62.2	62.7	Mean
	38.4	34.6	32.2	34.4	31.5	28.9	32.6	36.0	38.7	SD
HR Dems	69.9	71.5	72.6	77.6	74.3	69.3	65.7	79.2	77.8	Mean
	36.8	31.3	26.1	27.7	23.7	23.2	22.9	58.7	20.1	SD
E & L Dems	96.5	94.3	73.0	93.2	88.2	83.4	81.2	90.6	90.8	Mean
	6.7	11.2	17.0	13.1	11.5	11.5	12.5	10.4	11.9	SD
HR Reps	21.4	32.3	25.6	22.6	25.5	24.1	22.4	20.0	16.8	Mean
	21.9	22.4	19.2	23.5	18.7	17.4	17.4	17.1	62.7	SD
E & L Reps	26.6	35.1	29.0	34.1	32.0	29.3	18.9	23.7	15.1	Mean
	23.6	24.4	20.4	21.6	24.2	15.6	11.7	16.3	9.8	SD
	ACA/ACARI Scores									
Full HR	48.5	46.5	50.2	45.1	43.5	46.0	45.4	49.4	46.8	Mean
	36.7	28.6	31.7	30.4	32.6	31.2	31.4	30.5	32.7	SD
Full E & L	33.5	34.7	37.5	33.9	33.2	34.9	38.8	37.6	35.8	Mean
	37.7	30.7	30.2	27.5	29.7	28.7	32.1	30.3	31.6	SD
HR Dems	25.9	32.4	34.0	27.8	28.9	31.5	26.7	29.2	26.7	Mean
	30.2	26.1	27.7	24.1	26.7	25.1	20.5	22.7	21.9	SD
E & L Dems	4.8	14.0	16.2	15.4	16.5	18.8	17.4	15.0	14.8	Mean
	3.8	9.8	13.1	12.3	15.6	14.7	10.4	10.4	11.5	SD
HR Reps	78.2	65.0	73.6	67.4	72.9	75.0	77.6	75.1	78.9	Mean
	19.0	19.7	20.3	22.0	21.6	20.1	17.8	16.5	18.3	SD
E & L Reps	73.1	62.3	68.7	57.1	66.5	67.2	76.7	68.3	69.8	Mean
	24.6	26.8	18.4	23.4	21.8	21.6	19.2	18.6	22.3	SD

Sources: Author's calculations from Inter-University Consortium for Political and Social Research. Scores for the 98th Cong. are from *Congressional Quarterly Weekly Report*, July 14, 1984, pp. 1696-97, and April 20, 1985, pp. 748-49. COPE scores became AFL-CIO scores in 1980, and ACA scores became ACARI scores in 1982.

the practice of recruiting more liberal Democrats for Education and Labor continued into the Perkins era, although at a slowed rate. The comparatively high average ADA scores and the relatively low standard deviations suggest that, by this measure, committee Democrats largely were more liberal than were their House counterparts. The southern Democrats and other conservative party members who were not assigned to Education and Labor and thereby could not lower the averages. Moreover, a seemingly large number of committee Democrats scored in the upper ranks of the liberalism measure. Much higher proportions of Education and Labor members than of House members earned ADA ratings of 70 or more.

The labor union support scores, which were called COPE scores until the 96th Congress (1979-80), when they were revised as AFL-CIO support scores, also show that Education and Labor Democrats largely were more liberal than were their House counterparts. In all but one Congress (the 96th) during the period under consideration, over 90 percent of committee Democrats scored above 70 percent support for labor unions, compared with nearly two-thirds of the House. While House Democrats were inclined to side with union positions, House Republicans were not. Few Republicans scored above 70—under 8 percent in every term and none in the 95th through 98th Congresses, although generally, committee Republicans showed a higher degree of labor support than did House Republicans.

The ACA scores buttress the conclusion that Education and Labor attracted liberal members. The magnitude of the differences between House Democratic and committee Democratic means again are striking, and again they seemed to be declining in contrast to the Powell years, when they seemed to be increasing. They peaked in Perkins's first term as chairman, the 90th Congress (1967-68), after which Democratic members seemed to move toward being more representative of all the House Democrats. The Republicans continued a trend begun in the 89th Congress whereby committee members were less conservative than their House counterparts. Throughout the Perkins years, committee Republicans were rated as less conservative than their House colleagues.

The relatively high rates of turnover, the reversal of Republican status from earlier eras, and the declining differences in average House and committee ratings illustrate that the committee was moving toward becoming a microcosm of its parent body. Perhaps these factors also indicate decreasing salience of the issues under the committee's jurisdiction. Several institutional changes may have contributed to the moderation of the Committee on Education and Labor. The general atmosphere of the committee became more respectable when Perkins took the helm than it had been under Powell and Barden. Perkins worked to maintain the committee balance in his favor. A former staff member said: "Perkins had to lobby like hell to get people on the committee. Every time a new bunch came in, he would go over the list and try to canvass those he wanted. He wanted a Texan on there in the worst way. Wanted to keep it from being a New York committee. Had a great nest of New Yorkers on there. 'Them eastern seaboard boys,' he called them. They didn't give a damn about education. They were purely interested in labor" (interview). Perkins wanted members who would be inclined to vote with him, whose districts would benefit from the same formulas as his, and whose loyalty he could foster. He was afraid "them eastern seaboard boys" would override him.

The Republicans on the committee became more moderate for several reasons. Federal involvement in education had become an accepted practice, and they no longer had to wage an all-out war against it. Also, most of the big labor fights had been fought. Common site picketing was the only labor issue that engendered a significant degree of controversy, although labor issues always exacerbate differences. The last major labor battle had been fought in 1959 over the Landrum-Griffin Act. Furthermore, as a former staff member said, "Right-wing nuts didn't want to settle there very long. They wanted to serve their time and get out" (interview). Finally, and probably most important, the newly elected Nixon administration probably had a moderating influence generally on Republican behavior. Republicans had power in the White House, and they may have felt compelled to act a little more responsibly, since they had powerful help in getting their agendas considered or passed.

Voting Patterns

Examination of voting patterns conveys a sense of how cohesive or unified the members were in support of legislation, the frequency and intensity of conflict among members, and the degree of party unity. House party-unity votes show a relatively high degree of unity within each party. Voting patterns from 1967 to 1984 characterize the committee as having a high degree of conflict that generally split along party lines. Nevertheless, when the Rice Index of Cohesion is applied to roll-call votes in the committee, it is apparent that full committee cohesion levels increased from what they had been during the leadership spans of the previous chairmen. The percentages of committee party votes, on the other hand, manifest competition between the parties, particularly in the 1980s, when the Reagan administration targeted many of the committee's major programs for cutting.

The degree of partisanship apparent in the House and how reflective committee members were of their House counterparts can be gauged by party-unity scores, which were calculated for House roll calls only. The mean party-unity scores of committee members are compared with those of House members in table 5.5. Mean party-unity scores for committee

Table 5.5. Party-Unity Scores, 1967-1984

	Congress									
	90th	91st	92d	93d	94th	95th	96th	97th	98th	
Full HR	65.9	60.2	62.6	66.1	68.2	67.0	69.9	72.7	74.4	Mean
	20.4	18.1	19.7	17.8	19.6	18.2	18.2	42.9	15.6	SD
	51.7	35.2	44.8	51.5	56.2	52.8	58.9	60.9	71.5	% > 70
Full E & L	73.0	65.3	69.6	69.1	71.2	68.9	75.1	73.7	76.7	Mean
	16.6	17.7	13.1	15.0	17.1	16.3	11.5	14.9	12.5	SD
	56.3	48.6	56.7	59.9	61.6	55.6	72.3	70.6	74.2	% > 70
HR Dems	63.5	59.4	59.5	66.0	67.5	65.5	68.9	73.6	75.3	Mean
	23.2	20.1	22.2	19.7	20.7	19.1	18.4	55.6	15.5	SD
	50.8	37.8	41.1	55.7	56.3	52.1	56.4	59.7	73.3	% > 70
E & L Dems	80.3	69.1	74.4	76.9	76.6	71.6	76.0	80.1	80.3	Mean
	10.4	17.2	10.4	10.5	12.3	15.6	9.7	8.7	7.9	SD
	72.2	55.0	68.1	85.0	73.1	66.7	69.5	84.2	90.9	% > 70
HR Reps	69.1	61.1	67.1	66.3	69.6	70.0	71.8	71.4	73.1	Mean
	15.4	15.2	14.3	14.9	17.1	16.1	17.8	15.6	15.7	SD
	52.9	31.8	50.3	46.0	56.0	54.1	63.3	62.4	68.6	% > 70
E & L Reps	63.6	60.3	63.1	59.3	60.3	63.4	73.5	65.6	70.5	Mean
	18.7	17.7	13.8	14.1	20.5	16.8	14.4	17.4	16.4	SD
	35.7	40.0	40.0	26.7	38.5	33.3	77.0	53.3	46.2	% > 70

Sources: Author's calculations from Inter-University Consortium for Political and Social Research. Scores for the 98th Congress are from *Congressional Quarterly Almanac* 1984.

members exceeded the average scores of all House members in each of the nine Congresses under consideration. Committee Democratic means surpassed the average scores of their counterparts in the House in every instance. In addition, the variation in the House was far greater than the variation among committee Democratic scores.

Committee Republicans, on the other hand, seemed to be less partisan than their House Republican colleagues in every Congress under consideration save one, the 96th (1979-80). Moreover, committee Republicans party-unity scores generally varied more than did those of House Republicans. Whereas Republican leaders in previous years had tended to assign to Education and Labor the most conservative and partisan members they could find, after Perkins assumed the chairmanship that practice abated a bit. Given the higher standard deviations, the committee had at least a few Republicans who were less wed to their party's positions or more liberal than their predecessors. Interest group scores also indicated that the Republicans assigned to the committee had become slightly less extreme over the years.

Table 5.6. Committee Roll Calls Meeting Minimum Cohesion and Mean Rice
Index Scores, 1967-1984

| Congress | Year | N | Rice Index | | | Full E & L RI > 40 | |
			Full E & L	Dems	Reps	%	N
90th	1967-68	99	30.6	75.3	83.2	27.2	27
91st	1969-70	61	38.9	78.9	80.7	37.7	23
92d	1971-72	132	34.6	67.8	77.5	31.8	42
93d	1973-74	91	45.7	73.8	79.5	48.4	44
94th	1975-76	69	56.1	78.7	67.6	66.7	46
95th	1977-78	108	44.9	73.4	73.1	53.7	58
96th	1979-80	53	42.8	82.8	73.0	45.3	24
97th	1981-82	55	37.1	93.5	78.9	47.3	26
98th	1983-84	49	42.6	82.4	77.8	46.9	23
	Total	717					313
	Mean		40.8	76.5	77.0	45.0	
	Percentage						
	of total					43.7	

Source: Author's calculations from Committee on Education and Labor, *Minutes* 1967-84.

As a matter of course, Education and Labor Democrats boasted some
of the higher party-unity scores among House members. Larger percentages of committee Democrats had party-unity scores greater than 70 than
did House Democrats. In the 98th Congress (1983-84), more than 90
percent of the Democrats were highly partisan by this measure. Committee
Republicans, on the other hand, had smaller percentages of highly partisan
members than did the House. Their scores were consistently lower than
those of their House counterparts.

Not only were there substantially more roll calls during the Perkins
years than during his predecessor's, but voting generally was more cohesive. Members voted together, with a minimum of 70 percent of members on the same side, on 43.7 percent of all the roll calls during the Perkins
chairmanship, as compared with about 23 percent under Powell. Moreover, the average Rice Index Scores for all roll calls under Perkins generally
were higher than those under Powell, averaging 40.8. See table 5.6.

Rather than some cross-cutting consensus that led to near unanimity on
the floor as evidence of an integrated committee, the political parties
provided the integrating mechanism on Education and Labor that allowed
the committee to function. The conclusion that it was sufficiently integrated to satisfy its organizational maintenance needs and to get its job done
is supported by data gathered from committee prints, interviews, and
written studies illustrating that the parties were well integrated and delineated on this committee. Rice Index Scores based on roll-call votes in

Table 5.7. Percentage of Party Votes in Committee by 50-, 70-, 75-, and 90-
Percent Criteria, 1967-1984

Congress	Year	N	(number of qualifying roll calls in parentheses)			
			> 50%	> 70%	> 75%	> 90%
90th	1967-68	99	75.8 (75)	64.6 (64)	57.6 (57)	27.3 (27)
91st	1969-70	61	70.5 (43)	59.0 (36)	50.8 (31)	31.1 (19)
92d	1971-72	132	72.0 (95)	48.5 (64)	45.5 (60)	25.8 (34)
93d	1973-74	91	57.1 (52)	46.2 (42)	44.0 (40)	23.1 (21)
94th	1975-76	69	56.5 (39)	37.7 (26)	34.8 (24)	11.6 (8)
95th	1977-78	108	63.0 (68)	45.4 (49)	41.7 (45)	25.9 (28)
96th	1979-80	53	77.4 (41)	58.5 (31)	54.7 (29)	22.6 (12)
97th	1981-82	55	80.0 (44)	70.9 (39)	69.1 (38)	54.5 (30)
98th	1983-84	49	65.3 (32)	53.1 (26)	44.9 (22)	38.8 (19)
	Total	717	(489)	(377)	(346)	(198)
	Percentage of total		68.2	52.6	48.3	27.6

Source: Author's calculations from Committee on Education and Labor, *Minutes* 1967-84.

committee, controlled for party, provide a means to determine the extent of cohesion within each party on Education and Labor and, unlike party-unity scores, can be compared over time. In contrast to their voting behavior on the floor as shown by House party-unity scores, members of both parties, in committee, voted overwhelmingly with members of their own party much more often than not. Over the entire period Perkins was chairman (1967-84) the Democrats had an average Rice Index of 76.5, showing an 88-percent average cohesiveness. The Republicans averaged 77.0, meaning that they voted together about 89 percent of time. The indexes were high for both parties throughout Perkins's chairmanship, in keeping with the intraparty unity during the Powell era.

Interparty differences are reflected in the levels of party competition, which were relatively high on this committee throughout the Perkins years, although lower than they had been under Powell. When Powell was chairman, the parties opposed each other on about 75 percent of the votes. Under Perkins, just over half the roll calls qualified as party votes (see table 5.7). The issues Powell's committee faced in 1961-66 generated stronger partisanship, both in the committee and in the House. Nonetheless, committee programs faced severe cutbacks during Republican administrations, particularly during the Reagan years. The Democrats banded together to protect their vested interests—the liberal programs enacted in the mid-1960s. For all the assertions of "extremism" (Unekis and Rieselbach 1984), however, Perkins seemed to have had a moderating influence on the committee after Powell. Party voting levels on the committee decreased during the first ten years that Perkins was chairman, bottoming out in

1975-76, when Democrats opposed Republicans on 37.7 percent of the votes. The percentage of party votes began an upswing again in the 95th Congress (1977-78), peaking in the 97th (1981-82).

If the standard for integration is bipartisan consensus, the Committee on Education and Labor under Perkins once again could be characterized as a low-integration committee. This finding corroborates those of Unekis and Rieselbach (1984) and Parker and Parker (1985), who used different measures. Full committee integration grew during Perkins's tenure, partially, although not entirely, as a result of his stewardship. Nevertheless, the committee cannot be classified as highly cohesive. As it had in past Congresses, party provided the main integrating force once again on Education and Labor. With party voting as the norm, all three measures of partisanship indicate a high reliance on party in committee. But they also demonstrate a lesser degree of partisanship under Perkins than under Powell.

The party-unity scores pointed to committee Democrats as more likely than most of their other House colleagues to vote with the party on roll calls that pitted a majority of one party against a majority of the other. The Republicans, on the other hand, seemed slightly less likely to toe the party line on party-unity votes. The larger standard deviations for committee Republicans hint that a few may have had party-unity scores sufficiently low to bring down the mean scores among committee members appreciably, thus making the committee Republicans look less reliant on party than their House colleagues and than the committee Democrats. The Rice Index Scores are the strongest indicator of the partisanship in operation on the committee. They show that committee members were strongly inclined to vote with members of their own party in committee, but they mean little without being considered in the context of the proportion of times that the two parties were opposed. Not only were the index scores relatively high, but the proportion of votes on which the parties opposed each other was high as well, although not as high as it had been under Powell.

Committee fluctuations may be subject to a variety of interpretations. Some of the increased cohesion and slightly reduced partisanship might be attributed to the partisan split, since when the Democrats had the highest percentage of members (94th Congress, 1975-76), their voting cohesion was the highest, with 70 percent of the members voting together on two-thirds of the votes. But the Democrats never had 70 percent of the membership. To achieve the 70-percent minimum level of cohesion, some Republicans had to vote with the majority, or a fair number of Democrats had to vote with the Republicans in order to reach levels of minimal cross-party unity. At least four other factors entered the picture: the chairman's influence, the ideological composition of the committee, the imposition of additional committee rules, and the nature of the issues considered.

Politically, Perkins knew what would win. As one of his committee staff members said, Perkins "was good at getting his members to pull together," cajoling and persuading them frequently (interview). Perkins traded votes and support effectively in both parties, often managing to attract some Republicans. Early in his career he had mastered the art of easy-going persuasion, tugging at sleeves, and wheedling. He was relentless in pursuit of votes. His efforts paid off in committee as well as on the floor. His close friendships with a few of the Republicans helped, too.

Cohesiveness probably was facilitated by a more liberal minority. Until Powell's last year as chairman, the interest group scores showed that committee Republicans tended to be more conservative than the average House member. Beginning in 1966 the picture changed, so that the committee Republicans were slightly more liberal than their House colleagues, as were the Democrats, conditions that held true throughout the Perkins years. Perkins was more representative of minority philosophies than Powell had been. Minority members also may have been more willing to support the chairman because he had a reputation for being fair to them and he did a great deal of persuading on their side of the aisle. Characteristically, Perkins traded votes and made deals with the Republicans to bring them to his side.

The enactment of additional rules calling for more democratic procedures for the committee also promoted increased voting cohesion. Rules themselves are an integrating measure. They contribute to a universalistic rather than a particularistic method of operating and provide a way to organize conflict and keep it civil. As a former committee staff member said, "If everything is civil already, the rules are a way to structure the committee's business" (interview). The institution of rules and the chairman's enforcement of them reduced conflict over some of the procedural matters, thereby increasing integration in the process. Chairman Perkins realized that solving little problems often makes compromises on the more controversial issues easier.

Another factor that contributed to higher levels of cohesive voting on the committee was a change in the nature of the issues. Several had lost their partisan sting. Most of the battles over program authorizations had been fought by the time Perkins was far into his chairmanship, so all that was left were reauthorizations. The hard part had been done. Constituents of the Office of Economic Opportunity had been established in most members' districts. Federal aid to education monies were apparent all over the country. The Republicans, too, had vested interests in committee legislation. They had a more difficult time voting to cut existing programs that came out of their committee than they had had in voting against them in the first place. It is hard to vote against something that many perceive as working and that has established constituencies.

Committee Structure

Certain facets of committee structure are vital to the functioning of the committee: committee rules, committee size and party ratios, subcommittee structure and use, and committee and subcommittee staff. Changes in them from chairman to chairman show how each leader handled the committee differently.

Numerous committee rules changes were enacted after Perkins assumed the chair; however, most of the limits on his authority were in place when he took over. Although the chairman was affected by the House and Democratic Caucus reforms, he had far less to lose than other chairmen, since many of the House and caucus reforms were in effect on Education and Labor before they were applied to the House at large. In the last months of Powell's tenure, as a response to perceived widespread abuses of power and as an inoculation against future abuses, members approved several strict new provisions giving majority members more responsibility in committee operations. Perkins had been part of the cadre of committee members seeking to rein in the chairman and had few objections. In fact, he generally favored them and had voted for them in 1966.

As a result, the initial changes adopted when Perkins took the helm were relatively minor. Majority members already had given themselves control over the creation and jurisdictions of the subcommittees, although the effect of this provision was postponed until Perkins became chairman in 1967. It mandated due regard to committee seniority and to individual preferences, in effect almost guaranteeing choice subcommittee assignments and leaving little discretion to the chairman. Consequently, Perkins was little affected when the House Democratic Caucus adopted similar provisions applying to all committees in the 1973 "Subcommittee Bill of Rights."[6]

The 1967 committee rules prohibited subcommittee chairmen from sitting on more than one other subcommittee. They limited other members to three subcommittees and implied that subcommittees were to be appointed by the chairman, who was not mentioned specifically. Nor was the method of assignment set out—only that seniority and individual preferences were to be taken into consideration, insofar as practical. In contrast, Powell specifically had been authorized to appoint every committee member to at least one subcommittee. Perkins did the appointing in accordance with members' preferences.

Another new provision enacted when Perkins assumed the chair in 1967 allowed members to file, as part of the printed committee report, individual, minority, or dissenting views on any bill reported to the House by the committee. (A three-day time limit on the filing of these reports was imposed in 1973 to conform to Democratic Caucus reforms.) Another new

1967 clause stipulated that committee roll-call records indicate when a vote was cast by proxy, a practice that had been followed at least since the early 1950s. The 1967 rules also applied the committee rules to the subcommittee and gave subcommittee members the option of removing subcommittee personnel.

After Perkins's initial term as chairman, Education and Labor members adopted several major changes concerning committee operations in the 1970s. They also added others that reflected procedural changes of lesser significance, although they had the effect of furthering committee decentralization. A small number actually restored bits of authority to the chairman. Although most of the rules changes came about as the result of House or Democratic Caucus action, these were not the actions with the major operational effects on Education and Labor. The strongest impacts came from within the committee and set the course for other committees to follow.

The chairman initiated the operational rule change that had the most dramatic effect—the opening of committee meetings to the public. A senior staff member recalled the following scenario when the Republicans boycotted the mark-up of antipoverty legislation: "In one of his rare displays of indignation or perturbation, Perkins said, 'Just open those doors. Let the people in. And call the reporters. I want the people to see what's a-goin' on in here.' They opened the doors, called the reporters, and seven or eight Republicans filed out of the Republican cloakroom back there like little gentlemen and took their seats. I think that was the first open mark-up in any committee. When the vice president arrived at Perkins's birthday party on October 15, 1967, he referred to this 'open covenants openly arrived at' [one of Wilson's Fourteen Points]" (interview). The move was so successful at keeping a quorum and ensuring that members were on their best behavior that a provision requiring that committee and subcommittee meetings be open to the public appeared in the committee rules in the 91st Congress, four years prior to the 1973 stipulation in House rules that all committee and subcommittee bill-drafting sessions, with a few exceptions, be open to the public (House *Rules* 1979, rule II, cl. 2, Sec. 708).

As an internally initiated offshoot of 1973 House Democratic Caucus reforms, the chairman regained a few prerogatives when the committee majority caucus adopted rules giving the chairman authority to fill remaining Democratic vacancies on subcommittees, with regard to previous service and individual preference, subject to majority approval. The committee rules authorized the chairman to make temporary subcommittee assignments of any committee member to participate in committee matters outside of Washington, D.C. All members could question witnesses at public hearings of any subcommittee.

Committee majority members also amended the questioning provision, directing the chairman to recognize two Democrats for every one Republican called on to ask questions. The 1970 Legislative Reorganization Act (P.L. 91-510; 84 Stat. 1140) allowed the minority to call witnesses during at least one day of hearings on each bill, but until 1975 the committee rules provided for the chairman to initiate the questioning during hearings, followed by the ranking minority member and all other members, alternating by party. To keep the chairman from being overly accommodating of the minority, the new provision forced him to take into account the ratio of majority to minority members and to set the order of questioning so as not to disadvantage the Democrats. It also kept the Republicans from monopolizing the questioning.

An era of reform in the 1970s inspired numerous changes in House procedures, carried out in large part by the House Democratic Caucus. Many of these reforms trickled down to committees. One led to the 1973 adoption by Education and Labor of a rule concerning subcommittee appointment procedures. It required the chairman to appoint all Democratic members to subcommittees, pursuant to committee majority caucus rules, which entitled each committee member to a seat on one subcommittee of his choice as long as there were vacancies. In 1974 the House Democratic Caucus rule was amended so that no one was entitled to more than two assignments until all other members had made one choice and no one could be ranking majority member on more than one subcommittee, and subsequently the committee rule was likewise amended. In effect, this provision restored to the chairman the official appointment authority, which had been left unstated in previous rules. It also confirmed an existing practice on Education and Labor.

The prerogatives of committee chairmen were being challenged by reformers in the House, and nor were subcommittee chairs sacrosanct. Until 1975, Education and Labor Committee rules decreed that the ranking majority members be appointed to subcommittee chairmanships. As an offshoot of Democratic Caucus action, the 94th Congress committee rules gave majority members the right to bid for subcommittee chairmanships in order of seniority, with all bids subject to approval of a majority of those present and voting in the committee majority caucus. As an attempt to make subcommittee chairmen more responsive to their subcommittees and to the majority members of the full committee, the bidding procedure threatened the seemingly inalienable right of ranking majority members to be subcommittee chairmen. Its seeds were sown in the House Democratic Caucus, where the previous "right" of senior committee members to become chairmen was threatened by the 1973 adoption of automatic caucus votes on committee chairmen. Just as the chairman's authority was diminished by caucus rules requiring him to stand for election to his post, so was that of his subcommittee chairmen. Moreover, in recent years Education and Labor had stripped two chairmen of their prerogatives. Perkins would not allow himself to be the third. His staff recollected that the bidding procedure had little impact on the chairmen's behavior. It did not change noticeably after the caucus reforms (interviews).

Reflecting the reorientation of authorizing committees toward oversight and away from the approval of big spending programs, the committee responded to pressure from the House to step up its oversight activities.[7] In 1975, as an indirect result of the Legislative Reorganization Act of 1970, the committee adopted a rule directing each subcommittee to review and study on a continuing basis the application, administration, execution, and effectiveness of the laws or parts of laws under its jurisdiction (House *Rules* 1979, rule 10, cl. 2, sec. 692). The subcommittee was charged with determining whether these laws were being implemented in accordance with the intent of Congress; if the programs should be continued, curtailed, or eliminated; and if additional legislation was needed. The chairman was required to assign oversight measures to the subcommittees. The House granted a special oversight function relating to Education and Labor in the 93d Congress, directing the committee to oversee domestic education programs within the jurisdictions of other committees (House *Rules* 1979, rule 10, cl. 3[c]).

In 1975, when the House allowed the multiple or split referral of legislation, the committee followed suit. In a move restoring prerogatives to the chairman, committee members adopted rules allowing the chairman discretion in simultaneous referral of legislation to two or more subcommittees for concurrent or sequential consideration (Committee *Rules*, 94th Cong.). He also had the option of dividing legislation and referring the parts to the appropriate standing or ad hoc subcommittees. With the advent of this provision came the most discretion over referrals the chairman had had since the Powell years.

Another major procedural rules change adopted by the committee enlarged its investigative powers. Echoing House rules enacted in 1975, the 1977 committee rules included a provision enlarging the committee's investigative powers by authorizing the issuance of subpoenas on the approval of a majority of the present and voting members, with a majority present.[8] Subpoenas were to be signed by the chairman or by any designated member. Although this provision did not enhance or diminish the chairman, it certainly increased his stature vis-à-vis hearing witnesses and gave him equal standing with those few committees that previously had been the sole proprietors of the subpoena powers: Appropriations, Budget, Government Operations, Internal Security, and Standards of Official Conduct (House *Rules* 1979, rule 11, cl. 2, sec. 718, annotation, 413).

In 1984 a new committee rule directed the committee chairman, on request from any subcommittee chairman, to file with the appropriate department or agency head a formal objection to any final implementing regulation identified. The purpose of this rule was to suspend the effective date of the regulations in question and to ensure that regulations fell within the authority conferred by authorizing legislation.

The committee also adopted a host of important but less consequential rules changes. Since they largely concerned record keeping and the routinization of operating procedures, most of their impact lay within the committee. Several of these rules enhanced the chairman's prerogatives. One 1973 procedural rule change restored to the chairman the sole power to authorize committee-related travel for members and staff. In the prior Congress, the chairman or any subcommittee chairman could authorize travel funds. Largely confirming existing practice, this seemingly innocuous provision was the underpinning for a great deal of influence by the full committee chairman. The rules also required that the ranking minority member receive a copy of all written requests for travel. In 1973 the chairman also was authorized to approve international travel. As a safeguard against the repetition of past abuses, members had to submit a written report of their activities and of pertinent information gained on the trip.

The rules for the 92d Congress (1971-72) also revised the process for calling special committee meetings to enable the committee majority to circumvent an intractable chairman, at the same time giving him the authority to assemble recalcitrant members if they did not accomplish the committee's business in the normally scheduled meetings. Members reinstated a previously used provision allowing the chairman to call special meetings as he deemed necessary for the consideration of any piece of legislation or other item of committee business. This rule also empowered the members to petition for the call of a special meeting by filing a notice of intent with the committee clerk and apprising all members of the meeting time, place, and purpose.

In 1977 members made it easier to get a quorum and more difficult for Republicans to hold up committee business for lack of a quorum. A new rule provided that one-third of the members of the committee or a subcommittee, rather than a majority, constituted a quorum for taking any action other than amending the rules, closing a meeting from the public, reporting legislation, or authorizing a subpoena. This rule highlighted the difficulty of obtaining a quorum when members relied frequently on proxies, which were invalid in a quorum count.

Another 1977 rule prohibited consideration of a proposed change in committee rules unless the text of the change had been in the hands of all committee members for at least forty-eight hours prior to the meeting in which the change was to be considered. Of import only to committee members, this provision made it difficult for anyone to change the rules midstream to suit his purpose before other members could examine the impact such a rule change might have. It also served as fair warning for members to attend a meeting in which rules changes were to be discussed.

In 1971 minority members were given authority to call witnesses. In accordance with new House rules, the 1973 committee rules specifically set out hearing procedures generally pursuant to rule 11, clause 27, of the House rules. The chairman or subcommittee chairman was required to announce and publish the logistics and purpose of each hearing at least one week in advance. Witnesses were required to file with the clerk written statements of their proposed testimony at least twenty-four hours before their appearance. Also concomitant with House reforms, the 1971 committee rules delineated extensive provisions regulating media coverage of hearings. All media had access to full committee hearings, although access to subcommittee hearings was governed by majority vote of the subcommittee in question. The rules largely were designed to provide a minimum of interference in committee operations by regulating placement of cameras and other media equipment.

Although the chairman's statutory powers generally were weakened throughout the period that Perkins was chairman, the decline by and large was imposed externally, in contrast to committee-initiated reforms under the two previous chairmen. Most of the Education and Labor restructuring enacted before the Perkins era had been instituted by frustrated majority members. They had been chipping away at the chairman's traditional authority for ten years before Perkins became chairman. Having been subject to the abuses by the two previous chairmen, he had been part of the reform movement aimed both at Barden and at Powell and had voted for the rules crippling the chairman's power. Perkins knew all too well the problems that could occur without proper restrictions.

During his chairmanship, and particularly in the early 1970s, the chairman lost some of his standing at the hands of the House and of the caucus, but he was not alone. All other committee chairmen were subject to the same debilitations, such as being subject to caucus approval and being limited to chairing one subcommittee. This development was the result of an era of reform in the House substantially democratizing its committee decision-making processes.

From 1967 to 1984 most of the changes in the committee rules were relatively minor structural or procedural amendments, although they were of great import to committee members. The chairman-initiated opening of committee meetings to the public was perhaps the most significant reform, affecting the operations and the fate of legislation not only in Education and Labor (and possibly in the House) but later, in all committees. It almost forced attendance and attention to constituency pressures, because for the first time the constituents could see what their representatives were doing behind previously closed doors. The open-door policy fostered public accountability and aided interest group monitoring.

The size of the committee increased with the installation of a new chairman at the beginning of the 90th Congress in 1967, as it had when Powell assumed the chairmanship in 1961. Thirty-one members had been assigned to the committee under Powell. The committee picked up three slots in the 90th Congress and generally grew until the 95th, when, with fourteen new members, it peaked at forty members. It later leveled off at thirty-six members until the 98th, when it had thirty-eight.

The party ratios on the committee were similar to those in the House for every Congress between 1967 and 1984. Both the House and this committee were lopsidedly Democratic during most of the Perkins years, especially during the 94th through 96th Congresses (1975-80) when about two-thirds of the House membership was Democratic. The Watergate scandal seemed to have a national impact beginning in the 1974 elections, when the Democrats picked up nearly fifty seats in the midterm elections and maintained a heavy advantage until the 97th Congress (1981-82), when the Republicans gained thirty-four seats. Democratics regained most of them in the 98th Congress (1983-84).

During the years that Perkins was chairman, the House and Democratic Caucus approved a series of sweeping reforms aimed at decentralizing the committee system. Subcommittees all over the House increased dramatically in importance and autonomy (Davidson 1981b; Deering and Smith 1984; Sheppard 1985, 232-52). Changes in internal structures and procedures enhanced the ability to produce policy decisions more efficiently (Rieselbach 1975). They increased the flexibility of the seniority system by encouraging less-senior members to play more important roles in the legislative process. A summary of these reforms follows:[9]

1970 Legislative Reorganization Act

Provided that the ranking majority member would preside in the absence of the chairman. In practice on Education and Labor in 1966.

Encouraged open meetings unless majority voted to close them. In practice on Education and Labor in 1967.

Made roll calls available to the public.

Stipulated that committee reports must be filed within seven days.

Prohibited blanket proxies in committees.

Allowed three days for supplemental or minority reports to be filed for inclusion in the committee report.

Required one-third of committee's funds to be allocated for minority staff. Minority budget in practice on Education and Labor after 1966, but not necessarily one-third of the funds.

Provided that the minority be able to call witnesses during at least one day of hearings on a bill (nullified in 1971).

Permitted broadcast of hearings. In practice on Education and Labor in 1967.

1971 House Democratic Caucus Reforms

Prohibited members from holding more than one legislative subcommittee chairmanship. In practice on Education and Labor since 1967, although not written specifically into the rules.

Limited full committee chairmen to one subcommittee chairmanship. In practice on Education and Labor since 1967.

Required committees and subcommittees to have written rules. In practice on Education and Labor since 1957.

Permitted subcommittee chairmen to select one professional subcommittee staff member, subject to approval by the full committee majority caucus. In practice on Education and Labor since 1961.

1973 Democratic Caucus Reforms, "Subcommittee Bill of Rights"

Provided election of subcommittee chairmen by majority committee caucus.

Fixed subcommittee jurisdictions set by majority caucus. In Education and Labor rules since 1966.

Provided that party ratios on subcommittees be set to reflect ratio in the House. In Education and Labor rules in 1957, 1959, and after 1966.

Guaranteed adequate subcommittee budgets by majority caucus. In practice on Education and Labor beginning in 1967.

Guaranteed each member a major subcommittee assignment as long as there were vacancies. In practice on Education and Labor beginning in 1967.

Required full committee chairman to file committee reports within two weeks. In Education and Labor rules, chairman was directed to report bills "promptly" beginning in 1971.

1974 Reforms

Required committees with more than twenty members to establish a minimum of four subcommittees. Education and Labor mandated the establishment of subcommittees in 1957.

Provided that no member could be assigned to a second subcommittee before every member had chosen one subcommittee assignment (bidding).

Restricted members to membership on two subcommittees per committee assignment. Education and Labor rules limited members to three subcommittees in 1967.

A notable feature of Education and Labor is its autonomous subcommittee structure (Unekis and Reiselbach 1984, 150). Since 1967 majority members of the committee have controlled the creation, number, and jurisdiction of subcommittees. Formerly, and in all other committees, those prerogatives were reserved for the chairman.

During the first four terms of Perkins's chairmanship, the number of subcommittees fluctuated, although the committee always had a minimum of six standing subcommittees, and on occasion there were two or three special, select, or ad hoc subcommittees or task forces. These subunits were not specifically titled to indicate their jurisdictions. Instead, they were numbered or referred to by vague titles—general, special, and select subcommittees on education and on labor.

The implementation of the 1973 caucus reforms in the 94th Congress only slightly changed the subcommittee picture on Education and Labor. The committee replaced the vague titles of its subcommittees with more specific ones. It altered its subcommittees slightly over the next few sessions, changing names, adding units, or reorganizing as the issues or politics demanded, although not to the extent that the subcommittees of many other committees were altered.

Changes in the nature and salience of the issues before the committee dictated most of the subcommittee jurisdictional changes and reorganizations that appeared during the Perkins years. As issues became politically salient and appeared on the committee's agenda—such as the problems of juvenile delinquents, agricultural workers, and the elderly—subcommittees were created or reorganized to handle them. And their jurisdictions were increasingly specific in the rules.

Several structural rules changes reflected the shifting proportions of Democrats to Republicans in the House, mirroring the desires of the majority to increase its proportion of seats. These changes varied in specificity. In the early years, the ratio of majority to minority members was set at three to two on each subcommittee. Later it was changed to two to one. As the Democrats won more seats, they assigned an additional majority member to each subcommittee. In 1979, instead of setting ratios, committee rules set the precise number of members from each party entitled to seats on each subcommittee. Some subcommittees increased in size at the expense of others, echoing the changing committee size and jurisdictional salience.

The 1967 committee rules required that all members be appointed to one or more subcommittees in accordance with seniority and individual preferences and limited members to three subcommittees. Chairmen of standing subcommittees were restricted to one additional subcommittee. Ranking members of the majority party automatically would hold the chairmanships of the standing subcommittees. The full committee chairman could appoint any additional subcommittee chairmen, with due regard for seniority.

Not including the chairman, unless he chaired a subcommittee, or the ranking minority member, unless he had a regular seat on a standing subcommittee, the average committee member held between two and three subcommittee seats per term on Education and Labor. On the whole,

Democrats on Education and Labor were likely to hold a slightly higher number of standing subcommittee seats than were Republicans. Notwithstanding the committee rule limiting members to a maximum of three subcommittees, a member occasionally sat on four or five. There also were several violations of the rule stating that a chairman of a standing subcommittee may not be assigned to more than one other subcommittee. By tradition, the structure was sufficiently permeable during the Perkins years to allow any member desiring to participate (but not vote) in subcommittee deliberations to do so, even if he was not a member of that subcommittee. (A provision allowing such participation also was in the original committee rules adopted in 1957.)

Subcommittees were accorded little deference by the full committee. Frequently, battles fought and resolved (or not resolved) in subcommittees were fought again in full committee, although a good many bills were reported to the House in the form in which they left the subcommittee. Several characteristics of Education and Labor accounted for the lack of faith in subcommittee decisions. First, the controversial nature of the issues and the lack of necessity for expertise made the full committee the likely arena for many debates. Second, the contentious nature of many of the members was a contributing factor. If a subcommittee member did not get his amendments through the subcommittee, frequently he would try again in the full committee. Third, the Democrats frequently did not agree on the formulas for many of the programs. Chairman Perkins wanted his district to profit most, while the northern, urban, liberal majority of the Democrats wanted urban areas to get the lion's share of the benefits.

The committee rules required that every bill referred to Education and Labor be assigned to the subcommittee of proper jurisdiction within a week of its referral to the full committee, regardless of whether the sponsor was a member of that subcommittee (Committee *Rules*, 90th Cong.). Perkins generally followed this stipulation unless someone made a special request that a bill be sent to his subcommittee. Committee staff members who handled the referrals for the chairman did not remember the assignment of bills ever being an issue (interview).

The advent of specific subcommittees and mandatory referral, while not a new idea on Education and Labor, diminished the chairman's already precarious power a little further on paper but did not have a perceptible impact on operations. The primary result of these reforms was a name change for Education and Labor subcommittees. Perkins continued to operate as he had before the changes in rules and continued to follow committee rules regarding bill referral. The committee rule allowing the chairman to make multiple or split referrals of bills to subcommittees counterbalanced any loss of his authority. Perkins was much more democratic about running the committee than Barden and Powell had been, and

Table 5.8. Full Committee and Subcommittee Hearings, 1967-1984

Congress	Year	Days of full committee hearings	Days of subcommittee hearings	Total days of hearings	Percentage of subcommittee hearings
90th	1967-68	36	193	229	84.3
91st	1969-70	38	343	381	90.0
92d	1971-72	61	236	297	79.5
93d	1973-74	5	338	343	98.5
94th	1975-76	7	288	295	97.6
95th	1977-78	0	317	317	100.0
96th	1979-80	0	335	335	100.0
97th	1981-82	14	271	285	95.1
98th	1983-84	20	262	282	92.9
	Total	181	2,583	2,764	
	Mean	20.1	287.0	307.1	93.1
	Percentage of Total	6.5	93.5		

Sources: Compiled from Committee on Education and Labor, *Calendar* 1967-84; Committee on Education and Labor, *Activities* 1967-84.

the changes instituted before he took control blunted the impact of the 1970s caucus reforms.

Under Perkins, Education and Labor held frequent hearings at both the full committee and subcommittee levels. Between 1967 and 1984 just over 93 percent were held before subcommittees. Despite this high percentage, Perkins held more hearings in the full committee than Powell did, although in the 95th and 96th Congresses, Perkins held no full committee hearings at all. During Perkins's chairmanship, there were 181 days of full committee hearings, with an average of 20.1 per term (see table 5.8). On the other hand, for the three terms that Powell was chairman, the full committee held only 7 days of hearings, at an average of 2.3 days per term. The average number of subcommittee hearings during the Perkins years also exceeds that of the Powell years, as does the average total number of hearings per term. The Perkins committee held more hearings than did the Powell committee, just about any way they are compared.

Perkins relied largely on the full committee in his early terms as chairman to hold hearings on legislation he sponsored. The issues included amendments to and extensions of the Economic Opportunity Act of 1964, the Elementary and Secondary Education Act of 1965, and the National School Lunch Act. On several occasions the full committee held hearings on ranking minority member Albert Quie's (R-MN) education legislation as well.

It has been said repeatedly that Carl Perkins set out to solve unemployment problems single-handedly by hiring everyone who needed a job for his office or for the committee. As a result of this practice and for other reasons, the size of the staff varied markedly from month to month. Some stayed for years, and others for just a few months. Moreover, it is not always possible to determine how many staff members there were or whether they were classified as statutory or investigative. The record keeping and reporting procedures and practices varied throughout the years.

The Legislative Reorganization Act of 1946 (P.L. 79-601) allowed each committee four permanent, professional staff members and six clerical personnel. Minority allocations were not specified, because staff were supposed to be appointed without regard to political affiliation. Provisions for minority staff personnel were not written into the House rules until the Legislative Reorganization Act of 1970, which provided that one-third of the committee's investigative personnel funding, two of the committee's six professional statutory personnel, and one of the statutory clerical employees be allocated to the minority. Malbin (1980, 13) noted that both House and Senate Democrats ignored the one-third rule in subsequent years. In fact, the provision was repealed in 1971 and not reinstated until 1974, when the minority was allotted one-third of the eighteen professionals and twelve clerks and one-third of the investigative funds. In 1975 the House eliminated the 1946 requirement that professionals be nonpartisan and instituted prohibitions against discrimination on the basis of race, creed, sex, and age. That same year, subcommittee chairmen and ranking minority members were authorized to hire staff members, paid out of statutory or supplemental funds, to work on their subcommittees (House *Rules* 1979, rule 11, cl. 6, p. 439).

One of the hallmarks of Education and Labor staff members under Perkins (and Powell) was their party loyalty (Goodwin 1970; Morrow 1969). Despite the nonpartisan requirement, throughout both eras the committee staff was partisan. As one set of authors noted, "Party affiliation is a very important criterion in staff selection; here the minority staff services only minority members of the committees, while majority staff appointees serve only majority members of the committees" (Jewell and Patterson 1966, 242). There were physical barriers between the two staffs and little communication between them (interviews).

Prior to the guaranteed independent staffing of subcommittees implemented in 1971 (Deering and Smith 1981, 264), personnel considerations were limited by the committee budget. The chairman had the authority to employ and discharge additional majority committee and subcommittee staff members as the budget would allow. Under Perkins, however, many of the professional staff were on the House payroll and were not paid out of committee funds. Because the numbers of standing committee staff members were set by law, Perkins (and other committee chairmen) also relied on staff members paid out of investigative funds to do much of the work, including the staffing of subcommittees. Moreover, he allowed the minority part of these funds, but not necessarily one-third.

Until 1966 the authority of the committee to employ or discharge majority committee staff members was reserved for the chairman, while the ranking minority member had control over the minority staff. When Perkins became chairman, the subcommittee chairmen hired their own staffs, and the full committee chairman was responsible for the full committee staff. Perkins took advantage of his hiring powers to enlarge the investigative staff. Moreover, not only did he hire his own people, he hired friends of his ranking committee colleagues—Frank Thompson, Jr., Edith Green, John Dent, and James G. O'Hara, among others—sometimes giving them preference over his own people.

Although Education and Labor subcommittee staffs were not guaranteed prior to Perkins's chairmanship, they were authorized in the committee rules beginning in the 87th Congress (1961-62). The 1961 rules provided that the full committee chairman, in consultation with the subcommittee chairmen, would assign the duties and responsibilities of members of the staffs and delegate duties that he deemed appropriate. The ranking minority member had the same powers in regard to the minority staff, which was allocated by the grace of a merciful majority, since there were no statutory provisions for minority staff until the 1970 reform act. Although the Republicans had full committee staff they had few, if any, subcommittee employees throughout the Perkins years. It is difficult to tell from the records with any degree of certainty.

Under Powell, if a member desired staff assistance not usually rendered in the course of regular committee and subcommittee staff duties, he had to appeal to the chairman for such assistance. After Powell's departure, the committee rules for the 90th Congress (1967-68) borrowed a phrase from existing House rules that declared that "staff members shall be assigned to committee business and no other duties may be assigned to them" (Committee *Rules*, 1967, rule 11). This rule was honored more in the breach than in the observance, however. Under both Powell and Perkins, committee staff frequently handled district matters, according to some staff members (interviews).

By the end of the Perkins era, Education and Labor had a more complex structural configuration than it had had when it was chaired by Barden. It had more members, more subcommittees, and a larger staff. It was infinitely more decentralized than it had been in Barden's day, relying on subcommittees to a greater extent and allowing subcommittee chairmen a greater degree of influence in committee operations. As a forerunner in the decentralization of House committees, Education and Labor had institutionalized its own decentralization. Formal committee rules had increased in number, scope, and specificity and were followed more closely. In general, the committee was more egalitarian. All these strictures and developments had less impact on committee operations than might have been expected. Perkins had championed the reforms that devolved authority when Barden and Powell were chairmen and was able to manipulate committee activities to his liking despite them. The result was a more democratic, decentralized committee responding to its chairman's direction.

Jurisdiction, Work Load, and Function

The nature of the issues before Education and Labor changed during Chairman Perkins's tenure, as did the mission of the committee. The committee was no longer the bastion of innovation it had been in the early and mid-1960s. Throughout most of the 1967-84 period, Education and Labor was in a holding pattern. Budget cuts and a decreasingly salient jurisdiction forced it to concentrate on protecting the gains made in the Powell years.

The official jurisdiction of the Committee on Education and Labor remained largely the same as it had been under Powell. Nevertheless, new issues expanded its scope and shifted its emphasis. The programs covered within the vague issue areas delineated in the House rules changed in concurrence with issues on the political agenda. Most of the emphasis during the Perkins years was on education, although the major education laws had been enacted in the mid-1960s after years of bitter controversy. By the 1970s most of what Education and Labor did in education was by way of amending and extending the 1960s programs. A few new areas did emerge, however, such as day care, asbestos in schools, drug and alcohol abuse prevention and education, immigrant and refugee education, boxer safety, computer-related education, and, later, AIDS education. As far as labor was concerned, attention was diverted from union issues toward the formulation of job training programs for the disadvantaged. There were a few issues new to the political agenda, such as public sector pension and retirement plans legislation. The committee also dug deeper into occupational health and safety issues and manpower policies.

Education issues were prominent on the agenda at the outset of the Perkins years because of the recently passed Elementary and Secondary Education Act of 1965 (ESEA, P.L. 89-10) and the Higher Education Act of 1965 (P.L. 89-329). In the face of administration requests for large budget cuts in social programs, including federal aid to education, in Perkins's first year as chairman the committee authorized more than nine

billion dollars to extend and amend ESEA in the largest school aid bill in
U.S. history (P.L. 90-247). The bill consolidated library and instructional
resources as well as innovation and support services programs under
ESEA. In addition, it extended aid to federally impacted areas and expanded programs for the education of handicapped children. In other
legislation, members extended policies affecting higher education (P.L.
90-575) and vocational education (P.L. 90-576). In 1970 Congress enacted a
further extension of ESEA (P.L. 91-230), to the tune of $24.6 billion. The
program, which was overhauled and authorized again for four years in 1974
(P.L. 93-380), had expired but was kept intact by funding via a continuing
resolution. The revisions also consolidated several grant programs and gave
states more discretion over spending. They benefited poorer and more
rural states at the expense of wealthier urban states (*Congress and the Nation*,
4:383). In 1978, however, when the ESEA was amended and extended
again, Congress returned the emphasis to the urban, wealthier states, away
from the more rural South (P.L. 95-561).

The Education Amendments of 1972 (P.L. 92-318) responded to increasingly vocal opposition to busing students to achieve racial integration
by restricting busing and allotting two billion dollars for desegregation
efforts. Several amendments to education legislation in subsequent years
contained antibusing provisions.

The committee considered a variety of solutions to the rising costs of
higher education—a 77-percent increase between 1966 and 1976 (*Congress
and the Nation* 5:665). Ultimately the Education Amendments of 1972
authorized nineteen billion dollars to aid higher education and other programs. As part of these amendments, Congress approved Basic Educational
Opportunity Grants (BEOGs) to pay up to one-half the cost of higher
education for first-year college students. Congress also extended the higher
education programs in 1979. The 95th Congress defeated proposals for
tuition tax credits opposed by the Carter administration and approved
legislation expanding eligibility for BEOGs and decreasing the amount of
discretionary income required of qualifying families.

One major education measure escaped committee preview. The establishment of a cabinet-level Department of Education came under the aegis
of the House Committee on Government Operations instead of Education
and Labor.

With the coming of the 1980s, several other issues moved to the
forefront of the education agenda and consumed committee time. With the
rise of the New Right and the election of President Reagan, issues of prayer
in public schools and equal access to public school facilities by religious
groups resurfaced. Concurrently, questions of censorship of public school
textbooks (for "secular humanism") attracted attention. Questions con-

tinued on funding for elementary and secondary education, higher education, special education for the handicapped, and school lunch.

By the Perkins years, welfare and labor issues largely had been subjugated to education questions. Welfare concerns, a legacy of the Great Society, received little sympathy from subsequent Republican administrations. The influence of organized labor also declined (*Congress and the Nation* 2:618). With some notable exceptions, few significant labor laws were enacted between 1967 and 1984. After Chairman Powell had pocketed the situs picketing bill in 1966, thereby leading to its demise, Education and Labor approved it again in 1967, but it never reached the floor. When Congress finally passed a common site picketing bill in 1976 (H.Res. 5900), President Ford vetoed it. The next year, with a Democratic administration, Congress defeated a similar measure. It has yet to succeed.

Besides picketing at construction sites, organized labor largely concentrated its lobbying efforts on public service employment programs, extensions of unemployment compensation benefits, increased retirement benefits, and increased minimum wage (*Congress and the Nation* 3:703). President Nixon vetoed the committee's public service employment program, although one was approved in 1974 (P.L. 93-567) and another during the Carter administration (P.L. 95-44) to combat the recession. The committee was successful at getting Congress to increase the minimum wage (P.L. 93-259).

In the early years of Perkins's chairmanship, two major committee labor bills concerning worker protections were enacted: the Coal Mine Health and Safety Act of 1969 (P.L. 91-173) and the Occupational Safety and Health Act of 1970 (OSHA, P.L. 91-596). The mine safety act established safety standards for coal mines and approved financial compensation for victims of black lung disease (pneumoconiosis). The next year, Congress established the Occupational Safety and Health Administration to oversee a comprehensive job training safety program covering fifty-five million industrial workers, farmers, and construction workers engaged in interstate commerce. These two acts were amended and extended throughout the duration of the Perkins years and on into the late 1980s.

Throughout the late 1970s and early 1980s, although Congress amended and extended existing labor programs, it voted down other committee labor initiatives. In addition to legislation on picketing, the Senate killed a proposal that would have made it easier for unions to organize. Congress also defeated a measure that would have indexed minimum wage to inflation.

Manpower and training issues received considerable attention between 1967 and 1984. At the outset of Perkins's chairmanship, questions arose about the continued reauthorization of the Economic Opportunity Act of 1964, which contained the poverty program. Despite pressures resulting from Vietnam, inflation, and administrative problems to cut back Great Society programs, Chairman Perkins successfully shepherded the reauthorization through Congress in 1967. By the early 1980s, however, most of the poverty programs had been dismantled or cut back severely (Peters 1982, 241). The few that remained were parceled out to other agencies.

Largely as a result of high unemployment rates, and with a legacy of programs aimed at creating jobs, the committee worked on a number of other job training and employment opportunities bills throughout this period. In a major development in 1973, Congress approved one of the most controversial manpower acts since the WPA program of the 1930s—the Comprehensive Employment and Training Act of 1973 (CETA, P.L. 93-203). This act incorporated a comprehensive approach to job training and employment opportunities for the economically disadvantaged, the unemployed, and the underemployed. After being criticized and amended for several years, CETA was replaced by the 1982 Job Training Partnership Act (JTPL, P.L. 97-300), which was aimed at preparing youths and unskilled adults for entry into the labor force. JTPL also provided job training for the economically disadvantaged or for those who faced other barriers to employment (*Summary of Major Legislative Action*, 97th Cong., p. 16).

The committee was successful in efforts to amend black lung compensation laws, the longshoremen's compensation act, and the Manpower Development and Training Act several times. As part of the anti-poverty drive, it created the Domestic Volunteer Service Act of 1973 (P.L. 93-113), which gave statutory authority to the ACTION agency and included VISTA, the domestic Peace Corps. The committee reported and Congress approved the Emergency Jobs and Unemployment Assistance Act of 1974 (P.L. 93-567) to expand CETA. In addition, between 1967 and 1984, members voted on public pension plan legislation, including the Employee Retirement Income and Security Act (ERISA, P.L. 93-406) and the attempted Public Employment Pension Plan Reporting and Accountability Act.

Under Perkins's chairmanship, the committee's work load and success rates increased, as measured by the number of hearings held in full committee and subcommittee, the number of bills reported to the House, the number that passed the House, and the number enacted into public law (see table 5.9). The number of hearings by both subcommittees and the full committee rose. Part of the increase stemmed from the House's stepped-up emphasis on oversight, which resulted in all subcommittees being charged with oversight duties. The chairman's role perhaps was more important.

Table 5.9. Bills Referred to Education and Labor, 1951-1984

Congress	Year	Number referred	Number reported	Number passed HR	Number public laws
82d	1951-52	232	8	7	4
83d	1953-54	268	15	14	12
84th	1955-56	468	12	11	10
85th	1957-58	601	18	14	14
86th	1959-60	720	17	10	8
87th	1961-62	741	44	20[a]	18
88th	1963-64	713	25	14	14
89th	1965-66	959	51	32	28
90th	1967-68	836	38	33	23
91st	1969-70	855	26	24	23[b]
92d	1971-72	1,110	29	28	19
93d	1973-74	1,258	41	36	33
94th	1975-76	1,089	34	27	17[c]
95th	1977-78	1,113	40	37	31
96th	1979-80	521	34	25	13
97th	1981-82	433	33	17	7
98th	1983-84	488	55	43	19

Source: Compiled from Committee on Education and Labor, *Calendar* 1951-84.

[a] Includes six Senate bills.

[b] Three additional bills were enacted as part of the Elementary and Secondary Amendments of 1969 (P.L. 91-23).

[c] Two additional bills were enacted as part of the Education Amendments of 1976 (P.L. 93-482).

Carl D. Perkins, an active and permissive chairman, contributed substantially to the growth in hearings. In addition to scheduling regular hearings in Washington, the chairman frequently held hearings in his own and other members' districts. He also allowed other members to hold as many hearings as they liked. The general increase in the importance of subcommittees because of House and House Democratic Caucus reforms also may have contributed to more hearings. Some subcommittee chairmen may have been trying to carve a niche for themselves, a task that became easier when subcommittees gained importance in the House. The fact that Chairman Perkins himself took a subcommittee beginning in the 93d Congress (1973-74) accounted for the large jump in the percentage of subcommittee hearings. He used his subcommittee rather than the full committee for his forum, contrary to his predecessors.

While the committee was holding more hearings, it was producing somewhat less legislation. The number of bills reported dropped off slightly, from an average of 40 per term under Powell to 36.7 under

Perkins. This decrease can be explained in part by the eroding salience of the committee's jurisdiction under Perkins. By the time Perkins became chairman, Vietnam had become the top priority at the expense of domestic issues other than the economy. Another explanation for the decrease in the number of bills reported lies in the increased emphasis and time put into oversight.

Although the committee reported fewer bills per term under Perkins, its success rates on the House floor were substantially higher. Nearly 82 percent of the bills reported by Education and Labor passed the House as compared with the 55 percent that were approved under Powell. Once these bills reached the Senate, however, they sometimes were blocked by the difficulty of forging agreements with the Senate in a limited amount of time. There were several presidential vetoes.

Chairman Perkins was a factor in the relatively high rates of success the committee had between 1967 and 1984. Although by and large the measures considered by the committee under Perkins were not as critical as those handled during the Powell years, as chairman Perkins added prestige to the committee because of his honesty and seriousness. Perkins also worked diligently at building majorities for his bills. He was relentless in his efforts to win House support for committee bills, particularly his own. Committee concentration on amending and extending legislation enacted in the 1960s contributed to the higher number of bills passed and subsequently enacted. Moreover, many of the bills were of smaller scope and thus easier to pass.

On the whole, the Committee on Education and Labor's work load was not substantially different from what it had been during the Powell years. The flurry of activity increased, but the productivity, as measured by the number of bills reported, decreased. The functional shift the committee underwent during the Perkins years contributed to this change. An important point to remember, nonetheless, is that the success rate of committee bills on the House floor rose significantly, a development that can be attributed in large part to Chairman Perkins.

Concurrent with a change in the chairmanship, the committee function changed from spearheading presidential programs to maintaining earlier accomplishments. Under Powell, the committee had been the administration's vehicle for a large part of its domestic agenda, which included the War on Poverty programs and federal aid to education, two top priorities of President Johnson. By the time Perkins became chairman in 1967, many of the administration's programs were in place. Moreover, Vietnam had bumped poverty off the top of the public agenda. Funds from human resources programs were funneled to the war effort. In addition, the economy was in sad shape. As a result, Republican administrations came to power with objectives entirely different from the Great Society. They opposed large social welfare programs and set about to abolish them or replace them with cash grants. Nixon's impoundment of funds from the Office of Economic Opportunity overruled by the Supreme Court, is a prime example. Moreover, the Republicans also had different ideas concerning federal aid to education. Nixon favored a general revenue-sharing approach to restore discretion over education spending to the states. In addition, government spending was increasing, and efforts were under way to balance the budget, cutting federal education and welfare spending in the process.

Another factor in the functional shift of the committee was the declining power of its constituent interest groups. First and foremost, the decline of organized labor in membership, political and financial clout, and salience affected both labor and education. Unions had been heavy backers of committee programs. With the loss in labor influence, education programs were more vulnerable to attack, because labor had provided some of their strongest supporters. The education establishment maintained its strength, but it, too, met with resistance from the budget cutters.

As a result of the change in emphasis and concentration on budget cutting, Education and Labor shifted from activity and innovation to a holding pattern. A major goal of committee Democrats throughout the Perkins years was to hold on to gains they had made in the 1960s. Republicans, on the other hand, made large-scale efforts to cripple many of the committee programs, such as school lunch, scholarships, guaranteed student loans, and BEOGs. Chairman Perkins complained, "They're unreasonably gouging the Education and Labor Committee and the people in education and in labor. They've done so much harm" (interview). Although authorizations for education programs were increasing, there were large gaps between the amounts approved and the amounts appropriated. By fiscal 1973, Congress appropriated less than four dollars for every ten dollars it authorized (*Congress and the Nation* 4:384). To compensate for a jurisdiction declining in salience and power, the committee, according to the chairman, broadened its scope. It concentrated on issues new to the political agenda.

The 1974 budget act put the committee at the mercy of the Budget Committee and subsequent budget control acts, such as Gramm-Latta and Gramm-Rudman-Hollings. Education and Labor, led by Chairman Perkins, fought tooth and toenail to maintain its programs intact, particularly those in education. Members tried to keep secondary education, higher education, and vocational education reasonably supported, and they investigated alternative sources of funding, such as tuition tax credits. They also returned to race issues to deal with problems created by forced busing.

In sum, the committee's function under Perkins was to hold on to the gains made in the early and mid-1960s. During the years that Perkins was chairman, committee concerns were no longer at the forefront of the public agenda. Education and Labor continued to authorize large entitlement programs but met resistance from the budget cutters. As a former staff member lamented, "They keep trying to reinvent the wheel" by amending and extending existing programs and trying to keep them financially sound (interview).

6

The Chairmanship of Carl Perkins

The chairman of a congressional committee, within certain parameters imposed by House and committee environments, makes a difference in the behavior of his committee and in the outcome of the issues before it. This expectation certainly was true of Chairman Carl Dewey Perkins (D-KY), who had a unique impact on the operations and output of the Committee on Education and Labor.

A Portrait of the Chairman

"Carl Dewey Perkins was up there next to God in the Seventh District of Kentucky. He was a savior," according to one of his constituents who later worked for him.[1] He brought federal money, accompanied by jobs and roads, to one of the poorest congressional districts in the country, in the far reaches of Appalachia. After he died on August 3, 1984, between five and six thousand people attended his funeral in the Knott County High School gymnasium in Hindman, Kentucky, including a delegation of more than one hundred members of Congress and five former Kentucky governors as well as the sitting governor of the state. According to the *Troublesome Creek Times*, "The funeral probably represented the largest single gathering of national figures in Kentucky's history" (Daley 1984). Admirers later erected a statue to Perkins in Hindman and elected his son to fill his congressional seat.

In explaining some of the adulation, one of his obituaries quoted a highly placed official in the Johnson administration as saying, "It's safe to say that Carl Perkins has gotten more Federal money for his district, on a per capita basis, than any man on Capitol Hill" (Hunter 1984). Perkins helped millions of people, particularly the thousands of poor in eastern Kentucky, through the Elementary and Secondary Act of 1965, the Economic Opportunity Act of 1964, and Vocational Education Act of 1963, adult education programs, funding for libraries, black lung benefits for coal miners, flood-control projects, free school lunches for poor children, and other programs.

Born in 1912 on a farm near Hindman, Carl Perkins was the son of Dora Calhoun Perkins and James Perkins. His father, a lawyer, who also operated a livery stable, had come to Knott County from Grayson County, Virginia, in about 1880 (Reeves 1977). Hindman was a remote town, isolated by mountains. As a boy, Perkins earned money by taking a drove of horses to the railroad station in Hazard to pick up the lawyers and judges traveling the court circuit. For about $1.50 per person, he would guide them up the Kentucky River valley, over the mountains, and back along Troublesome Creek to Hindman.[2]

After attending the Hindman Settlement School and the county schools, Perkins was a student at nearby Caney College, now Alice Lloyd College, in Pippa Passes, Kentucky. After two years, he took a job teaching school for about fifty dollars a month (Hunter 1984).[3] He commuted on horseback, traveling over the mountain instead of by the road, which was twice as far (Glickman 1972, 2). For a time Perkins also attended Lees Junior College in Jackson, Kentucky. He had a less than spectacular academic record and never graduated from college.[4] Later he graduated from the Jefferson School of Law in Louisville.

Subsequently, Perkins held a number of public offices. In 1939 he served an unexpired term as Commonwealth attorney. The next year he was elected to the Kentucky General Assembly. Perkins served as the Knott County attorney from 1941 to 1948, even during the time he served in the U.S. Army in Europe. In 1948 Governor Earle Clements appointed him counsel for the Kentucky Department of Highways.. Also that year Perkins first won election to Congress.

Carl Perkins married Verna Johnson, and they moved to Washington to be near Congress, although Perkins never called any place home but Hindman. In 1954 Carl and Verna had their only son, Carl C., whom they called Chris. When Carl Perkins died in 1984, Chris was elected to his father's seat largely on the strength of the Perkins name, which was highly revered in eastern Kentucky. He retired in 1992 after the legislature passed a redistricting plan that pitted him against formidable GOP opposition.

Ultimately encompassing twenty-three counties in eastern Kentucky, the Seventh District is largely a jumble of mountains and steep valleys, except where it gentles out into a few counties in the state's famed Bluegrass region. At the onset of Perkins's congressional service, roads were generally poor, television was unknown, and radio stations were few and far between. Outside the county seats telephone communication was marked less by its presence than by its dearth. There was (and is) only one city of any consequential size, Ashland, which had 29,000 people in 1970 and declined to 27,064 in 1980. The Seventh District of Kentucky was and is one of the poorest congressional districts in the United States. According to the Ralph Nader Congress Project's research on Perkins, the 1968 average per-capita income in the Seventh District was $1,332. This figure compares with a statewide average of $2,614 and a nationwide average of $3,159. The Nader Project described it as the "most thickly-populated rural area in the country despite a ten percent population loss during the 60s" (Glickman 1972, 2).

The local economy depends on the coal industry, which was depressed severely during most of Perkin's congressional service. Increased mechanization of Kentucky mines and the ease of mining western coal, which was less harmful environmentally, resulted in fewer jobs for coal miners. Moreover, many companies increasingly relied on strip mining, which requires fewer workers than does deep mining. As a consequence of these factors and the dangers associated with mining, many miners abandoned the Seventh District for promises of a better financial future in industrial places like Akron, Flint, Toledo, and Detroit, where there were factory jobs (Glickman 1972, 2; Barone, Ujifusa, and Matthews 1977, 326). Many district residents also relied on tobacco farming for their income. In 1972 over half of the district's farms, more than thirty thousand of them, grew at least some tobacco. In addition, livestock, petroleum refining, and primary metal industries fueled the economy.

Also in 1972 about 80 percent of the residents lived in rural areas, and 70 percent were blue-collar workers, almost double the national average. Blacks and foreign born composed only 2 percent of the district's population (Glickman 1972). At one point, Committee on Education and Labor staff members reported that school superintendents under federal pressure to integrate their schools complained that there were not enough blacks to go around to satisfy an order from the Department of Health, Education, and Welfare.

The residents of the Seventh District traditionally have been Democrats as a result of New Deal reforms and the influence of the United Mine Workers (UMW). As of 1972, the voter registry listed 65 percent of the voters as Democrats and 34 percent as Republicans. In Perkins's first election, the Taft-Hartley Act was the major campaign issue. Perkins took the side of the miners, although he did not have their union's endorsement. He had, however, represented more than a few miners in workmen's compensation cases. He won the election with 60.5 percent of the vote (Glickman 1972, 2). In every election after that, the UMW was solidly behind him. Despite the declining importance of the labor unions, the district remained largely Democratic and loyal to Carl Perkins, even after his death.

Not only the miners in the Seventh District and in Kentucky, but union members all over the United States considered themselves constituents of Carl Perkins. He had come along at the appropriate time to prevent legislation abhorrent to organized labor from being reported from his committee. He had been on the side of labor from the moment he entered Congress in 1949 and was one of the few members involved in the House-Senate Conference Committee on the Landrum-Griffin Act in 1959 who would not sign the conference report. In the 1930s and 1940s mine owners and UMW members fought bitterly over union wages and benefits, but the struggle later was replaced by one between the mining industry, particularly strip mine operators, and environmentalists (Glickman 1972, 2). The battle still rages in the 1990s. Strip mining became one of the major issues of the district elections, and several groups antagonistic to strip mining formed during the 1970s. Generally, environmentalists did not support Perkins.

The education establishment supported Perkins, who, in turn, was one of its biggest supporters. Before he was chairman, he gained its backing by his work on the Elementary and Secondary Education Act of 1965 and the Vocational Education Act of 1963. The teachers' unions found good in Perkins from both the educational and the union perspective. He was a champion of teachers and of public education.

When he became chairman of the Committee on Education and Labor in 1967, Carl Perkins came in contact with a broader, but not fundamentally different, constituency. It consisted of the poor people of the nation, the beneficiaries of the social welfare programs enacted with the help of the committee in the 1960s. They lived all over the country, in large cities and ghettos, in small towns, in rural areas. Thousands of these people—poor, uneducated, unemployed, and unskilled—happened to live in the Seventh District of Kentucky. *Disadvantaged* was the word used to describe them. They made up his real constituency. Rather than regarding himself as an advocate of the disadvantaged nationwide, as some perceived him to be, Perkins was devoted to the people of the Seventh District, truly being one of them himself. Throughout his congressional career, he fought tirelessly for programs to improve the quality of life in this poor Appalachian region.

Although those who knew him well knew better, on the surface Perkins appeared to many to be a fumbling, bumbling bumpkin who whistled through his teeth when he talked.[5] Tom Bethell described him in the *Rural Coalition* newsletter as "a great, shuffling, bear of a man who has never paid attention to changing fashion. . . . He has enormous hands that look as though they remember what manual labor was like. He doesn't televise well, and he lacks the quick wit and glibness that today's politicians seem to need" (cited in Furguson 1984). One of the committee staff members wrote to a constituent: "It has now been nearly 30 years since Carl came to Washington. But it is as if he has been placed under a glass bell, for urban life, Potomac Fever, or Congressional grandeur have never rubbed off on him. He is still the same plain, unaffected, old-fashionedly polite Kentuckian he was when he set foot in the place" (Reeves 1977).

Perkins did not join the Washington social scene. Frequently he did not even tell his wife about generally coveted invitations to the White House and to other affairs. Most people jump at the chance to dine at the White House, but not Carl Perkins. One time when he and his wife, Verna, were invited to the Johnson White House for dinner, the chairman asked a staff member to "go down there and represent me." The last time he had gone, "They didn't get supper on the table 'til after 10 o'clock." The women had gone with Mrs. Johnson, and the men had sat and talked with the president, who told one Sam Rayburn story after another. Perkins had not enjoyed the previous occasion and did not relish a repeat performance (interview, staff).

Perkins had the reputation of being exceedingly honest. He earned great respect among his colleagues for this trait. On one occasion, the Kentucky AFL-CIO tried to present him with a color television as a token of appreciation. He would not go near it. He did not want even the appearance of accepting gifts.[6] He also paid for his personal telephone calls made from his office and put postage on personal letters instead of relying on the readily available congressional frank. Perhaps his caution in this respect was heightened by the prison terms meted out to two of his eastern Kentucky predecessors for financial malfeasance.[7]

A telling factor regarding his financial caution was his refusal to accept campaign contributions from anyone, including his staff, for the greater part of his congressional career. His campaign expenses were minimal and came out of his own pocket. Beginning sometime in the Nixon administration, he began to accept a few contributions, albeit not large ones. By that time it had dawned on him how much television air time cost and how many stations he had to buy from to get his message to constituents in his district (interviews, staff).

Perkins's district was such that he did not need to spend large amounts of money campaigning for reelection. Mass media were limited in his rural, mountainous district; thus political advertisements on radio or television were minimally effective. He did buy some television time, but it was expensive, and he did not consider it as efficient as some of his personal campaign practices. Perkins spent time instead of money campaigning, thereby negating the need for most financial contributions. He made the long trip back to his district almost every weekend and traveled the territory meeting with everyone he could. He went way back up in the "hollers" to visit constituents and to see if they had any problems that he could help them solve. Perkins also worked long hours attending football games, horse shows, fairs, and other social functions where he had maximum access to large numbers of constituents. Years after he died, the *Congressional Quarterly Weekly Report* characterized Perkins as having a "blend of informal 'hillbilly' manners and deal-cutting skills" that made him "an influential legislator unassailable at the polls" (January 25, 1992, p. 189).

Orientation of the Chairman

Since his rough edges never wore off and he never became a part of the Washington establishment, Perkins truly was one of the people of the Seventh District. They could have had no better representation in Congress. Perkins was noted, both at home and throughout the country, for aiding his district. There was no one able or willing to fight harder for the benefits of his constituents, and they knew it. By his persistence and maneuvering, he managed to gain a strategic position that could bring large amounts of money to the poverty-stricken area of eastern Kentucky. As chairman of the Committee on Education and Labor, he had control over legislation that targeted the underprivileged areas of the nation, and he used his position to funnel funds to his own people.

Out of devotion to the people in his district, he worked hard for the Elementary and Secondary Education Act of 1965, the Vocational Education Act of 1963, and the poverty program even before he became chairman. He made sure that the formulas were written to the benefit of his constituents. These three programs directly improved the quality of life for the people of the Seventh District. Between 1964 and 1968 Kentucky received the fifth highest amount of War on Poverty funds in the country, preceded only by the much larger states of California, New York, Texas, and Illinois (U.S. Bureau of the Census 1969, 331).

Kentucky also received among the highest amounts of federal education funding. It ranked fifth in the amount of higher education grants and loans, seventh in Teacher Corps funds, ninth in elementary and secondary education money, and thirteenth in vocational education financing (U.S. Bureau of the Census 1969, 134). Had Carl Perkins not been influential in the creation of the formulas, Kentucky probably would have been way down the list. It surpassed several much larger states whose cities alone should have merited higher rankings. One committee member cited eastern Kentucky as "the model for everything" (interview). Another said, "He let ——— run the labor side of the committee. As long as we started from the Seventh District and worked from there in the education formulas. Give Carl what he wants and cut the rest up" (interview). Another committee member referred to this aspect of Perkins's leadership as his "regional agenda" (interview).

Perkins improved his standing at home and advanced his agenda by routinely taking congressional delegations to his district for hearings. He wanted his fellow members to see how badly his people needed help, and he tried to make sure that all the new committee members went to Kentucky to attend hearings on black lung. It was important to Perkins that members of Congress understand the distress of his constituents suffering from the only recently recognized disease. After one such trip to the Seventh District, one committee member said, "If you ever had a doubt [about black lung legislation], go into a drafty high school gymnasium. Hear the witnesses talk and the people coughing in the audience. You'll come back supporting it" (interview). In questioning a victim witness about black lung's ravages, Perkins sometimes could be embarrassingly clinical. "Mr. ———," he would say in his country lawyer voice, "tell this committee what color you spit up." The witness graphically would describe the product of his cough. Perkins was satisfied, and the assembled committee was quite willing to let it go (interview, staff). To accomplish his goal of getting other members to his district, Perkins frequently held hearings in their districts. He also made them look good to their hometown crowds.

Because of his success at bringing millions of dollars in federal money to his district and his hands-on, personal contact with his constituents, Perkins was highly regarded in Kentucky. His constituents respected him for his persistence, his position, and his successes, and many loved him for his down-home, personal concern for their welfare. He was reelected by large margins every time after 1956. Few had the courage to oppose him in the Democratic primary, and on several occasions no one filed, although the Republicans always put up a candidate. His victories in the general election were overwhelming.

Despite large electoral margins in his favor, however, he never felt secure about his seat. He was afraid that he would be defeated, and he worked tirelessly for the benefit of his district. In turn, his constituents almost worshiped him. A staff writer for the Louisville *Courier-Journal* described Perkins and the attitude of his constituents toward him: "Tough and persistent but disarmingly gentle in manner, the wily Knott County native had showered his mountain district with enough dams, social programs and constituent favors to rank, as one Eastern Kentuckian put it, 'just about a half-notch below God'" (Brown 1988). One member who knew Perkins well said that he had never seen anyone who could so diligently and effectively protect his parochial interests while being a national legislator: "Carl has a tremendous impact on his district. It makes the difference between getting an education and not getting an education, and eating and not eating. They are the best-taken-care-of people from the congressional standpoint that there ever were" (interview).

When Carl Perkins died, the members of Congress who went to the mountains of eastern Kentucky to pay their respects and to see the Seventh District of Kentucky were surprised at the extent of the pride and admiration Seventh District denizens held for their congressman. More than one member was overheard saying, "Now I understand."[8] Other attendees who had not visited the district for many years were amazed at the improvements, particularly in the roads, that had been made.

Some people judged Carl Perkins to be liberal, and others judged him to be conservative. The best indicator of Perkins's ideology is the benefits that accrued to his district. He was regarded as a liberal because of his wholehearted support of the social welfare programs of the 1960s aimed at helping the poor and otherwise disadvantaged. He fought for federal aid to education and on the side of organized labor—two liberal mainstays. And he was one of the few southern Democrats to vote for the Civil Rights Act of 1964. He was a liberal in that he thought that government was meant to help the people and the otherwise disadvantaged. One editorial writer wrote, "The idea of government as a helping hand has never been more embodied in one man than in Carl Perkins" (Furguson 1984).

He was regarded as conservative in other aspects. An Education and Labor staff member who knew him well stated, "There really wasn't anything liberal about Carl Perkins. He looked to his conservative southern Democratic friends to tell him how to vote" on issues that were not under his committee's jurisdiction (interview). His son, Chris, concurred: "My father was basically very conservative, but he had a social agenda that would be considered liberal. He believed in feeding and educating children, in giving students the opportunity to attend college, and in taking care of mothers and children. He believed in causes associated with human need" (interview). Most of the chairman's best friends were among the southern conservatives, such as William Natcher (D-KY). Perkins also took the conservative position on some social issues, such as allowing students who wished to congregate for religious purposes equal access to public schools.

Chairman Perkins did not think "liberal" or "conservative" consciously. He thought Seventh District. Being one of its people, he knew the problems and did everything he could to help. One of his obituaries said, "He wasted no time on futile arguments over whether legislation was liberal or moderate or conservative—his only criterion was whether it was good for the people. He was a resourceful, tireless and tenacious fighter for his causes. Those causes were invariably the ones that were important to the people of his beloved 7th District" (Reeves 1984). He worked for improved health care, having known the critical need for it personally. He lost his only brother to peritonitis or appendicitis in about 1930 because no medical facilities were nearby. Perkins himself had a brush with death when he was young. His appendix burst, and "he was stiff as a board by the time they got him to the little clinic at Ary for surgery" (Reeves 1977). His liberal attitude toward government spending on health care was a result not of his philosophy, but of his understanding of the needs of his constituents.

Vocational education was another of Perkins's favorite issues considered liberal by many. But in fact it resulted from his childhood classes in manual training at the Hindman Settlement School and had little to do with political philosophy except in its potential benefits for the people of the Seventh District. He appreciated and saw the benefits of the manual skills that vocational training could produce. He frequently mentioned someone in Knott County or in Floyd County who was "one of the finest carpenters I ever saw" (Reeves 1977). He put some of his interest into practice in his sponsorship and support of the Vocational Education Act of 1963 (P.L. 88-210) and later the Carl D. Perkins Vocational Education Act (P.L. 98-524).

School lunch, or "feeding programs" as he called them, was another of the chairman's favorite causes. One of his friends was quoted as saying: "Literally millions of kids are getting fed every day because of him. Maybe it would have happened without him, but he was the one who found the handle to do it. He believed in getting something going, not just talking" (quoted in Furguson 1984). To Perkins, ideology did not matter as long as he could help the poor people of the Seventh District. The badly needed roads, schools, training programs, flood-control projects, and miners' protections financed by massive amounts of federal money poured into his district stand as monuments to the "ideology" and persistence of Carl Perkins.

In generally accepted surrogate measures of ideology, such as interest group scores, Perkins generally ranked somewhere toward the liberal end of the scale. He looked like a moderate in comparison with his committee Democratic colleagues, however, despite generally reflecting the positions of House Democrats (see table 6.1). On the other hand, the labor unions, usually considered liberal, supported him wholeheartedly, as did education groups. His scores on the labor scales indicate that he returned the favor most of the time; they were always higher than the average House Democratic ratings. When he died, his overall labor support record was 89 percent favorable to organized labor. Out of a lifetime 320 votes considered critical to AFL-CIO, Perkins voted "wrong" on only 35 roll calls ("Rep. Carl Perkins Mourned" 1984). To show their respect when he died, the miners put a black "miner's wreath" of mourning at the entrance to the UMW headquarters in Washington ("Rep. Carl Perkins Mourned" 1984; York 1984). This honor usually is reserved for victims of mine accidents or for deceased UMW officials.

Table 6.1. Perkins's Interest Group Ratings Compared with the Average Scores of Other Members, 1967-1984

Group	Year	Perkins	E & L Dems	HR Dems	Full E & L	Full HR
ADA	1967-68	62.7	80.9	56.3	55.4	38.7
ADA	1969-70	40.0	78.0	51.7	54.3	38.3
ADA	1971-72	50.5	73.0	51.5	53.2	37.7
ADA	1973-74	51.8	73.2	55.1	54.4	39.8
ADA	1975-76	59.0	71.7	58.5	55.6	45.1
ADA	1977-78	42.5	61.6	50.3	49.2	39.7
ADA	1979-80	57.0	70.7	57.3	53.6	42.9
ADA	1981-82	65.0	76.0	64.1	56.8	43.9
ADA	1983-84	71.5	79.7	70.4	57.6	49.3
COPE	1967-68	100.0	96.5	69.9	67.2	48.9
COPE	1969-70	76.5	94.3	71.5	68.9	54.6
COPE	1971-72	95.8	73.0	72.6	63.4	53.4
COPE	1973-74	100.0	93.2	77.6	66.9	53.6
COPE	1975-76	93.5	88.2	74.3	69.5	58.1
COPE	1977-78	79.8	83.4	69.3	65.4	54.2
AFL-CIO	1979-80	74.6	81.2	65.7	58.7	49.8
AFL-CIO	1981-82	88.7	90.6	79.2	62.2	53.3
AFL-CIO	1983-84	93.2	90.8	77.8	62.7	54.4
ACA	1967-68	18.0	4.8	25.9	33.5	48.5
ACA	1969-70	19.5	14.0	32.4	34.7	46.5
ACA	1971-72	26.2	16.2	34.0	37.5	50.2
ACA	1973-74	16.7	15.4	27.8	33.9	45.1
ACA	1975-76	20.0	16.5	28.9	33.2	43.5
ACA	1977-78	19.0	18.8	31.5	34.9	46.0
ACA	1979-80	21.7	17.4	26.7	38.8	45.4
ACARI	1981-82	27.6	15.0	29.2	37.6	49.4
ACARI	1983-84	21.0a	14.8	26.7	35.8	46.8

Sources: Scores for Perkins, and for all members in 1983-84, are from *Congressional Quarterly Weekly Report* 1967-85. Other than for Perkins, ratings from 1967 to 1982 are from Inter-University Consortium for Political and Social Research.

a Perkins died in August 1984 and was not rated by ACARI for that year. The score presented is the 1983 score.

ACA scores, generally presumed to indicate the degree of conservatism in a member's voting behavior, reflect a decidedly nonconservative bent to Carl Perkins. Although he did not score in the top reaches of the more liberal ADA scores, neither did he rate even moderate scores in the conservative-oriented ACA rankings. According to ratings by this group, Perkins voted the ACA position slightly more often than did his Democratic committee colleagues, but less frequently than did the average House Democrat.

Perkins's interest group scores bear out the assertion in his obituary

Table 6.2. Perkins's Party-Unity Scores Compared with the Average Scores of Other Members, 1967-1984

Congress	Year	Perkins	E & L Dems	HR Dems	Full E & L	Full HR
90th	1967-68	89.0	80.3	63.5	73.0	65.9
91st	1969-70	83.0	69.1	59.4	65.3	60.2
92d	1971-72	81.0	74.4	59.5	69.6	62.6
93d	1973-74	83.0	76.9	66.0	69.1	66.1
94th	1975-76	83.0	76.6	67.5	71.2	68.2
95th	1977-78	82.0	71.6	65.5	68.9	67.0
96th	1979-80	83.8	76.0	68.9	75.1	69.9
97th	1981-82	72.3	80.1	73.6	73.7	72.7
98th	1983-84	86.2	80.3	75.3	76.7	74.4

Sources: Scores for Perkins, and for all members in 1983-84, are from *Congressional Quarterly Almanac* 1967-84. Other than for Perkins, ratings from 1967 to 1982 are from Inter-University Consortium for Political and Social Research.

cited above that he was not interested in whether an issue was considered liberal, conservative, or moderate. He voted the best way he knew how to benefit the Seventh District of Kentucky. Nevertheless, the bulk of the legislation he supported, such as federal aid to education programs and prolabor policies, generally was seen as liberal. He supported government intervention to help the poor, particularly in eastern Kentucky, not the minimal government favored by most conservatives.

Another aspect of the chairman's orientation is illustrated by comparing his party-unity scores with those of his fellow committee members and House members. As shown in table 6.2, with the exception of one term (1981-82), when he was chairman Perkins voted more frequently with the majority of Democrats on party votes than did the average committee member. His scores were higher in all but that one instance than were the averages of the scores of his fellow Education and Labor Democrats; they had been since 1951, except when they were identical in 1955-56. In addition, Perkins's scores were higher for every Congress between the 90th and 98th except the 97th than were the averages of all House Democratic scores. In all but the 97th Congress (1981-82), Perkins voted with the Democrats against the Republicans on over 80 percent of the roll calls on which a majority of Democrats opposed a majority of Republicans. In his first term as chairman, he supported his party on nearly 90 percent of the party votes.

By most standards, and compared with his predecessors, Perkins was a loyal Democrat; he seldom voted against his party. Barden and Powell both had relatively low party-unity scores. While chairman, Powell had voted with the Democrats on just over half of the votes. Barden had averaged only 38 percent Democratic unity. Not only were there more party votes

Table 6.3. Perkins's Support for Democratic on Committee Party Votes, 1967-1984

Congress	Year	Party votes (> 70% opposition)	With Dems N	With Dems %	Party Votes (> 50% opposition)	With Dems N	With Dems %
90th	1967-68	64	55	85.9	75	58	77.3
91st	1969-70	36	29	80.6	43	33	76.7
92d	1971-72	64	59	92.2	95	84	88.4
93d	1973-74	42	36	85.7	52	39	75.0
94th	1975-76	26	26	100.0	39	39	100.0
95th	1977-78	49	44	89.8	68	54	79.4
96th	1979-80	31	28	90.3	41	37	90.2
97th	1981-82	39	39	100.0	44	43	97.7
98th	1983-84	26	26	100.0	32	32	100.0
Total		377	342		489	419	
Percentage of total				90.7			85.7

Source: Compiled from Committee on Education and Labor, *Minutes*, 1967-84.

between 1967 and 1984 (3,549), but Perkins showed higher rates of party unity than did either predecessor, with an average of about 83 percent for the entire period.

Therefore, both party-unity scores and interview data characterize Perkins as a loyal Democrat. An examination of the chairman's voting record in committee illustrates that his relatively high rates of support for Democratic positions in fact did extend to his committee behavior. The chairman's support of a majority of Democrats is shown in table 6.3 for votes on which 70 percent of one party opposed at least 70 percent of the other. His record of support for bare majority opposition is shown for purposes of comparison. The data in this table show that Perkins, for the most part, had a similar rate of party voting in committee and on the floor of the House. When party votes at the 70-percent level are counted, Perkins overwhelmingly supported his fellow Democrats against the Republicans. His levels of support compare favorably with Powell's. Overall Perkins voted with committee Democrats on about 91 percent of the party votes (70-percent level), whereas Powell voted with his fellow party members on about 94 percent.

Table 6.4 shows the extent of Perkins's support for the Democrats on all committee votes, not just on those considered party votes. Most of the time he voted with his party. He rarely opposed a majority of his fellow Democrats. His low levels of support for the Republicans on party votes (9 percent) bears out that assertion.

Table 6.4. Perkins's Support for Democrats on All Committee Roll Calls,
       1967-1984

Congress	Years	Roll calls	With > 70% Dems (%)	With > 50% Dems (%)
90th	1967-68	99	76.8	80.8
91st	1969-70	61	78.7	80.3
92d	1971-72	132	72.7	90.9
93d	1973-74	91	76.9	82.4
94th	1975-76	69	81.2	89.9
95th	1977-78	108	72.2	83.3
96th	1979-80	53	84.9	92.5
97th	1981-82	55	96.4	96.4
98th	1983-84	49	85.7	98.0
Total		717		
Mean			80.6	88.3
Percentage of Total			78.7	87.3

Source: Author's calculations from Committee on Education and Labor, *Minutes* 1967-84.

These statistics lead to the conclusion that Perkins was likely to support the Democrats at the expense of the Republicans. On occasion he supported the minority, but not often. His floor behavior and his committee behavior were similar. On committee party votes in three Congresses (94th, 97th, 98th), he did not side with the minority in a single instance.

Not only did the chairman vote frequently with the Democrats, but he voted most often on the winning side. Such success is not surprising given the Democrats' control of both the committee and the House and Perkins's penchant to support Democrats. Table 6.5 illustrates his success record on committee votes, an average of over 84 percent during the period he was chairman. Perkins's average was slightly higher than Powell's winning average on all committee votes.

Perhaps because he voted more often with the Democrats, Powell had a slightly better record for winning on party votes. On party votes at the 70-percent level, Powell was successful about 89 percent of the time, Perkins on about 87 percent. Although he generally voted with the Democrats, a few of Perkins's wins were at the Democrats' expense, although in no discernible pattern. Powell, however, rarely voted with the Republicans on party votes, and Perkins's casting his ballot with the minority more frequently probably is reflected in his lower overall win rate on party votes. Nevertheless, in several Congresses, Perkins won on over 90 percent of the party votes. Perkins's success rates were high on his committee, more than double those of Barden, albeit lower than Powell's. Perkins also served as

Table 6.5. Perkins's Votes on the Winning Side in Committee, 1967-1984

Congress	Year	Roll calls	Chair Wins N	Chair Wins %	Party votes*	Chair Wins N	Chair Wins %
90th	1967-68	99	85	85.9	64	55	85.9
91st	1969-70	61	54	88.5	36	32	88.9
92d	1971-72	132	97	73.5	64	49	76.6
93d	1973-74	91	77	84.6	42	33	78.6
94th	1975-76	69	58	84.1	26	25	96.2
95th	1977-78	108	91	84.3	49	44	89.8
96th	1979-80	53	48	90.6	31	28	93.5
97th	1981-82	55	52	94.5	39	38	97.4
98th	1983-84	49	44	89.8	26	24	92.3
Total		717	605		377	328	
Percentage of total				84.4			87.0

Source: Compiled from Committee on Education and Labor, Minutes 1967-84.

*Party votes are defined as roll-call votes on which at least 40% of the Democrats opposed at least 70% of the Republicans.

chairman nearly three times as long as Powell did, and the committee cast over three times as many recorded votes (377 under Perkins to 125 under Powell).

In sum, although his support for the Democrats was strong, Perkins was oriented more toward his district than toward any particular party or philosophy. He wanted to improve the lot of the people in the Seventh District of Kentucky, where the state of the coal industry had left many citizens destitute. Perkins was in a position to help and did so at every turn.

Although Perkins lived in Washington for thirty-five years, it never seemed to rub off on him. The rough edges remained: he still walked and talked like a mountain man from Kentucky. Behind that country facade lay a clever man who knew how to get the most out of government for his people. He also was expert at getting the most out of his colleagues. Many people mistakenly thought that because he was unpolished he was stupid and that they easily could take advantage of him. In turn, he ran rings around them in the legislative arena. He ended up owning many of their votes because of naive bargains they had made.

Perkins did not consider himself a liberal or a conservative but had good friends in both camps and few enemies. He was a moderate compared with most of his fellow committee members, although many outside the committee considered him a liberal because of his support for big-spending liberal social welfare programs. He generally voted with the Democrats but occasionally strayed to the minority side of the aisle.

The Seventh District of Kentucky was the guiding force of this chairman of the Committee on Education and Labor. Everything he did revolved around his constituents. He did not take advantage of many of the perquisites available to him because he did not want his people to think badly of him. He brought the weight of Congress to bear on improving the conditions in eastern Kentucky. Benefits to other areas that had similar problems were a by-product of Carl Perkins's efforts at helping his own. The Seventh District of Kentucky defined Carl Perkins.

Leadership: Institutional versus Personal Resources

Each committee chairman reacts to constraints imposed by the committee, the House, and external factors, by developing available institutional and personal resources. As a consequence, the chairman has a unique impact on the committee. In this study, the way a chairman led is inferred from the way he tapped the resources at hand—the institutional prerogatives that accrue by virtue of the office and whatever personal resources he may have brought with him.

The parameters of acceptable behavior differ from committee to committee and have become more restrictive over the years. Education and Labor was in the forefront in forging more stringent rules. Because of the excesses of Barden and Powell, members had adopted a host of measures designed to limit the institutional prerogatives of the chairman and to enable members to operate in his absence. Each of the two previous chairmen had abused the behavioral expectations. In turn, each had been subject to revolts of the majority membership, which imposed rules to curtail his discretion. As their legatee, Perkins operated within a significantly more constrained committee environment than had Barden and Powell. On assuming the chairmanship, Perkins inherited fewer leadership resources than did his predecessors and most other committee chairmen. Instead of possessing a healthy reserve of official prerogatives, he had to rely on his wits to get his way to a greater extent than did most of his fellow chairmen.

Writing about committees between 1955 and 1966, Fenno referred to the chairmanship of this committee as "institutionally feeble" (1973, 287). The abundance of rules adopted to hog-tie Powell in his last year as chairman instead constrained Perkins, decentralized the committee structure and operations, and forced the chairman to resort to ways to exert his influence that would not conflict with the committee rules—largely by way of personal factors. Fortunately for Perkins's leadership, his goals coincided with those of most of the majority members, thereby reducing the levels of conflict. He was willing to play within the committee rules, and he agreed with his majority committee colleagues on the direction that education and labor legislation ought to take; thus Perkins had few problems. Since he cooperated with his colleagues and they with him, the committee was not under sufficient stress to necessitate a third revolt to disarm the chairman.

Perkins employed what institutional resources he had, however, differently than his predecessors had. This individualized resource deployment was reflected in his use of subcommittees, conduct of meetings and hearings, influence over the committee agenda, treatment of the minority, dispensation of rewards and sanctions, movement of legislation, and control over the budget.

Some chairmen strictly limited the use of subcommittees. For instance, Ways and Means had no subcommittees for years, allowing the chairman to have full control of all the legislation referred to the committee (Manley 1969). In Judiciary, Chairman Emanuel Celler (D-NY) often used his discretionary power to avoid referring legislation to the appropriate subcommittee, leaving bills to die without consideration (Schuck 1975, 48). Although the Judiciary subcommittees determined their own jurisdictions, Celler co-opted many bills that might have gone to other subcommittees, directing them instead to his own (Schuck 1975, 51).

Perkins, on the other hand, had less discretion over the use of subcommittees than did other chairmen. His authority over assignments had been reduced to appointments to ad hoc subcommittees, since seniority dictated who would serve on standing subcommittees. Also as required by the rules, he duly assigned most Education and Labor bills to the requisite subcommittee, whose members could determine how the bill would be treated. On many occasions, however, the bills were not finally marked up in subcommittee but reported back to the full committee for mark-up. If a significant number of the members were interested in a bill, the mark-up was done the first time in full committee to avoid marking up a bill in subcommittee and again in full committee. Moreover, on several occasions, the full committee discharged the bill from the subcommittee if members could not reach an agreement on how to proceed. Perkins kept close tabs on what was going on in his subcommittees and usually attended meetings when the chairmen needed him for a quorum. Some major bills were kept for consideration by the full committee.

In general, Perkins adopted a permissive stance toward subcommittee operations. He allowed the subcommittees to hold whatever hearings members wanted and, for the most part, to schedule them wherever they wanted. In addition, he held all the full committee hearings that his members requested. As one staff member said, "Perkins never turned down a hearing in his life" (interview). He gave everyone's witnesses a chance to speak, sometimes to the point that it seemed to both members and staff that the hearings would never end. Perkins generally favored whatever measures would help his members in their policy or reelection goals. He tried to keep his membership satisfied. The only thing he did not tolerate was some other member's conducting an investigation or a hearing in the Seventh District.

A former Education and Labor staff member characterized Perkins as a floundering presiding officer: "He was so fumbling that everybody wanted to help. It was the secret of his strength" (interview). He appeared to be so helpless that members frequently came to his rescue, in the process giving him what he wanted. Many people were uncomfortable watching a great hulking man whistling through his teeth and blundering with the procedure. But as the chairman said, "I'm a pretty good feller for playin' dumb" (interview).

In this respect, Perkins was a stark contrast to Adam Clayton Powell, the master orator and preacher. Powell could run a meeting efficiently and speak eloquently on just about any subject, even if he knew nothing about it. Perkins, on the other hand, just bumbled along, sometimes running roughshod over the rules for committee meetings and hearings. The reaction of the other members was a shrug, a shake of the head, and a "Well, that's just Perkins." He never appeared to be doing it on purpose. He acted the same way at least once when he chaired a conference committee. When asked what the impact would be of the House instructions to the conferees, Perkins responded, "Well, we'll try to follow the spirit of it" (Gladieux and Wolanin 1976, 192). According to many people, Powell had been an excellent presiding officer. He had run the meetings efficiently and with a sense of order, something that was an anathema to Perkins. A staff member said, "Order was the antithesis of what Perkins was trying to do—get his way. He succeeded by virtue of his awkwardness" (interview).

Committee chairmen must operate within certain boundaries of acceptable behavior imposed by the congressional environment; they have little authority per se. They cannot control the decisions or actions of others via commitments to organizational values and purposes. What little authority chairmen do have over committee colleagues is circumscribed by democratic values dictating member equality and collegial decision making. The chief institutional resource remaining to the chairman is the authority "to arrange and order the consideration of business" (Cooper 1977, 147).

Nevertheless, for many reasons, Perkins had little direct control over the committee agenda. His practice of referring bills to the appropriate subcommittees and then letting the subcommittees decide which bills to consider sapped his authority. For his first two terms as chairman, Perkins did not chair a subcommittee. As a consequence, he kept major legislation in the full committee to protect it. There were few serious objections to such actions because he and the majority generally were in agreement. In addition, if the chairman wanted a bill, few subcommittee chairmen were willing to fight him for it.

Although he could not control the agenda absolutely, Perkins exercised his influence by concentrating the full committee efforts (or his own subcommittee's) on legislation with potentially large impacts in his district. Particularly in his early days in power when he was one of the few chairmen to allow television cameras in his committee room, Perkins could command national attention in this television-dependent society by granting access to the media. He held numerous hearings and had the committee consider bills that other chairmen might not have chosen. In these endeavors, he had the full weight of the administration behind him when a Democrat was in the White House.

Much of each administration's domestic legislative agenda came under the jurisdiction of Education and Labor. With difficulties in the international arena, the Johnson administration was eager to shift the public focus to domestic issues. Perkins exploited the opportunities fully. A staff member commented that it was a happy coincidence that Perkins was chairman of such a committee when his type of poverty was in vogue (interview). Perkins also headed the committee when its social programs were the target of the budget-cutting ax of several Republican administrations. He affected the agenda by drawing attention to the people who would be hurt if these programs were cut back or eliminated.

Perkins's persistent efforts to obtain support for his programs shaped the agenda as well. He brought national attention to coal mine safety by holding lengthy televised hearings on coal mine disasters and black lung disease that affected so many of his constituents. He repeatedly focused the committee's efforts on the need for vocational education and school lunch programs. As the first chairman to open committee mark-up sessions to the media, he used their coverage to revitalize poverty issues. As he had done when he was a subcommittee chairman considering the Youth Conservation Corps legislation in 1962, Perkins would hold hearings just to keep an issue alive.

When Republicans won the White House and targeted programs under the committee's jurisdiction for elimination or severe cutbacks, Perkins fought tenaciously to keep them properly funded. He refused to let his causes die, and the committee concentrated on bills that would improve the lot of the disadvantaged, often when other issues were more salient. As Perkins's son said, "He was an unrelenting type of force who would not accept no for an answer. You could beat him, but you couldn't stop him" (interview). A fellow committee member recalled Perkins's counting his votes and saying, "We're not a-gonna let 'em do it."

The chairman's influence with the House leadership was a handy agenda-shaping tool. His friendship with the Speaker as well as his membership in the establishment enabled him to collude with the leadership in getting particular bills assigned to his committee or to others. If Perkins wanted a measure passed or killed, he went to the Speaker and asked that it be referred to whichever committee was likely to do what he wanted with it. That was not always his committee. Sometimes it was to his advantage not to decide on a bill, although this situation did not occur frequently. Such decisions might have been politically disadvantageous or divisive for his committee or his district. Moreover, he traded these favors with other chairmen.

Many members believe that the chairman is responsible for protecting the committee's jurisdiction from impingement by other committees. Unless for some reason he wanted a bill to go somewhere else, Perkins fought for his committee's turf with gusto, something not always done by Education and Labor chairmen. According to a chairman of another committee, Perkins could (and did) make a case that every bill with even a minor impact on "his people" should be referred to Education and Labor. Frequently he won.[9] Perkins made essentially the same arguments for his constituents as did a chairman of the Committee on Post Office and Civil Service who stated that his committee ought to have jurisdiction over every bill affecting a federal worker (interview). In effect, this attitude gave him license to consider just about all the bills introduced in the House.

By and large, the committee agenda was imposed by forces external to the committee. The chairman could and did influence the committee's work, however, by strategic selection for consideration of issues important to him. He commanded public attention by opening the committee to the media, particularly to television news cameras, and by making people aware of congressional actions and possible cutbacks in federal programs. His persistence in pushing his programs helped design the committee agenda. Moreover, although he did not pen the bills, Perkins significantly molded legislation and the distribution formulas, largely to the benefit of his constituents and others in similar circumstances.

According to the minority staff director of Education and Labor, Perkins generally treated the minority generously. He gave them their own budget and their own staff and worked cooperatively with them. While this more equitable treatment was begun during the Powell years, Perkins expanded it greatly. Majority members complained in many instances that Perkins was too fair to the Republicans. He allowed them to ask all the questions they wanted, let all their witnesses be heard, and gave them many concessions. Majority members considered him too closely in cahoots with ranking minority member Albert Quie (R-MN) on many occasions (interviews, members and staff).

Perkins was the first Education and Labor chairman to give the minority adequate funding and staff allowances. He saw no need to haggle with the minority over nonpolicy matters as his predecessor had done. Under Powell, one Republican had boarded himself into his office to protect the minority's office space (Jewell and Patterson 1966, 242-43, 254; Lewis 1963, 97-98; Fenno 1973, 87). Perkins, in contrast, gave the minority a large portion of the committee perquisites.

Nevertheless, the Republicans did not regard him as fair all the time. They often objected strenuously to his conduct of committee meetings when he packed the witness list with people favorable to his cause and forced the committee to listen (or at least to be present) for the duration of their testimony. They also accused Perkins of fostering extreme partisanship on occasion. Like many other members, he often manipulated the questioning to his advantage. In the hearings on the funding reauthorization for the Economic Opportunity Act of 1964, Representative William Steiger (R-WI) was quoted as complaining that "Perkins led witnesses 'down the primrose path' in an attempt to prove the Nixon Administration was bent on bombing the poverty war" (Edstrom 1969). A journalist accused the chairman of bringing on "partisan wrangling" as the committee opened hearings on the future of the antipoverty programs, saying, "He attacked Republican committee members with zest, and they fought back" (Burks 1969). One Democrat commenting on Barden's treatment of the minority said, "When the battle lines were clear, he ran right over them. So does Perkins" (interview, staff).

Under Perkins, Education and Labor continued to be one of the most partisan committees on the Hill, but not nearly as partisan as it had been under its previous chairman. Perkins manipulated the partisanship to his advantage. On many occasions he contributed to the partisan atmosphere by refusing to compromise on legislation affecting his district. He resented the Republicans' trying to cut federal spending at the expense of his constituents. By focusing so much attention on big social welfare programs and their reauthorizations, he repeatedly alienated Republicans. On the other hand, many of the Republicans who had been on the committee for years had a stake in maintaining these policies too. Education and Labor programs had been implemented in their districts and had created constituencies and jobs. Consequently, it was hard for the Republicans to vote against reauthorizations or to vote for funding cuts.

By and large, Perkins got along well with the minority members of the committee. There were a few whom he thought were unduly nasty or partisan, but he was friends with most of those who had been on the committee for a while. Occasionally he looked to Republicans to tell him how to vote on noncommittee matters.[10]

The chairmanship also offers influence in the form of control over certain rewards and sanctions. The chairman has several tools at his disposal, although not as critical as agenda control, including scheduling, appointment powers, and authority over travel money and other perquisites. As John Manley noted, by themselves the rewards available for the chairman to dispense are of little significance, and some are even trivial, "but cumulatively, they are of inestimable importance to the functioning of the Committee" and to the chairman's place in it (1967, 136). They can be of major importance to members as well, since they might generate favorable publicity, constituency approval, or other desirable opportunities. By the time Perkins became chairman, the institutional prerogatives that governed his ability to dispense rewards and sanctions had been curtailed. Nevertheless, Perkins took advantage of other options that his predecessors had not. He utilized his ability to help members in electoral campaigns and his influence with the leadership and other committee chairmen.

With rare exceptions, Perkins used rewards almost to the exclusion of sanctions. His son said, "He preferred the carrot to the stick" (interview). This practice became standard operating procedure on Education and Labor, although it did not apply to all committees.[11] In part, his reliance on rewards perhaps was the result of constraints imposed by the committee rules that left him little authority to deny perquisites or positions of power to committee members who did not go along with him. On the other hand, it was not his nature to use sanctions. When someone had gone back on his word to the chairman or had done something to displease him, Perkins never retaliated, although he could have. On several occasions, members of his staff encouraged him to strike back at some member for undercutting his authority or for reneging on a promise. Perkins refused, realizing that he might need that member's vote on legislation in the future, and opted not to start a fight. He was not confrontational.

The scheduling authority provides the chairman with control over certain rewards and penalties that members respect. If a member does not comply with the chairman's wishes, there is the implicit threat that legislation important to that member will be left by the wayside or will be scheduled at a time when passage is not likely. Implicit in the scheduling power is the authority to choose when to refer bills to subcommittees, which subcommittees to send them to, and when to take up legislation reported back to the full committee.

On Education and Labor, the committee rules adopted in 1966 curtailed both the timing of consideration and the referral aspects of the chairman's scheduling power. For the most part, Perkins abided by the stipulations requiring bills to be sent to the appropriate subcommittees, whose jurisdictions were set out specifically in the rules. The rules also required that the full committee consider bills reported by the subcommittees in the order that they were reported. Few people, however, wanted to challenge the chairman when he sought to rearrange the agenda. Moreover, he usually went along when other members wanted to change the order of consideration. Consequently, the chairman retained his influence over the order of bills taken up in committee as well as over favorable scheduling of committee bills in the House, a prerogative that never was questioned.

Although the chairman's appointment powers also were constrained by the rules, he still had some influence over subcommittee and conference committee assignments. He was allowed to appoint members to ad hoc subcommittees and extra members to conference committees. The rules also did not specify the size of the conference delegations, leaving that up to him to recommend to the Speaker. Perkins followed the committee rules concerning various appointments, letting the majority members do the appointing of subcommittees until the bidding system was imposed by the House Democratic Caucus in 1973 in the 93d Congress. He also complied with the committee rule directing the chairman to designate subcommittee members as members of conference committees in order of seniority. He used these appointments as a reward, exceeding the requirements by appointing more members than was necessary. In many instances he designated the entire subcommittee although he need have appointed only the two or three most senior members. He remembered how he had felt when he had worked hard on a bill and Barden had refused to appoint him as a conferee: "It cuts you deep when you get yourself prepared and can't go to conference" (interview). Perkins and the ranking minority member always attended conferences.

As directed by the rules, Perkins also let the subcommittee chairmen appoint their own staff members. And although Chairman Perkins retained control over the appointment and duties of the full committee staff, he allowed several committee members to put their own people on the full committee staff. One member said: "The committee was enthusiastic about having Perkins as chairman. He lets the subcommittees run. He holds a tight, but proper, rein. He knows how to go about discipline. . . . Subcommittee chairmen can hire whomever they want. Total freedom. And there is greater full committee staff input under Perkins. He lets other members be privy to selection of staff. Lots of committee chairmen give their subcommittee chairmen problems when staffing their subcommittees—like Teague, Staggers, and Sullivan. Perkins never did" (interview). Representatives Frank Thompson, Jr., James G. O'Hara, John Dent, Edith Green, and William Lehman all chose full committee staff members, including some of the chairman's top advisers. In addition, they decided who would be on their subcommittee staffs. Perkins, however, generally controlled most full committee staff appointments.

He also maintained control over staff activities. As chairman, Perkins was the despair of the staff because staff titles on the organizational chart remained something of a mystery to him. When he had something on his mind, he unloaded on the first staff member who came into view. Once, when he believed the staff was getting a little ahead of its authority under

Chief Clerk Robert McCord, he declared, "Bob McCord thinks he's a-gonna run that committee. But as long as I'm chief clerk, *I'm* a-gonna run that committee" (interview, staff). The committee staff answered to the chairman, although several had close ties to other members.

Perkins also used travel as a reward, although he did not withhold it as a sanction, as he could have. He was not averse, however, to making people sweat for it every once in a while. On one occasion, a new committee Democrat voted against the budget resolutions from all the committees, including Education and Labor. The next year, when he asked Perkins to authorize the money for him to travel to the southwestern United States to investigate Indian education, Perkins hesitated, saying, "I don't know. We don't have a lot of money to work with." The member did not find out until the last minute that Perkins had approved his travels (interview, member). A staff member said that Perkins never turned down anyone's request for money: "He never held up anything, but he did quarrel around with some things ――― wanted to do; he thought they were right at the edge of propriety" (interview).

Another tool Perkins relied on as a reward was campaign assistance. In many instances he traveled to a member's district, making campaign speeches and talking to people. Moreover, although he accepted few campaign contributions himself (and none for years), he was not above suggesting to lobbyists that they might want to give money to a particular member. He wrote letters to the teachers' unions in various places, urging them to "help a great friend of education, Congressman ―――." He campaigned for committee member Ike Andrews (D-NC), among others. Another committee Democrat said that Perkins had gone to his district and "made me look like the most brilliant man in Congress. The news media had enough sound bites for three or four days of news. Perkins was very good to his members" (interview). Perkins also contributed time to members who were not on Education and Labor. He went to North Carolina to make speeches in support of Governor Terry Sanford's campaign for the U.S. Senate. He also provided campaign help to Andrew Jacobs, Jr., (D-IN) and Robert Edgar (D-PA).

Committee chairmen usually go along with other chairmen (interviews, members and staff). As a member of the elite group of House leaders, Perkins used his influence with other chairmen and with the House leadership as a reward or as a method of banking political favors. Not uncommonly, he would confer with the Speaker or some other House leader on behalf of one of his members. He also helped his committee members with their bills in other committees. He was glad to talk to Ways and Means chairman Wilbur Mills or Appropriations chairman Jamie Whitten or Appropriations subcommittee chairman Tom Bevill for the benefit of an ally or a committee member. In addition, many other members owed him favors. Perkins had helped many members when he served on the Committee on House Administration. Furthermore, he supported other members' public works projects and appreciated their support for his.

Perkins refused to campaign against members who usually opposed him. He was loyal to his committee members of both parties. He became angry when an opponent of Representative Philip Crane, a committee Republican from Illinois, came to his office and asked for support in his race to unseat the incumbent. Perkins easily could have worked to undermine Crane's support. Instead, according to a staff member, Crane's opponent nearly ran from the office (interview). Perkins even took positive action to help some of the Republican members of Education and Labor. He went to one young member's district for hearings, and in front of his Democratic opponent, a labor leader, Perkins told the audience, "You have sent a great representative. He's very effective" (interview, member).

In sum, Perkins avoided sanctions. He was loyal to those members who helped him and rarely punished those who crossed him. He used his influence in the House to work for members' bills, he rewarded members with travel money, and he campaigned for his friends. He used the few official prerogatives available to him as chairman to help those who helped him.

The chairman can facilitate or hinder the committee's business. Barden had used every tactic available to prevent the enactment of liberal legislation. By his hands-off manner, Powell had facilitated the passage of many of the Great Society social welfare programs that were on the agenda during his tenure as chairman. He lacked, however, the stature in the House to be a driving force. Perkins, on the other hand, did not just facilitate; he pushed. And he pushed tirelessly. He fought for the programs that would help the people of his district and other disadvantaged areas.

As chairman, Perkins wanted to get the legislation out of committee and to the House with dispatch. One member compared him to the sausage factory employee assigned to stuff the sausage into the casings: "The chairman wanted to stuff as much legislation through the committee as possible and move it on to the next stage" (interview). Although Perkins let everyone have his say, he wasted little time in his efforts to grind out the legislation and put it into the appropriate casing. Such actions greatly affected the committee operations.

The conference on the Education Amendments of 1972 provides an example of the chairman's leadership. More than anything, Perkins wanted to emerge from the conference with a bill in hand. He was quoted by several people as saying repeatedly, "We gotta get a bill." With his reputation riding on whether a bill was reported or not, he brought his sausage-stuffing mentality to bear on the conference. One of his staff members said: "When Carl Perkins undertakes to do something, he generates phenomenal psychological drive to get it done. This is his Baptist-Calvinist-Puritan ethic. He drives and drives and drives. If there are frustrations and road-blocks, far from defeating him, they just energize him even more" (Gladieux and Wolanin 1976, 170). When Perkins had the gavel in his hand, he would not let members quit negotiating until an agreement was reached. A staff member commented, "No one wants to adjourn the conference if the chairman wants to forge ahead" (interview). The same held true for Education and Labor meetings.

Perkins wielded the gavel power effectively. It allowed him to stop the proceedings if he wished and to allow his constituents to testify on some completely different issue (such as black lung, which was taken up in the middle of education hearings because some of the chairman's constituents showed up and wanted to talk). It also enabled him to keep members negotiating at all hours of the night if he thought that was the best strategy. He could wear down the opposition with his gavel and routinely did. The gavel also proved useful to Perkins because it helped him structure the issues. As presiding officer, he could set the course for the debate. He could decide whether to proceed on a technical or a philosophical basis. He could decide what to bring up first and what to skip. He used these assets effectively to satisfy his legislative goals.

When Perkins assumed the chairmanship, he was subject to a spate of committee rules concerning the budget. Even though the rules had been enacted in the previous session, no budget had been adopted. Given the abuses of the past chairman and some of his staff, Perkins was careful to convey the appearance of propriety in all of his operations, particularly the financial aspects. He hired one adviser to "come tell me where the money's a-goin' to" and appointed another staff member to oversee the committee's budget (interview, staff). The committee budget officer, Marian Wyman, was so strict with the money that several members complained that she had too much influence with the chairman over committee funds. Although Perkins himself never withheld committee funds, his money manager sometimes did. In effect, he had someone to do the dirty work for him. On the other hand, Wyman's decisions were not based on punishment or on the denial of rewards. When she denied a member's request, it usually was because of a question of legality or propriety.[12] Since Perkins always supported her position on why she denied some member the funds he requested, most members gave up asking him to overrule her. With Wyman in charge of the money, every penny was accounted for and documented. One member commented that "Marian Wyman was protective of the chairman. Powell had run the committee so loosely. Perkins wanted a tightly run committee, and he did it very well" (interview).

Some chairmen freely authorize their staff members to travel on committee business with the members. Perkins would have none of that. Few Education and Labor staff members under Perkins went on the "junkets" that other committee staff (and Powell's staff) had the opportunities to take, particularly the trips abroad. Nor did the chairman go himself. He did send some of his top committee staff to investigate coal mine disasters or to attend meetings where the committee needed to be represented. Most of those trips were not of the glamorous variety.

Another aspect of the chairman's budgetary duties concerns allotments for committee operations. Perkins commonly asked for two or three times the amount he needed to run the committee and always received adequate funds. The committee never was short of money toward the end of the fiscal year. On other committees, such as Judiciary, the chairman had a tight-fisted attitude and did not ask for funds sufficient to carry out the committee's business. As a result, Judiciary did not have adequate staff support for its work load (Schuck 1975, 53-54). Its chairman used his small budget as a tool for failing to consider and thereby obstructing legislation he opposed. Perkins did no such thing, always requesting money so that his subcommittees could operate effectively and be adequately staffed.

Only occasionally does a chairman have to rely on manipulation of the rules to achieve his goals within his committee. In anticipation of potential rewards or sanctions, as well as for other reasons, most members will try to find ways to accommodate him. More than one committee member said, "Most members don't want to confront the chairman."[13] He has the resources, diminished though they may be, and the influence with other members to make their lives easier or more difficult if they run up against him too often. When forced to make a choice between voting his conscience and voting with Perkins, one member said that he went to the doctor and avoided the vote rather than opposing his committee chairman on the floor (interview). Since many of the chairman's prerogatives had been stripped by the 1966 rules enacted to control Adam Clayton Powell, Perkins had to rely largely on unstated advantages often formulated as the occasion arose. In general, the majority party members concurred in his exercise of informal institutional prerogatives.

The other major component of a chairman's leadership is his reliance on personal resources, including his expertise on the rules and on the subject matter, his reputation among his constituents and peers, and any other personal traits or leanings that may affect how he operates the committee. The chairman's reliance on personal resources interacts with his reliance on institutional prerogatives to determine how he leads.

Expertise on rules and subject matter and reputation are elements of leadership because they are among the tools with which people gain influence. Some members are considered leaders because of their knowledge or their ability to manipulate the rules.[14] This was not true of Chairman Perkins. Although Perkins had more expertise on the committee rules than most Education and Labor committee members, he rarely used this knowledge for leadership purposes. He was more likely to employ his skill as a deal maker and his tenacity to achieve his ends than to outmaneuver his opponents by manipulating the rules. On occasion, however, he was crafty in designing parliamentary maneuvers to steer his legislation through the House or conference committees.

Perkins also did not draw on a wellspring of knowledge about the committee's subject matter as a source of leadership strength. His expertise apparently was spotty. Over the years he came to know a good deal about the Elementary and Secondary Education Act of 1965, Title I in particular. Title I concerned education for disadvantaged children, a great many of whom were in his district. He did not know much about labor legislation, with the possible exception of coal mine labor laws, and relied on his staff to help him on labor issues. Several other committee members were perceived as more expert than Perkins on education or on labor legislation. Edith Green (D-OR) and John Brademas (D-IN) were regarded as more expert on education matters, while Frank Thompson, Jr. (D-NJ) and John Dent (D-PA) outshone him on knowledge of labor laws. Nevertheless, Perkins was acknowledged as a near genius on the formulas that best would benefit the Seventh District of Kentucky.

Although he was an attorney himself, Perkins did not write the legislation that bore his name. Much of the education legislation he sponsored was prepared by his committee staff attorneys in collaboration with the education lobbies, such as the National Education Association, the old American Federation of Teachers, or the Association of Land-Grant Colleges. Labor legislation frequently came from the Department of Labor or from Perkins's friends at AFL-CIO, who worked closely with committee attorneys. Andrew Biemiller, the chief lobbyist for AFL-CIO, and Kenneth Young, Biemiller's second in command, had tremendous influence with the chairman. Hartwell Reed, a committee attorney, wrote a large part of the Elementary and Secondary Education Act of 1965, and Donald Baker, another committee attorney, was largely responsible for the Economic Opportunity Act of 1964, the antipoverty program.

According to some of his staff members, Perkins paid little attention to the details of legislation unless he could manipulate them to the benefit of his constituents. He quickly lost interest in the details of a bill if he thought they were not going to have any effect on his district or on Kentucky. On what benefited his people, one of his colleagues referred to him as "a master legislative mechanic" (interview, member).

Perkins had two distinct reputations among his peers in Congress. One of his staff members described them aptly: "Among new members without much exposure to him, he was thought of as a hayseed. Those who had been around and had had their pockets picked two or three times by him took him seriously" (interview). Some members considered him to be stupid, a belief that worked to his advantage in most fields. Because of his mountain accent and his disheveled appearance, people who did not know him frequently assumed him to be a polite but unsophisticated hillbilly. He did nothing to change their attitudes. In fact, he worked to enhance this reputation and laughed about it, saying, "The papers were a-wondering whether I could handle the chairmanship" (interview).

Among veteran members and his friends, Perkins also had a reputation of being honest; he was honest and gave the appearance of absolute integrity. He also was regarded as politically astute in predicting political developments. Even though members may not have liked what they heard, when he told them what he thought politically, they knew it was the truth. He would not steer someone in the wrong direction intentionally. Those who knew him also considered the chairman to be crafty but reliable. He earned this reputation by making deals with everyone he could and always following through on his end of the agreement. Expressing a sentiment echoed by many members and staff, a former employee said, "I don't believe in the thirty-six years he was there that anybody could outscheme, outmaneuver, or outdeal him" (interview).

One of the most pronounced aspects of his reputation among his peers was his tenacity—particularly in getting money for his district. In comparing him with Powell, one member said that the two were totally opposite. He said that whereas Powell lacked persistence, "Perkins digs and digs and digs and hangs in there" (interview). A former assistant to the chairman remarked: "When it came to getting legislation passed, nobody was willing to work as hard as Perkins. He didn't embarrass. He was willing to go back time after time until it was easier to give in than to have an arm grabbed one more time" (interview).

Late one afternoon, when Indianapolis mayor Richard Lugar came by Perkins's office on his way to the airport and home, Perkins saw an opportunity to get expert testimony on the reauthorization of the poverty bill at hearings the next morning. Acting as though he did not hear Lugar's repeated protests that he had important meetings scheduled, Perkins just assumed the mayor would come. Unable to get his refusal accepted, Lugar reluctantly appeared before the committee at nine o'clock the next morning (interview, staff). When the poverty bill reauthorization had cleared the House late one Friday night, Perkins called Senator Joseph Clark, chairman of the Senate Committee on Labor and Public Welfare, at 6:00 A.M. on Saturday to say, "That little bill passed the House last night. Can you be ready to go to conference at about nine o'clock this morning?" (interview, staff).

Perkins also was widely known for getting everything he could for the Seventh District of Kentucky. A *New York Times* obituary stated: "Even before becoming chairman of the Education and Labor Committee, Mr. Perkins gained the reputation in Congress of being highly adept at dipping into what is called the Federal 'pork barrel' to aid his 23-county district, one of the poorest in the nation, gaining Federal money for a variety of projects" (Hunter 1984).

Although Chairman Perkins's reputation among his peers was a useful instrument of leadership on occasion, his manipulation of it in shaping an image probably was more important. A reputation for honesty assures colleagues. A reputation as an astute judge of politics generates confidence in predictions. A reputation for following through on bargains makes others more willing to trade. And a reputation for tenacity makes others less willing to challenge leadership. Perkins's colleagues' view of him as a possessor of all these qualities probably contributed to his ability to lead.

Perkins's canny political skills and sense of timing constituted an outstanding characteristic of his leadership. He was renowned as one of the greatest political bankers of the House, storing and trading political credit with other members. He continually did favors and traded votes on a variety of issues. Frequently he would trade a promise made to him by one member to another member in exchange for another promise. When he called in his chits, he generally had substantial support for his cause.

Perkins could be crafty in getting his legislation passed. When bills important to him were scheduled for House consideration, the chairman usually arranged with the Speaker to have a friend, often William Natcher (D-KY), presiding over the House. When Perkins lacked the parliamentary expertise himself, he could count on numerous friends for help in using or manipulating the chamber rules to his advantage.

Two incidents aptly illustrate Perkins's political acumen. On one occasion, one of his major bills had been amended and passed by the Senate. Committee Republicans and others were waiting for it to be reported back to the House so they could sabotage it. At a time early in the day when the House was passing routine measures by unanimous consent, Perkins arranged for his old friend Frank Albert Stubblefield (D-KY), a renowned mumbler, to have the bill taken from the clerk's desk and passed. With one of Perkins's friends acting as Speaker, Stubblefield stood up and mumbled something intelligible only to the clerk, who had a copy of the motion on his desk. Because no one could understand the motion, the bill passed without objection. Later, when the chairman's staff members came to warn Perkins that there would be trouble when his bill came up on the floor, he grinned and said, "Oh, that already passed. I had Frank Albert bring that up this morning" (interview, staff).

On another occasion, an important committee bill concerning formulas for money to disadvantaged children had reached the conference stage. Several House members and senators with large urban constituencies formed alliances to manipulate the formulas so that their constituencies would benefit most, at the expense of Kentucky's Seventh District and other districts like it. At about eleven o'clock at night, after the conference had gone on for hours, the first vote on the matter was tied. Perkins asked that the second vote be postponed because he had some other business to do. He then rounded up Sam Gibbons (D-FL) and arranged for the Speaker to appoint him to the conference. When Perkins returned to the conference with the tie-breaking vote in tow, he announced, "Now we can have a vote on this" (interview, member).

Perkins reportedly employed another shrewd tactic on more than one occasion. When an Education and Labor bill was scheduled to come up in the House on the consent calendar, Perkins looked around the floor for members who were likely to object. When he found one, he rushed over to him, put an arm around him, and physically "got right in his face" to prevent the member from objecting (interview, member).

Along with his political shrewdness, Perkins also had an uncanny sense of timing. He knew what would be acceptable and when to raise the issue. His chairmanship of conference committees provides several examples. In an understanding between the House and Senate committees with jurisdiction over education and labor issues, conference committee chairmanship alternated between the chambers on education and labor. By this arrangement, the House chairman would preside over one labor bill, and the Senate chairman would preside over the next labor bill to go to conference. The same arrangement would hold for education. Part of Perkins's strategy was to make sure that he presided over the conference that dealt with bills important to him. If necessary, he would ensure that a minor bill would go to conference ahead of his major bill so that his turn would come on House bills.

When his turn came, Perkins exercised his political skills and sense of timing effectively. The conference committee that considered the Education Amendments of 1972 provides a striking example.[15] At the beginning of the conference, Perkins established the tone and the order of procedure by starting on page 1 of the "Blue Books" instead of by focusing on the widely known philosophical differences between the House and Senate versions.[16] By first addressing the bill line by line in a technical manner instead of arguing about the big philosophical issues, Perkins facilitated compromise instead of conflict. When members could not reach agreement with relative ease, the chairman moved on to the next issue and saved the controversies for later, thus avoiding deadlocks early in the process. By working on the smaller differences first, members established a rapport with one another. In addition, many members attended sporadically. Perkins curried favor by arranging to consider issues important to them when they found time to attend. Since by this time most people had invested a considerable amount of time in the bill, they wanted to reach an acceptable compromise. They also had particular programs that they wanted to see approved. What is more, the ability to reach an acceptable compromise on a major bill was a source of pride to many members.

Another episode from the same conference also illustrates Perkins's political acumen. Shortly after the conference began, Edith Green (D-OR) complained on the House floor that the Senate was "rolling" the House in the conference. Her speech was tantamount to saying that Perkins was not doing his job and was knuckling under to the Senate. The House then instructed its conferees on the actions they should take, another insult to the chairman. Green's implied criticisms and the resulting instructions led Perkins to declare, "That God-damned lady is no gentleman!" (interviews, staff). The next day Perkins brought up the issue of sex discrimination and put Green, an emphatic advocate of women's rights, in an awkward position because she had to fight against the stronger anti–sex discrimination provisions in the Senate bill (Gladieux and Wolanin 1976, 170-71). Perkins called on some of the anti-Green forces, notably Frank Thompson and John Brademas, and garnered the support to "roll" Green. This episode was the only specific instance that anyone interviewed for this study could remember of Perkins's retaliating for anyone's actions against him.

As chairman of Education and Labor, Perkins could decide when to call votes. He always had his votes counted before he brought a proposal to a vote or asked for a roll call. If he opposed something, he would order a roll call to defeat it. One Republican member recalled a relatively minor amendment that he had introduced one day in a mark-up session. Shortly after he began his explanation of why he was offering such a proposal, Perkins interrupted, "Will the gentleman yield?" Thinking that the chairman wanted to ask him a question, he yielded, whereupon, much to his surprise, Perkins called for the yeas and nays on the amendment (interview, member).

In a way, Perkins's strategy was similar to that of Chairman Barden, who, according to Perkins, never called a meeting until he had the votes. Perkins, however, made sure that he never thwarted the will of the majority. He kept a little notebook with the vote tally in it. He would go to different delegations and canvass his votes. He said that he held up bringing the amendments to the Elementary and Secondary Education Act of 1965 to the floor until he had the votes to approve it. He said, "I was my own whip. I relied on my own count. When we got in good shape, we moved along" (interview).

Perkins's Leadership in Retrospect

Since the chairman's institutional prerogatives largely had been curtailed by 1967, Carl Perkins had little choice but to rely primarily on his personal resources for the bulk of his leadership strength. His task was made easier by the fact that he generally agreed with a majority of the majority party and acted to preserve the members' trust, thereby precluding a revolt similar to the ones both of his predecessors had endured. In spirit he played by their rules, and for the most part, they did not challenge him.

Perkins's leadership can be characterized as strategic, calculating, and manipulative. A former staff member described him as "strategically scheming" (interview). He used his institutional and personal resources selectively to enhance his attainment of goals. He was a driving force behind committee legislation, particularly his own. His canny sense of politics and timing and his colleagues' recognition of it enabled him to get legislation adopted that otherwise might have failed.

All of this was accomplished by a man who often appeared to be bungling and disorganized but who, at the same time, was wily and sometimes brash. Many of his colleagues respected his honesty, his political judgment, and his tenacity. Those who thought him to be a bumbling farmer or a hayseed were ripe for his picking. In whichever light his colleagues pictured him, Perkins took advantage of it. After listening to Perkins bellow a campaign speech in a crowded stadium one night, a reporter lamented: "That's the unspeakenest poor son of a bitch that ever tried to speak" (William "Snooks" Crutcher, publisher of the *Morehead News*, Morehead, Ky, 1955). Perkins went out of his way not to dissuade anyone from this impression. He used it effectively and persuasively, appearing to be so inept that people rushed to help him and to give in to him. He took advantage of the wealth of opportunities this impression afforded him. "Dumb like a fox" was a simile frequently used to describe him.[17] He used his gentlemanliness and country image to run rings around those who considered him slow.

His strategic operation of the committee contributed to its integration. He granted free rein to his subcommittee chairmen to work on legislation important to them. Moreover, he supported them in their efforts. The subcommittee chairmen were grateful for a minimum of interference from the full committee chairman. He granted almost all the requests his members made and let them do what they wanted as long as he was able to achieve his goals. In committee meetings and in hearings, Perkins let everyone voice an opinion. He believed that all members ought to have a chance to be heard, although not all ideas deserved equal weight. He made his members, particularly the minority, feel better by affording them a hearing before the Democrats "rolled" them. Moreover, he called all the hearings anyone wanted and let everyone's witnesses testify.

Having resented Chairman Barden's blocking techniques and Powell's lack of concentration, Perkins found rewards a better strategy than sanctions in eliciting support from his members. He chose to make resources available to members of the committee and to keep his members apprised of what was going on in the areas under their jurisdiction. Some chairmen keep the information to themselves; Perkins shared it with his colleagues. He rarely used sanctions; in fact, other than the maneuver to retaliate for Edith Green's criticism on the House floor, it was difficult to find an example of his punishing anyone. Personally nonconfrontational, Perkins often avoided controversy by delegating authority to staff members, in particular to his budget officer, thus remaining on good terms with everyone.

The chairman dealt with the committee members on a personal basis rather than by relying on inspirational oratory to motivate them. He concentrated his efforts on making individuals happy and beholden to him. He did not hesitate to use his political prowess and influence with the House leadership to advance his own agenda or to aid his committee members on their legislation.

Although in one way Perkins's strategic leadership and his tendency to accommodate members of both parties contributed to bipartisan committee integration, in another way his generally pro-Democratic stances detracted from it, enhancing committee partisanship. His continuous efforts on behalf of his constituents usually led him to vote with the Democrats. Nevertheless, in setting the tone for committee deliberations, he seemed to be conciliatory to the minority, particularly on education issues. Labor issues evoked more fundamental differences between the parties.

Perkins was a master of political bargaining. His political timing and skills were unsurpassed. Although strongly partisan, on numerous occasions he managed to elicit the support of minority committee members and others who opposed his programs. He maneuvered to his advantage without making enemies of his opponents. At the same time Perkins operated with integrity and loyalty in his dealings with other members. A combination of integrity and political prowess made him one of the most effective political bankers and bargainers in Congress.

When he took over as chairman of Education and Labor, most members thought that neither the poverty program nor the elementary and secondary education bill had a remote chance of being reauthorized. Perkins said, "I had to bring through those two bills to show I wasn't a weak chairman" (interview). When the Economic Opportunity Act was under consideration, Perkins went around to all the southerners and said, "Now look here, I'm a southern chairman, and it would look like hell if I got beat on my first time out as a chairman with a major bill." He managed to persuade nearly all of them to help him. The Republicans were flabbergasted when the normally conservative southern Democrats lined up behind Perkins. Even L. Mendel Rivers (D-SC), the conservtive chairman of Armed Services, marched down the aisle to vote with Perkins. When the

Republicans asked him why, he quipped, "It's a new coalition—southern Democrats and northern Democrats" (interview, Perkins and staff). The southern Democrats cast their ballots with the chairman on all of the amendments, and when he had amassed the votes for passage of the re-authorization, they voted against it on final passage, lest it be held against them back home in their districts. Perkins had a better rapport with the southerners after he became chairman than he had before, frequently having referred to them privately in the past as "them Ku Kluxers" (interviews, staff). According to a former staff member, when Perkins became chairman, he rose in stature in southern eyes. He had more influence in the House and thereby more to trade. He also "played up his southernness to the southern committee chairmen," an important element of House leadership (interview, staff).

With the help of a few friends, Perkins also managed to get the Elementary and Secondary Education Act of 1965 reauthorized. The tide of public opinion had turned against it by the time Perkins became chairman. He succeeded in getting it reauthorized by his doggedness and by his reminders to his colleagues that "I'm talking about my little people down there" (interviews, members and staff). A former committee staff member said that after public opinion turned against the education program, "it was the legislative know-how and the whining, begging, and pulling at elbows" that led to the reauthorization of that bill (interview). Regarding his maneuvering on poverty legislation, Perkins said, "None of the rest of them could have passed the Poverty Bill in 1967 when it came up for renewal" (interview).

A hallmark of Perkins's leadership was his perseverance. It benefited him on several pieces of legislation, including the elementary and secondary education and the poverty bills, which had poured money into his district; these bills were tailor-made for districts like Kentucky's Seventh. His persistence paid off time and again. It was one of his most successful leadership resources. He just wore down the oppostion.

Largely on the basis of his personal resources, Perkins built a base of political support so strong that he was nearly unbeatable. Most of the younger members, as well as the old and influential friends he had accumulated throughout the years, would have supported him. Despite the rules imposed on him because of the abuses of his predecessors, Perkins managed to operate effectively and to use his committee as a tool to facilitate social programs aimed at helping the disadvantaged. A former staff member noted that "on paper, they took away his power. But they knew that if they wanted to fight him on the floor, they wouldn't have a chance in hell" (interview).

7

Leadership and Development on Education and Labor

The prevailing view of institutional leadership is that individual leaders have minimal influence on the organizations they head and that organizations are shaped by their environments. To determine if this view is correct as it relates to chairmen of congressional committees, this study examined the leadership of three disparate chairmen—Graham Barden (1950-52, 1955-60), Adam Clayton Powell, Jr. (1961-66), and Carl D. Perkins (1967-84)—who headed the Committee on Education and Labor for most of its existence. This study has demonstrated that as far as this committee and its chairmen were concerned, the prevailing view was incorrect. As each chairman conducted committee business in a markedly different manner, he contributed to changes in committee operations and to alterations in committee structure, function, and output. He helped shape the committee's metamorphosis to an extent not ordinarily attributed to chairmen in studies of congressional committees or leadership. The influence of each, along with other factors, made the committee a different organization at various stages in its development. The study also showed that the committee developed in stages roughly equivalent to each chairman's tenure rather than evolving smoothly.

The findings here do not suggest that a chairman's leadership is the only factor in committee development or that the environment is unimportant. They highlight the impact of the chairman as committee leader, a leader whose actions directly contribute to alterations in the committee. What is more, each chairman generated changes not only in the committee but in its environment—the House of Representatives.

The Role of Committee Chairmen

The first question posed in the introduction dealt with the role of the chairmen in shaping the structure, operations, function, and outputs of the committee and the extent to which each chairman was a unique leader and had a different impact. This study provides substantial evidence that the chairman had an important influence on the committee. It also reveals that each chairman exercised leadership differently. In reliance on institutional prerogatives—use of subcommittees, management of committee meetings, control over the agenda, treatment of the minority, employment of rewards and sanctions—and dependence on personal resources, each made a difference. The result was dramatic change in the committee from Barden to Powell to Perkins. The chairmen's impacts were not uniform, however; each chairman did not have an effect of equal magnitude on the same aspects of the committee as his fellows had. Because of his orientation and leadership, modified by the environmental constraints under which he operated, each left a unique imprint on the committee.

The degree of reliance on institutional prerogatives—those available by virtue of a leadership postion—varied among the three chairmen and progressively deteriorated. Barden had an abundance of formal resources and made full use of them as chairman. In his early years he had seemingly unlimited power over the committee. There were no written rules other than those enacted as part of the Legislative Reorganization Act of 1946. Eventually, Barden's unwillingness to respond to members' concerns resulted in his institutionally derived prerogatives being taken away from him by an angry majority.

Powell, to whom a little of the discretion (over bill referral) was restored, used his institutional prerogatives in a positive manner for most of his tenure, facilitating the passage of the Great Society legislation. Late in his service, however, when the House refused to act to his satisfaction on antidiscrimination measures (and on his committee operating budget), he began using his chairman's authority against the committee majority and against the House. The committee reacted by removing those resources from the hands of the chairman. The House reacted by stripping him of his seniority and, thus, his chairmanship. When Perkins succeeded Powell shortly thereafter, he was left with few formal prerogatives and relied on them to a substantially lesser extent than did his predecessors.

In Education and Labor, each chairman's conduct made a substantial difference in the formal resources available to successive chairmen. Such developments emphasize not only the importance of a leader's personal attributes but the necessity of maintaining majority support. They could serve as a lesson for present and future chairmen who may be tempted to ignore their fellow committee members.

The three chairmen employed subcommittees to varying degrees, but in general, the use of subcommittees increased over time. Barden relied little on subcommittees. Until the committee revolted in 1957 and adopted written rules, there were no standing subcommittees, only ad hoc units. Most of the committee's work was done in full committee, where Barden could watch over it closely. He called few meetings, appointed few subcommittees, and referred little legislation to those he did appoint.

When Powell took the chair, the committee relaxed controls it had imposed on Barden. Although the rules maintained the standing subcommittees, provisions were deleted that specified subcommittee jurisdictions and required that bills be referred to the appropriate subcommittee. Contrary to the actions of his predecessor, Powell relied on the subcommittees fully. For the most part, he referred bills to the subcommittees where their sponsors or promoters served. He also established some ad hoc subcommittees and chaired a few dealing with issues of particular interest to him, such as de facto school segregation. In addition, he chaired the Subcommittee on the War on Poverty Program, which considered the major domestic legislation of the 88th Congress (1963-64) and let other members chair subcommittees of special interest to them.

Perkins had little discretion over whether he used subcommittees. By the time he became chairman, rules mandating the use of subcommittees were in place. Because of the actions of his predecessors, he was required to refer all bills to the appropriate subcommittees, whose jurisdictions were defined in the rules. He had to take up bills in the full committee in the order in which they were reported. Although he generally followed these stipulations, for the first few terms Perkins kept some of the major legislation at the full committee level, effectively using the full committee as his subcommittee. There were few outright objections to this practice, because Perkins did not chair a subcommittee himself and all members could participate in the full committee mark-ups. Moreover, few members wanted to challenge the chairman. Because of his general agreement with the majority, he was able to exercise substantial influence inside and outside the committee. Even without the formal authority granted to an earlier chairman, Perkins skillfully used his personal resources to influence committee operations. His actions illustrate that personality and leadership often can overcome formal requirements without detrimental consequences to the leader's influence.

Nowhere is the difference among the three chairmen more apparent than in their convening, attending, and conducting sessions of the committee. Perkins differed from his predecessors by attending and voting at regularly scheduled committee meetings. He was absent occasionally, but absence was not the norm as it had been under Barden and Powell. Barden had absented himself regularly so members could not have meetings, resulting in the adoption of committee rules requiring regularly scheduled sessions. Nevertheless, when Powell became chairman, he missed many of the meetings that were held.

As presiding officers, the three chairmen also differed markedly. According to members and staff, Powell was an excellent presiding officer. He was smooth and articulate. He moved things along and tolerated no dilatory tactics from his members. He was not always fair to the minority, but even they admitted that he presided over meetings and hearings effectively. Barden, too, used his prerogatives as presiding officer skillfully, although less frequently. He tailored the situation so that it usually came out to his benefit. He stacked the witness lists at hearings and manipulated the time that witnesses had to speak. He managed to have little time to hear the opposition. In other instances, he recognized his allies and used other dilatory tactics to prevent his opponents from bringing up legislation. According to members and staff, Perkins also could be an effective presiding officer at times, but often he appeared to be fumbling. Generally, he enforced the five-minute rule; however, if a member wanted to speak on a subject for longer than the allotted five minutes, he could arrange with the chairman to do so.

Barden's unwillingness to call regular meetings and his biased conduct of what sessions there were frustrated members, thwarting their expectations of participation. It diminished their influence in the policy process, possibly depriving them of the opportunity for taking credit for programs at election time. Consequently, they reacted by depriving Barden of control over the scheduling of meetings, a deprivation that constrained future chairmen. Powell's absences undermined his leadership. After a while members adopted rules enabling them to proceed without him. In contrast, Perkins's faithfulness enhanced his reputation for reliability. Members possibly felt less need to circumvent him on committee matters since he demonstrated commitment to committee goals. Moreover, his willingness as presiding officer to accommodate members increased his capacity to bargain.

Even after the rules substantially diminished the chairman's authority, all three chairmen managed to find ways to exert their influence over the agenda. Previously, Barden had had complete control over what the committee considered. He decided which bills the committee would take up, which he would refer to subcommittees, and which would languish untouched. After the committee rules were adopted, Barden's authority declined, but he still managed to decide which bills would get favorable treatment. He created ad hoc subcommittees for particular legislation, such as the joint subcommittee on labor reform legislation established to keep labor ally Carl Perkins from having complete jurisdiction over it. Barden also decided which bills the full committee would consider after the subcommittees had reported the legislation. Moreover, he determined the timing of bills sent to the House. He still had friends on the Rules Committee who were more than willing to accommodate him.

Powell managed the agenda to some extent because of his broad discretion over bill referrals. He could keep the ones he wanted in the full committee and direct the others to subcommittees. In addition, he could establish ad hoc units to consider particular items. At the same time, the administration's interest in Education and Labor programs overshadowed Powell's discretion somewhat. Presidents Kennedy and Johnson pressured him to move their legislation forward. Ultimately, in his third term as chairman, Powell exercised control over the agenda by holding some legislation hostage until certain conditions were met. Sometimes these conditions included the enactment of other legislation by the House and by the Senate.

As a consequence of the actions of his two predecessors, Perkins had less control over the committee's agenda via his institutional prerogatives. But he too managed to maintain a substantial amount of influence over it. Until he took a subcommittee in the 93d Congress (1973-74), he kept much of the important legislation at the full committee level—to protect rather than to defeat it. Beginning in 1973 he assumed the chairmanship of a subcommittee that considered much of the most important legislation and was the most active. Perkins also influenced the agenda by bringing public attention to the committee's bills or deliberations. He allowed the media into mark-up sessions in 1967 and was one of the few chairmen to permit such access prior to the House reforms of the 1970s. He also molded the agenda by holding numerous hearings on issues important to his constituents and by allowing other members to do the same. Perkins used his influence with the leadership as another agenda-shaping tool. He often argued effectively that certain bills should be referred to Educaton and Labor, particularly after the advent of split, sequential, and multiple referral. He diligently protected his committee's turf.

The behavior of these three chairmen illustrates the ability of leaders to employ personal skills to advance particular aspects of an organization's agenda. In his own way, each chairman shaped the committee's agenda at one of its three stages.

Another aspect of the chairman's leadership is reflected in his treatment of the minority. Barden had been allied closely with the minority. For the most part, he treated the Republicans better than he did the Democrats, although he disparaged their ability to run the government. But since they agreed with him concerning labor and several aspects of federal aid to education, he was inclined to make deals with them for support of his positions. Barden voted with the Republicans more often than he did with his own party.

Powell, on the other hand, paid little heed to the minority. He gave them staff allowances but evicted them from their committee offices (Fenno 1973; Lewis 1963; interviews). In the 88th Congress he locked the minority members out of the committee room while the Democrats marked up the poverty bill. He rarely voted with the Republicans against the majority members.

Perkins accommodated the minority more than Powell did. According to minority members and staff, Perkins treated them fairly. He went out of his way to let everyone be heard, although it may not have made a difference in the outcome. An examination of the rules shows that he may have been too fair for the tastes of the majority. Members adopted a rule requiring him to recognize two Democrats for every one Republican to question hearing witnesses. Also, Perkins counted a few committee Republicans among his good friends. He even voted with them occasionally.

The three chairmen of Education and Labor between 1951 and 1984 differed dramatically in their dispensation of rewards and sanctions. Of the three chairmen, Barden, who had the most formal powers at his disposal, relied the least on rewards. Every once in a while he favored his allies with the sponsorship of important legislation. The Landrum-Griffin Act, for which two junior colleagues (one Democrat and one Republican) got credit for sponsorship, is the prime example. Occasionally he appointed his friends to subcommittee chairmanships. During one session, Cleveland Bailey (D-WV) chaired three subcommittees, and Carl Elliott (D-AL) headed two.

Powell's position was such that he had to rely on rewards to get what he wanted. One of his tactics was to use bill sponsorship as a basis and as a reward for support. He had made enough enemies during his years in the House that his name on a bill was tantamount to poison. By letting the more junior members have their names on major legislation, he looked magnanimous at no personal cost.

Perkins adopted rewards as a leadership strategy with regularity. In addition, he used a different variety of rewards from his predecessors. He had few subcommittee chairs to give away, so he had to find something else. He employed many tactics to achieve his goals: scheduling bill consideration at the most propitious time; distributing travel funds generously; appointing to a conference committee all members of the subcommittee concerned rather than just a few senior members; appointing other majority members' patronage to the full committee staff, sometimes in senior positions; sharing information so that all members looked good to their colleagues as well as to their constituents; and providing campaign assistance to members, sometimes even to the minority, by appearing in their districts and directing contributions their way. Perkins used any legal and honest means that he could think of to help his fellow members (interview, staff).

Barden's use of sanctions consisted mainly of withholding rewards. The most notable example was his refusal to appoint his second-ranking member, Powell, to a subcommittee chairmanship to which his seniority entitled him. Nor would he allow Powell to speak in committee meetings and hearings on a number of occasions. He skipped Powell and recognized third-ranking Cleveland Bailey and others (Hickey and Edwin 1965, 184). Barden also withheld travel vouchers as sanctions, although he is said to have given Powell all the vouchers he wanted so he would go away.

Powell, too, used sanctions. A principal one related to bill referral. Although he reportedly offered Phil Landrum a subcommittee chairmanship, Landrum declined because of a well-founded belief that it was unlikely that any significant legislation would have been referred to him (Lewis 1963, 94). Powell also used his discretion over bill referral to assign bills without regard to tradition or interest despite an understanding with his members that he would refer legislation to the sponsor's or the promoter's subcommittee. Moreover, knowing the difficulties of securing a rule for Education and Labor bills, he manipulated the scheduling of legislation to be reported (interview, staff).

Perkins relied on rewards and incentives largely to the exclusion of sanctions. Part of this emphasis on favors may have resulted from constraints placed on his ability to use sanctions or to deny perquisites. On the other hand, it was not in his nature to punish. He rarely used sanctions when he had the opportunity, not wanting to jeopardize future alliances.

In sum, the three chairmen's reliance on institutional resources varied markedly. Barden, who had the most tools, used them, for the most part, in a negative manner. Powell, who had fewer tools but increased discretion over bill referral, also used some of his authority in a negative manner, although on the whole he facilitated the passage of legislation. Perkins, who had the fewest institutional prerogatives, relied on other means to accomplish his goals. Barden worked against the system. Powell let the system work itself for a while and then worked against the system. Perkins worked through the system.

Galloway referred to committee chairmen as "lord proprietors" (1953a, 289), and Smith and Deering termed the period between 1947 and 1964 as "the era of strong committee chairs" (1984). Both Barden and Powell fit these classifications. Because the rules placed fewer constraints on them, they relied on the institutional resources available to chairmen to a much greater extent than Perkins was able to do later. Perkins, however, was effective because of his superior strategic use of personal resources.

Froman (1967), Hinckley (1971), and Smith and Deering (1984) contended that a chairman's views usually correspond with those of his majority members, thereby negating the need to resort to "strong-arm tactics" (Smith and Deering, 1984, 27). Barden deviated in this respect; he did not agree with his majority much of the time, particularly after the Speaker had liberalized the committee, and he persisted in "strong-arm tactics." When Barden's almost exclusive reliance on institutional prerogatives put him on a collision course with his committee majority, members rebelled, adopting rules limiting his institutional prerogatives. He maintained his effectiveness by relying on his personal reserve of political prowess and a bountiful supply of conservative friends, such as Carl Elliott (D-AL) and Rules Committee chairman Howard W. Smith (D-VA). On the rare occasion when Barden could not prevent his committee from reporting a bill, he looked to his friends on other committees, notably Rules, to block it. He would ask the Committee on Rules not to issue a rule or, if it did, to allow an open rule permitting unlimited floor amendments. Still, until the last two terms of his chairmanship, he relied heavily on institutional resources.

When Powell took the chair, he was saddled with most of the constraints the committee had placed on Barden, although he had discretion over the referral of bills. His abuse of his formal powers led to his downfall. Had he not been stripped of his chairmanship or barred from his seat, he too would have had to look to his personal resources for help. But in some ways, partly because of racial prejudice against him, Powell had fewer personal resources at his disposal than did Barden and Perkins. He had few friends to help him among House members, and he had been deprived of some of his patronage and office space because of his support for Eisenhower in the 1956 elections (Hickey and Edwin 1965, 136). Moreover, he had not built a reputation for himself based on diligence and knowledge of the subject matter, thus diminishing his effectiveness. Additional detracting factors were his penchant for accusing his opponents of being racist and for injecting race into every issue. On the other hand, his considerable personal attractiveness and magnetism, his ability to think on his feet, and his oratorical skills worked in his favor.

Perkins took the chair under Powell's legacy—an "institutionally weak" chairmanship (Fenno 1973, 288). Most of the official prerogatives had gone down the drain with Powell. Perkins had little choice but to rely on personal resources, which included his reputation for honesty, tenacity, and political acumen and his de facto honesty, tenacity, influence, and political acumen. Although he held the chair more than twice as long as each of his predecessors, he had few problems because he generally agreed with the committee majority.

Perhaps not realizing what a wily chairman they would have and seeing that he would not fight them, the members responsible earlier for initiating the rules changes may have thought that they could manipulate Perkins and have the committee operate to their advantage. He appeared to let them have the run of the committee, as long as he accrued as many benefits as possible for his district. Several of these members acknowledged that

Perkins substantially influenced the legislation reported from subcommittees. They noted later that unlike Powell, Perkins had his fingerprints on almost all the legislation that came out of Education and Labor during his chairmanship (interviews).

At the onset of his chairmanship in 1967, many members underestimated him, an opinion that Perkins turned into a political asset. They did not consider him sophisticated enough to handle the leadership of such an important committee (Barnes 1984).[1] Some thought he was stupid and then had the misfortune of finding out the truth about Carl Perkins. Part of his strength was that his foes thought they were smarter than he was. One Kentuckian who had frequent dealings with Perkins for many years said, "The political graveyards of East Kentucky are full of people who thought they were smarter than Carl Perkins."[2] Several members of Congress found themselves inadvertently in his debt because they had underestimated him. Among those who knew him, he had a reputation for being wily and crafty. One former committee member said, "When you talk to Carl, check for your wristwatch. He'll have it. Your wallet, too. He's good at legislating" (interview). Another member was quoted as saying, "When you get into a conference with Carl Perkins, you may end up not having any furniture in your office. He is awesome" (in Fenno 1989).

Although the institutional resources largely were gone, Perkins maintained considerable respect. He still had influence with other chairmen and with the leadership, and he continued to control committee travel money. In addition, he retained a good deal of his authority over the scheduling of committee business, and when he violated a rule on the sequence of bill consideration, few members challenged him. He was a master at timing consideration of measures on the House floor. He would ensure that a bill would not come up unless he had the votes. When the bill reached the conference stage, he would maneuver so that it was his turn in the rotation with the Senate to chair the conference committee, even if it meant reporting another bill slightly different from the Senate version.

Like Barden, Perkins relied heavily on his friends in the House. He used them to move bills through the House, unbeknownst to his political opponents. Representative Frank Albert Stubblefield's (D-KY) mumbled motion to suspend the rules and pass one of Perkins's bills before anyone realized what it was is a prime example. Perkins's recessing a conference with the Senate until he could get an additional conferee appointed to secure a vote for his position is another. When committee bills were scheduled to be taken up in the House, Perkins frequently arranged to have one of his friends acting as Speaker so as to have an ally with the gavel. In addition, he could depend on a host of other friends he had accumulated over the years. He had a kindly, ingratiating way about him. He spent a great deal of time on the floor of the House, cultivating friendships among members, old and new. He particularly worked on new members whom he thought he might be able to attract to his committee. Many members of both chambers were quite fond of him and thus were willing to support him on many occasions.

One of Perkins's most valuable personal resources was his tenacity. He secured passage of many bills by sheer perseverance. Unlike Powell, who reputedly had a fleeting attention span (Bolling 1966, 98), Perkins wore down his opponents by sheer persistence. He snatched several major programs from the jaws of defeat by not knowing when to quit. He earned the respect of his members and of others for his relentless pursuit of passage of Education and Labor bills. In the process, he gained a reputation for being one of the great bargainers of the House and one of its most effective members. He traded chits all over the House.

These three chairmen used their resources in different ways to get the committee to do what they wanted, and their actions resulted in three different committees. Within the institutional context and guided by shifts in the salience of the committee's jurisdiction, the committee leadership was responsible for many of the changes in the committee. Barden's use of his formal powers to achieve his ends overshadowed his use of personal resources. His leadership was characterized by his use of his institutional prerogatives in a negative, obstructionist manner. His refusal to call meetings, his refusal to appoint standing subcommittees, his refusal to appoint Powell as a subcommittee chairman, his actions in declaring the lack of quorum for meetings when he knew that in a matter of minutes one would be present, his weak reliance on rewards, and his conspiracies with his conservative friends on the Rules Committee all amounted to negative exertions of authority or influence. His actions in contravention of the majority's will produced negative reaction and sharp curtailment of the institutional prerogatives of the chairman.

For the most part, Powell's use of his institutional and personal resources resulted in a permissive and facilitative leadership that contributed to a committee more productive than it had ever been. Members worked out compromises and reached agreements that would not have been possible under Barden, who rarely let the committee meet and thus avoided considering legislation. For most of Powell's tenure, the negative exercise of power came at the expense of the Republicans, whom the chairman locked out of the poverty bill mark-up, evicted from their staff offices, and routinely "rolled" on committee votes. He might have wanted to be authoritarian toward the majority, but he did not have the leadership backing or popularity among other House members to carry it off. A staff member said that Powell had a "siege mentality." He thought that his majority members were out to get him (interview). In many ways, he was correct. A former member said, "We wanted the committee to be immunized from

Powell. He was uneven. It was easy to take advantage of his status in the House" (interview). According to former members, Powell had an implicit agreement with his members: he gave the subcommittees free rein, and they allowed him to retain the perquisites of the chairmanship and to do largely what he wished, as long as he did not interfere with the will of the majority. In Powell's third term as chairman, his imperious ways got the better of him. He reneged on his end of the agreement to refer bills to the subcommittees of the sponsor or promoter. In addition, his expenditures of committee funds were excessive and embarrassing. But the catalyst in his downfall was his decision to impede the progress of three major pieces of legislation. Powell shifted from a permissive and facilitative leadership to a high-handed one.

Perkins combined his institutional and personal resources to produce a strategic, calculating leadership that was the driving force behind committee legislation. In Barber's terms (1972), Perkins could be characterized as an "active-positive" chairman. His son described him as "activist in the things he believed in" (interview). He stayed well within the bounds of his majority's approval on most issues, and he worked diligently to see that committee programs were reauthorized and adequately appropriated. He worked at building coalitions in the committee and on the floor. He used rewards almost to the exclusion of sanctions.

While Barden and Powell had their strongest impacts on the structure and operations of the committee, Perkins's impact was most pronounced on the committee product, the legislation it reported. That is not to say that Barden's obstruction had no effect on legislation; it did. It prevented it. And as Fenno (1973, 130) noted, Powell's primary contribution to decision making was his movement of legislation through the committee and to the floor as rapidly as possible. Both Barden and Powell violated the trust and will of the majority, deeds that resulted in structural and operational changes. The committee never returned to its old ways. In every Congress after 1957 the committee adopted written rules. In all of those terms there were standing subcommittees. Staff sizes grew, along with the size of the membership. The number, scope, and complexity of the committee rules also increased dramatically. For example, whereas there were twelve rules beginning in 1957, by 1984 there were twenty-four. Moreover, the first rules could be printed on one page. Subsequently, they have been published in booklets; the committee rules for the 98th Congress (1983-84) ran to nineteen pages.

The actions of both Barden and Powell resulted in a more democratic and decentralized operation, not because the chairmen aspired to democratic goals but because of their thwarting of the committee majority. The participatory practices became institutionalized over the years. Power was fractionalized and dispersed among the majority members. The majority preempted some of the chairman's prerogatives as well. Others were exercised jointly by the chairman and his colleagues. The subcommittee chairmen shared in this dispersion of authority and had greater influence under Perkins than they had under the two previous chairmen. In the 1970s, when the House and the House Democratic caucus adopted many of these reforms and procedures became institutionalized in other committees as well, Education and Labor was in the forefront, largely because of the actions of its chairmen.

The extent to which the committee reflected the chairman's leadership may be inferred from alterations in the committee's function, which changed dramatically over the three periods under scrutiny. That it shifted under each chairman is shown by the amount and the different types of legislation produced under each chairman, although he was not the only influential factor. The function by and large coincided with the chairman's agenda, although the committee was more productive and harmonious when the chairman's agenda melded with the majority will. During the Barden years, little legislation at all, and particularly not any that favored organized labor, was reported by the committee. Under Powell, the committee produced much new, progressive social legislation. After Perkins became chairman, national public policy emphasis shifted to defense and economics, thereby forcing the committee to concentrate on maintaining the gains of the past.

During the Barden years, the committee's function was to prevent so-called liberal legislation from being enacted. Liberal legislation included anything favorable to organized labor and any federal aid to education measures that would penalize states allowing segregated schools. In addition, federal aid to religious institutions was on the verboten list. Chairman Barden effectively used the committee as a vehicle for preventing passage of such bills. By refusing to call meetings, to appoint subcommittees, to assign legislation to subcommittees, and to allow the committee to act, Barden blocked consideration, and thus passage, of progressive or liberal legislation.

Under Powell, the committee came into its own. It was charged with laying the groundwork for large portions of the administrations' domestic agendas in the Kennedy and Johnson years. Fortunately, for the most part, these agendas coincided with that of Chairman Powell, who did not intercede to prevent most bills from passing. In fact, he helped immensely by not interfering with his subcommittee chairmen and by keeping his name off the legislation. The committee's function was to consider, report, and see enacted large parts of the Great Society programs.

Under Perkins, the situation shifted away from enacting new programs toward preserving the gains already made. Vietnam had deflected attention and funds away from the poverty program and federal aid to education issues. Other than the war in Indochina, the economy became the top priority. With a few exceptions, the committee enacted little new, far-reaching legislation. Its mission became to safeguard the liberal gains made in the Powell years. This mission became more difficult by the 1980s, when President Reagan's budget-cutting operations were in full swing and the president had little sympathy for Education and Labor programs. The committee, however, was bent on amending and extending its programs—in the words of one staff member, trying to "reinvent the wheel"—and it had to protect existing funding from being cut completely.

Not only did the chairmen of Education and Labor affect the committee, they left long-term legacies in the House. Some reforms, particularly the financial restrictions, were applied to the House in part as a result of the actions of the chairmen of this committee. Education and Labor's accounting procedures, begun under Chairman Perkins to track where "the money's a-goin' to" after he took over from Powell, were adopted for most committees. Powell also was the catalyst in the 1970 establishment of the House Committee on Standards of Official Conduct, commonly known in the 1980s and 1990s as the House Ethics Committee. Proponents had been worried about previous violations in ethics, and the Powell affair precipitated action (*Congressional Quarterly Almanac* 1966, 524). In addition, the public disclosure of private interests was an offshoot of Powell's actions. Other committees now routinely have open meetings and bill mark-ups (a Perkins contribution), standing subcommittees with fixed jurisdictions (an anti-Barden legacy), and bill referral to subcommittees (a reaction to Barden) largely thanks to the chairmen of Education and Labor.

Shifts in Committee Composition and Policy Outputs

A second question addressed by this study concerned the relationship between shifts in regional and ideological composition of the committee and policy outputs. Brady (1978) advanced the thesis that major shifts in the composition of Congress produced major changes in policy output. The present study examined whether his argument is applicable to committees as well. Data on members' districts and interest group scores and information on the amount and scope of the committee's legislative actions and output support the thesis that major shifts in committee membership produce major policy changes. Education and Labor's policy output changed when its composition changed. Other factors, such as a new chairman anxious to benefit a national constituency of blacks and a president who placed education and labor issues high on his agenda, undoubtedly also contributed to the shift in the committee's output.

Although patterns in the committee's seniority and proportions of new members did not change substantially, the committee increased in size over the years, and its regional and ideological composition shifted dramatically. In the Barden era its membership came principally from southern and Middle Atlantic states. In contrast, by 1960 the committee was dominated by northern, urban liberals, particularly by those in the North and East. A number of members from large urban areas in Illinois, Michigan, and California also joined the committee. Few new southerners were appointed.

In the early Barden years, the committee was a bastion of conservatism. Ultimately, the Speaker interfered and gradually stacked the committee with liberal Democrats, thus changing its ideological complexion. The Republicans sent some of their most conservative members to Education and Labor in the 1950s and early 1960s, but after 1964 most Republicans on the committee were no longer envoys of the extreme right wing of the party. Their average interest group scores were more liberal than those of all House Republicans after 1964 for the duration of the period under study. There were a few archconservatives, such as John Ashbrook of Ohio, but they were counterbalanced by more moderate Republicans, such as Ogden Reid, Charles Goodell, and Peter Peyser, all of New York. Reid and Peyser later became Democrats. As a result of the regional and ideological shifts, the committee membership no longer reflected House membership.

The metamorphosis of the committee from an ideological microcosm of the House into a committee with a strong liberal bias resulted from several factors, some external and some internal. First, the Speaker's refusal to appoint conservative Democrats, and southerners in particular, and the influence of organized labor in getting assigned only those members who were sympathetic to unions accounted for part of the pattern. Second, according to several persons interviewed, the fact that the committee chairman in the early 1960s was black probably kept a number of southerners off the committee. Third, by the time the Great Society's programs were in full swing, the committee was known for its liberalism, and conservatives had little incentive to be a part of it. Fourth, the members on this committee built up constituencies through program benefits that emanated from Education and Labor and thus felt obliged to defend them. Finally, the nature of the jurisdiction of this committee also attracted the more liberal members, particularly those from urban constituencies that would benefit most from its programs.

A shift in the composition of the committee was one of several factors that contributed to changes in committee output. The chairman, the president, and the general salience of the committee's issues had varied impacts. The committee output changed markedly when Barden left the committee in Powell's hands; the scope and quantity of Education and Labor legislation increased. The number of bills reported rose dramatically, and federal aid to education legislation and other liberal proposals finally had a chance. The composition of the committee was tailor-made for this. The House leadership had stacked the committee, thus enabling the liberals to keep an effective majority and facilitate the passage of legislation, much of it of major significance.

Also indicative of a relationship between committee composition and policy outputs were the experiences during the Perkins years. The actual composition of the committee changed, but the regional and ideological makeup remained comparatively stable. Subsequently, there were few major policy shifts, thereby lending support to Brady's theory and highlighting the role of the committee composition. Most of the legislation considered amended or reauthorized existing programs.

Committee Development

A third question of this study concerned whether, in its efforts to adapt to internal and external pressures, the committee developed in stages or in smooth, incremental transitions. The evidence shows that it developed in stages. The committee during its first stage—one that might be compared with childhood—was small, uncomplicated, and relatively unproductive, and it operated under a strict patriarch. In its adolescence, it rebelled. As it matured it took control of its own affairs and contributed substantially to congressional output and long-term policies. In its old age it tries to maintain its vigor and status by adding new areas of activity, fearing all the while that its glory days are largely in the past.

As organization theory predicts, the structure of the committee became more complex, more formalized, and more decentralized over the years. Evidence supporting this conclusion includes a more complex configuration reflecting more members, increased and permanent subunits, and a rise in the number of committee and subcommittee staff members. Membership grew from twenty-four during Barden's first term as chairman to forty in the 94th Congress (1975-76), declining slightly thereafter. Subcommittees were ad hoc until 1957, when standing subcommittees were instituted. Subsequently, the number of standing subcommittees grew from five to eight under Perkins. Data on staff size are imprecise; nonetheless, it is apparent that staff size fluctuated and expanded dramatically overall. There were ten staff members in 1951 under Barden and more than a hundred later under Perkins. The addition of subcommittee and minority staffs as well as the growth of oversight activities accounted for a significant portion of the increase.

The institution and subsequent institutionalization of rules indicate that the committee became more formalized. Until late in Barden's chairmanship no written committee rules existed, and the chairman almost entirely controlled committee activities. Rules adopted in 1957 required weekly meetings, the establishment of standing subcommittees with fixed jurisdictions, and referral of all legislation to the standing subcommittees. These units were empowered to hold hearings, receive exhibits, take testimony, and report to the full committee. The next term, members refined the rules to required, among other things, that every committee member be appointed to at least one subcommittee. Rules changes adopted in 1966 preempted most of the remaining prerogatives of the chairman. The adoption and expansion of rules institutionalized their application and produced a more formalized committee.

Greater decentralization is reflected in the fractionalization of power— subcommittees gaining a voice in committee decision making and operations. They did most of the work, held most of the hearings, and considered most of the bills. Subcommittee chairmen were given control of their staffs, some responsibilities for budget preparation, and an expanded work load. Standing subcommittees, which had been nonexistent under most of Barden's chairmanship, took on new importance under Powell and continued to be major components under Perkins.

The impact of the 1970s House and caucus reforms on this committee's structure were mitigated by actions of the committee membership itself. The committee's "naughty child" orientation generated internal reforms that accomplished most of what House and caucus reforms later did. By and large, most requirements already were in place on Education and Labor by the time they were applied to other committees. Standing subcommittees had been established for more than a decade, although reforms altered the method of appointing chairmen and members. In addition, subcommittees considered most legislation, except that held in the full committee by implicit agreement between the chairman and his majority. The committee instituted accounting procedures after Powell's troubles. Committee meetings had been open to the public for several years before the reforms. All in all, Education and Labor was affected only mildly by the 1970s House and caucus reforms that undoubtedly were precipitated in part by committee problems and solutions.

Some aspects of the committee's operations, such as procedures, work load, and voting behavior, changed while others remained stable. Procedures became much more democratic. Both the expanded member participation in the decision-making process and several rules changes are evidence of greater democracy. The new rules diffused power previously belonging to the chairman by delegating authority to establish subcommittees to majority members, authorizing minority questioning of witnesses, and requiring the assignment of every member to a standing subcommittee, among other things. Thus, each member became more influential in the Education and Labor policy-making process.

The committee work load increased over the three periods. The number of bills assigned to the committee grew, the number of hearings increased, and more bills were reported. Bill referrals generally rose until multiple sponsorship was allowed in 1975. The number of hearings went up as well. Moreover, more bills were reported by the committee, passed by the House, and eventually enacted. Many of these increases largely resulted from external forces, such as the general growth of the congressional work load and the renewed emphasis on oversight. But increases in a few of the indicators, such as the rise in the number of hearings or in the number of bills reported, also were influenced by internal committee factors. Powell's and Perkins's permissiveness with subcommittees contributed to the rise in output and hearings.

Stability and change in committee operations is reflected in patterns of full committee and party cohesion on committee roll calls. Full committee voting cohesion remained stable and low, and partisanship remained stable and high. There was little full committee cohesion under Barden, particularly during his last term as chairman. In fact, as the number of committee roll calls went up, voting cohesion decreased. During the Powell years, the average full committee Rice Index Scores rose, although they still indicated a fairly divisive committee. In addition, the percentage of minimally cohesive votes (70-percent cohesion) grew as well. When Perkins assumed the chair, the mean cohesion scores and percentages of minimally cohesive votes rose further, although by no means could Education and Labor be considered a unified voting bloc.

Several factors may have affected the rise of voting cohesion on Education and Labor during the Perkins years. First, Chairman Perkins probably had some mitigating effect on the controversies surrounding the issues. He worked hard at building coalitions. Second, the membership of the committee was not as philosophically extreme as it had been in earlier years. The Republicans were more liberal than their House counterparts, and the Democrats were becoming more representative of theirs. Third, by the time Perkins became chairman, most of the great fights had been fought. The degree of controversy may have subsided as the salience of the issues declined. Also, some of the Republicans had an interest in maintaining the committee's programs. Their constituents benefited, and thus they may have been inclined to vote with the Democrats a bit more often.

Party voting was moderate during the Barden years. It increased markedly when Powell took the chairmanship and stayed high throughout his tenure and into the beginning of the Perkins years. The percentage of party votes generally decreased somewhat from Powell to Perkins. After the 90th Congress (1967-68), levels of party voting decreased until 1980, a presidential election year, when the proportions rose to more than 70 percent.

Party voting cohesion was moderate for both parties in the 1950s and high in the 1960s. It began to decrease for both parties in the 92d Congress (1971-72), although levels remained fairly high for the duration of the Perkins years. Democrats were particularly unified in the 96th, 97th, and 98th Congresses (1979-84). The decrease in party cohesion scores coincided with increases in the average full committee cohesion scores from the Barden and Powell years.

For the most part, the extent of party voting in Education and Labor bore little relation to the degree of party voting in the House. Nor did mean party-unity scores appear to resemble party cohesion or party voting in the committee. The exceptions were the 96th, 97th, and 98th Congresses. The relatively high rates of party voting in the committee during these Congresses correspond to higher levels of party voting in the House found by Dodd and Oppenheimer (1989).

Party voting on the committee was at its highest during the period that Education and Labor was the vehicle for a large part of the president's domestic agenda. When the issues were at the peak of salience, members fought for their interests. The legislation that incited most of the partisan differences in the 87th Congress (1961-62) related to school construction, NDEA, and impacted areas policies. The high number of roll calls indicates conflict, albeit not necessarily along partisan lines. In the 88th Congress (1963-64), the War on Poverty legislation generated a substantial amount of partisan controversy. The Johnson administration threw its weight behind the Democrats, almost forcing the issues to be partisan. Moreover, the fact that the committee had jurisdiction over such salient and visible issues contributed to the divisiveness. Party voting was somewhat less prevalent, although still present, in the 89th Congress (1965-66), when the committee emphasized education legislation. Members were able to work out compromises on aid to elementary and secondary schools that had been a highly partisan issue in the past.

Partisanship also was high in the last part of the Perkins years. Beginning in the Carter administration, Education and Labor programs increasingly were threatened with large budget cuts or with abolition, exacerbating controversies already present on the committee. Democrats fought to keep the gains they had made in the early and mid-1960s. About the same time, the country was in the midst of a rising tide of conservatism that brought Ronald Reagan to the White House. The conservatives continued with renewed vigor the budget cutting begun in the Carter administration. Although there was no discernible pattern of partisanship on the issues themselves, the committee and subcommittee recommendations to the Budget Committee for financing programs under the committee's jurisdiction split along party lines on every vote.

Other Findings

Certain other findings of interest emerged from this study concerning the salience of the issues before the committee, the degree of specificity in the committee structures and rules, the role of the chairman in committee decentralization, and committee integration. The issues before the Committee on Education and Labor have waxed and waned in salience. They did not become prominent until the early and mid-1960s, when there was enough impetus in the environment for making major policy changes, at least insofar as the issues before this committee were concerned. The added salience of Education and Labor issues lasted into the early 1970s, when social welfare concerns were replaced or supplanted by more pressing needs. Many of the problems confronted during the 1950s and 1960s were no longer issues. They were solved in some sense or another. There was no major disagreement anymore over whether the federal government should provide aid to education or whether schools should be segregated or integrated. The problem of whether to aid public schools only or to include parochial schools faded as a pertinent issue, although it is unlikely to stay faded. What is more, federal aid became an even smaller percentage of the money spent on education than it was when the ESEA was enacted. Nor was poverty any longer a prominent issue. Bargaining and minimum wage concerns were not at the forefront of the public agenda. Curtailment of labor unions belonged to an era of the past. The salient labor issues fell under the jurisdiction of other committees, such as Ways and Means, as tariffs, import quotas, and cheap labor superseded the fights over situs picketing, secondary boycotts, and minimum wage.

In the latter part of the Perkins era, the committee was the victim of the double whammy—a less salient issue jurisdiction and the threat of reduced program funding. Its main constituents, organized labor and the poor, declined as political forces. At the same time, the committee as an organization became institutionalized and continued to maintain itself in the face of less salient issues of narrower scope. Led by its chairman, it fought not only dying interest in its issues but budget limitations and cuts.

The problems of Education and Labor are symptomatic of those faced by most of the authorizing committees. The committees concerned with financial and defense issues have taken precedence over most of the others. One pair of researchers has termed it the new "committee oligarchy," consisting of the money committees, Rules, Armed Services, and Energy and Commerce (Dodd and Oppenheimer 1989, 48-50). This oligarchy arose out of a need for centralization of the decentralized subcommittee government created by the 1970s House and caucus reforms combined with attention to the enormous federal deficit, forcing a reduction in new programs and old funding levels. The agendas of the authorizing committees have been forced to fit into the budget projections. The budget and its reconciliations are the major domestic legislation considered by Congress.

Education and Labor was hit hard by the emphasis on budget cutting. Chairman Perkins complained bitterly about not being able to "help poor people." He was angry that the programs authorized by the committee were not fully funded and that their very existence was threatened. His job as the guardian of the 1960s social welfare and education gains became increasingly frustrating (interview). In addition, since a large part of the power on Capitol Hill is vested in the "committee oligarchy," the authorizing committees, including full committee chairmen and subcommittee chairmen, have less authority.

Contrary to what Smith and Deering (1984, 168) argued, when committee structures and rules were vaguely defined, as in the Barden era, the chairman tended to rely more on his institutional prerogatives than on his personal resources for influencing the committee structure, operations, function, and outputs. Where the structures were clearly specified, as when Powell presided, the chairman had little choice but to rely on his personal resources, since his institutional prerogatives had been preempted by the committee majority. On Education and Labor, when structural arrangements were loosely defined, the chairman could establish the structure and operations, within limits, according to his view of the world. Institutional prerogatives offered the most efficient and least risky ways of being effective. If the structures and procedures were defined clearly, the chairman had little discretion over their shape. He had to depend on his personal arsenal to work within or around existing structures or operations.

Another finding that emerged from this study is that the actions of the chairmen of this committee largely were responsible for its decentralization. The reforms were adopted primarily at the end of Barden's and Powell's tenures as chairman. Most were instituted because the chairman had flouted the will of the majority. They supplanted the will of the chairman with the will of the majority. They fractionalized and diffused the power to ensure that the majority would have a voice in committee operations and structure. These reforms were adopted years before they were applied to the standing committees at large. Education and Labor members had more influence over what went on in their committee long before members of most other committees could claim such influence.

An unsurprising finding was that Education and Labor was not highly integrated. A number of studies have characterized Education and Labor as one of the least integrated committees in Congress. Most conceptualize integration in Fenno's (1966, 191) terms as a "meshing" among its subunits and roles or as the minimization of conflict. Several arrived at their opinions on the basis of some form of measurement of voting cohesion (Unekis and Rieselbach 1984; Dyson and Soule 1970). Others based their conclusions concerning this committee on interview data (Munger and Fenno 1962; Fenno 1962, 1966, 1973; Manley 1965). This study has done both. If the standard for integration is full committee cohesion, this study supports judgments that Education and Labor was not highly integrated, although the degree of cohesive voting increased during the Perkins years. The aforementioned authors did not consider, however, that parties and rules are integrating mechanisms, both of which were in abundance on Education and Labor.

Several factors contribute to the relatively low cohesion levels on Education and Labor compared with some other committees. Fenno (1966) discussed those facilitating integration on the Committee on Appropriations. First, the money men apparently place a high value on internal integration in the committee. This value is conveyed via the norms of reciprocity, unity, minimal partisanship, and compromise. Second, members of Appropriations have a consensus on committee goals, particularly in protecting the power of the purse. Third, Appropriations makes decisions in dollars and cents instead of in philosophical terms.

None of these conditions prevailed on Education and Labor, which practiced none of the listed norms. In fact, members did almost exactly the opposite. Compromise, unity, and minimal partisanship were infrequent visitors. There was no cross-party consensus on goals. Democrats tended to support government aid or intervention in labor matters and in education, whereas Republicans tried to protect the Treasury and keep federal involvement in education to a minimum. In labor relations, Republicans almost always sided with management and voted to restrict unions, whereas many Democrats were union men. Third, the decisions made on Education and Labor were at the very heart of the philosophical differences between the parties, subjects that divide by their very nature instead of unifying and promoting integration. Some of the great philosophical battles, such as that over federal aid to education, were fought in Education and Labor.

Fenno (1966) mentioned a few other conditions that contributed to smooth operating conditions on the Appropriations Committee. First, the chairman and the ranking minority member served as ex officio members of every subcommittee and worked closely together in the process. On Education and Labor, although the chairman and ranking minority member were ex officio members of all subcommittees, unless they were particularly interested in an issue under consideration they generally stayed out of subcommittee affairs. While this practice may have promoted integration on Appropriations, it added little to Education and Labor, other than an extra vote when needed. Fenno (1966) also commented on the minimization of conflict on Appropriations. While all conflict cannot be eliminated in Congress, it can be contained. The containment of conflict on Appropriations was aided by the practice of reporting bills with no minority reports, which were seen as visible symbols of committee disunity (Fenno 1966, 203). In Education and Labor, on the contrary, there was no effort to contain the conflict. Committee rules included a provision specifically allowing members to file minority, individual, or supplemental reports along with committee reports, beginning in 1971. The signs of conflict were published for all to see. Many members wanted their constituents to know that they had opposed these big-spending bills.

An apprenticeship period may have contributed to integration in some committees, but there was no such apprenticeship in Education and Labor. New members could begin their service square in the middle of the committee's disputes. When Perkins assumed the chairmanship, he began assigning freshmen and other subcommittee members to conference committees. The appointment of freshmen or low-ranking subcommittee members to conference committees would have been a rarity on Appropriations. The lack of apprenticeship on Education and Labor contributed to minimal integration. That lack could make each member feel more competent and thereby more assertive, since he would gain experience early in his committee career, while members on other committees watched instead of participating. Immediate participation also removed potential rewards from the hands of the chairman, such as appointments to conference committees as rewards for biding time. If subcommittee members automatically were designated as the conferees, the chairman had little discretion over whom to appoint. Moreover, it removed incentives for members to cooperate with the chairman, since they likely could serve anyway.

In addition to the integration problems faced by Education and Labor, it had some integration strengths. Conflict structured along party lines enabled the committee to carry out its functions successfully, particularly when the majority was large. Also, the committee had numerous rules to contain the conflict. In the words of a former staff member, "Rules are a way to organize conflict and keep it civil. If everything is civil already, rules are a way to structure business" (interview). Further, even though Education and Labor was not highly integrated under any of its chairmen, all seemed to have ways of making it work to their satisfaction. The fact that the Republicans did not filibuster the committee also testifies to some degree of integration. True, they offered numerous amendments to Democratic legislation, but they did not work against the process, an indication that the committee could work together.

Each chairman's leadership contributed to integration, as well as detracting from it. Education and Labor was integrated sufficiently to be able to survive several threats to its existence as one committee instead of two and to accomplish its work. If it continually reported legislation that was too extreme for the House to approve, it would have been "reorganized" to suit the needs of the House. But it adapted to the pressures and demands from its environment.

Understanding Congressional Committees

The aim of this study was two-pronged. First, its goal was to enhance the understanding of how committees operate and what effects certain internal and external environmental influences have on their operations, outputs, and development. Second, and integral to the first goal, this study was directed at narrowing the gap in knowledge of committee leadership. For decades scholars and others have pointed to committee chairmen as among the most powerful members on the Hill. But few have carried the torch in their research. This study highlights the importance of and the abilities of individuals in affecting the structures, operations, and outputs of congressional committees.

In recent years, many congressional scholars have emphasized the institutional context in determining how committees and their leaders act. But that picture is not complete. Although the institutional context is significant, the current study underscores the importance of individual chairmen in the actions and development of congressional committees. Moreover, not only can chairmen affect the committee, but they also can affect the House, as was illustrated by the three chairmen studied here. More attention might profitably be paid to the proactive influences of committee chairmen.

This study also has implications for the selection of committee leaders. One might expect a different modus operandi from a chairman who is held accountable by election or by implicit threat of removal than one who ascends to the office by virtue of seniority and assumes himself safely ensconced. The former would be more responsive to the wishes of the majority caucus as well as to committee members. Committee leadership determined by seniority lacks accountability to the membership by virtue of its universalistic character. Minus a threat of overthrow, the committee chairman has little incentive, other than some quirk of personality, to cater to the wishes or goals of committee members except to further his aspirations.

Also important for understanding congressional committees is the impact of the committee's historical development on the current committee. Care should be taken in selecting aspects to be compared, because two committees may not be in the same stage of development. Committee A might be in its infancy, whereas Committee B might be in a relatively mature stage, with institutionalized traditions, structures, and operations. One may not understand certain norms or ways of doing things without a good idea of how the committee developed and why it developed the way it did.

Another implication of this study is the importance of the committee composition—of the individuals who make up the committee. Drawing on Brady's thesis (1978) that major policy shifts result only from major shifts in the composition of Congress, this study suggests that changes in membership composition can affect committee output. The individuals on a committee, including the chairman, can have a marked effect on its output.

Another important factor in understanding congressional committees is the salience and divisiveness of the issues in a committee's jurisdiction. The jurisdiction of Education and Labor was relatively unimportant in the early stages of its development; then it peaked during its teenage years under Powell and waned under Perkins, although the latter did everything in his power to maintain the gains made in the early 1960s. Other committees undoubtedly endure cycles of salience, something that should be considered when studying them.

Like many organizations created to serve this broad and diverse country, Congress is a multifaceted and, indeed, a many-splendored thing. The more we understand the pieces that tessellate that grand mosaic, the greater will be our appreciation of the entire institution. The author hopes that this study of the Committee on Education and Labor and its three disparate chairmen has illuminated one facet of this mosaic in a way that limns the whole Congress.

Notes

Chapter 1. The Committee during the Barden Years

1. For example, in 1952 the Senate held hearings pertaining to Communists in labor unions. The Communist Control Act of 1954 (P.L. 83-637) prohibited Communist party members from holding union offices or from representing an employer before the National Labor Relations Board (*Congress and the Nation* 1965, 598). In 1954 Senator McCarthy held hearings in the Senate Government Operations Committee to investigate possible Communist infiltration of the State Department, the Voice of America, and the army. Education and Labor considered the issue of loyalty oaths on several occasions during the decade, including in the 1958 National Defense Education Act, in the Landrum-Griffin Act, and in several other efforts to repeal the latter. See *Congress and the Nation* 1965, 1669-70; and Puryear (1979, 133-34).

2. The Taft-Hartley Act formally is entitled "The Labor-Management Relations Act of 1947" (P.L. 80-101).

3. The act is formally entitled "The Labor-Management Reporting and Disclosure Act of 1959" (P.L. 86-257).

4. Interviews; also documented by a number of new members to Education and Labor who also held seats on other committees, such as Merchant Marine and Fisheries, Interior and Insular Affairs, Banking and Currency, Public Works, and Agriculture. The chairman of Government Operations also sat on Education and Labor.

5. The number of times each member voted for and against each group's position was printed in the *Congressional Quarterly Weekly Report* at various times throughout the decade.

6. For example, if a member voted correctly on twenty of the twenty-seven roll calls chosen by the AFL, he would rate a support score of 74.0. Whether he voted against the AFL position or did not vote at all is irrelevant, since neither action would constitute support for the AFL's position. One drawback to this measure is that it penalizes members who were not in Congress in all of the terms in question; however,

if they were not in Congress, they could not support that pressure group's position on the selected roll calls.

7. See Fenno (1969, 292-93, 296). This assertion was also substantiated by the author in interviews with former members and Education and Labor staff. Bolling remarked that the Democratic Study Group helped change the composition of committees by working to persuade the party leadership to fill vacancies with liberals from time to time: "Notable success has been achieved in changing the complexion of the Education and Labor Committee from deep conservative to liberal" (1966, 57).

8. See Fenno (1969) for a discussion of the effect of membership changes on federal aid to education legislation.

9. Until now, no one has been able to document systematically these allegations because the roll-call records were not available for the early years of the committee's existence. The staff of the Committee on Education and Labor was kind enough to allow this author access to all the committee minutes and roll calls taken since Barden assumed the chairmanship in 1950. Records for 1953, 1954, and 1957 are missing.

10. Party-unity scores represent the percentage of party-unity roll calls on which each member voted with his party against a majority of the other party on House floor votes.

11. The Rice Index of Cohesion (Rice 1928) represents the absolute difference between the percentage of yea votes and the percentage of nay votes. Scores on individual roll calls can be averaged to yield mean scores. This index can be applied to voting with parties as well as voting between parties. See Anderson, Watts, and Wilcox (1966, 32-35).

12. See Fenno (1969, 292-93, 296) and Cater (1964, 160). The assertion regarding stacking the committee was also supported in several interviews.

Chapter 2. The Chairmanship of Graham Barden

1. This section draws heavily on a thorough biography of Barden by Elmer Puryear (1979).

2. The constituency information is drawn largely from Puryear (1979).

3. Much of the following information was drawn from interviews with members of Congress and with staff members of the Committee on Education and Labor. In addition, Puryear (1979) provided many of the details about Barden's attitudes and the reasons for them.

4. These tallies were printed in the *Congressional Quarterly Weekly Report* at various times throughout the 1950s.

5. Party-unity scores are printed in each year's *Congressional Quarterly Almanac*.

6. See Jones (1981) for a discussion of contextual versus personal perspectives on leadership.

7. Another way to approach leadership is through classifications of leaders into categories. For some notable examples, refer to Barber (1972) for classifications of presidents, March and Simon (1967) for modes of conflict resolution, Unekis and Rieselbach (1984) for the voting patterns of House committee chairmen, Manley (1967) for a discussion of task-oriented versus affective leadership, and Burns (1978) for a discussion of transactional versus transforming leadership.

8. A notable exception was the creation of a subcommittee on staffing matters by

the majority of Education and Labor in response to "Chairman John Lesinski's highhandedness" in the 81st Congress; see Goodwin (1970, 145).

Chapter 3. The Committee during the Powell Years

1. Much of the information in this section can be found in various *Congressional Quarterly* publications. Committee prints of the House Committee on Education and Labor also provided much of the information on committee accomplishments and activities.

2. Scott's ADA scores ranged from 0 to 12 from 1960 to 1966, his COPE scores from 0 to 27, and his ACA scores from 60 to 83. His party-unity scores ranged from 4 to 29 for the same period.

Gibbons had COPE scores of 73 in 1963-64 and 77 in 1965-66 and comparatively high party-unity scores: 76 in 1963 and 93 in 1966. He really did not fit the stereotype of the southern congressman. He was younger and more progressive than many of his colleagues and came from Tampa, an urban instead of a rural area. Voting for federal aid to education and other "progressive" measures did not appear to be as much of a hardship for Gibbons as for some other members, such as Scott.

3. The ideological composition of the committee throughout the Powell years is inferred both from interest group scores and from the impressions of members and observers of the committee. Whereas for most of the 1950s *Congressional Quarterly* printed the number of "right" and "wrong" votes cast by each member according to the particular interest group, the 1960s scores were calculated by the interest groups.

4. The questionable travel expenses include sixty-five trips to Miami or San Juan, Puerto Rico, that were all billed as "official travel." One trip to San Juan was scheduled in the name of Leon Abramson, the committee's chief counsel for labor management, and the other was charged to Michael Schwartz, the assistant counsel to the Antipoverty Subcommittee. See Loftus 1966b. Several other staff members were subpoenaed to provide information on trips that were billed to the committee in their names but that they never took (interviews).

5. The chairman's estranged wife, Yvette Marjorie Flores, who lived in Puerto Rico, was one. See Jacobs (1973, 250) for the specifics.

6. Now the House Stationery Store will not pay cash for returned merchandise.

7. Various statements made in interviews conducted for this study conveyed that impression.

Chapter 4. The Chairmanship of Adam Clayton Powell, Jr.

1. For a more thorough treatment of Powell's background, see Hamilton (1991) and Gunther (1985).

2. Overall, as chairman, Powell missed 26 percent of Education and Labor's meetings. His attendance ranged from 36 to 88 percent of the committee's meetings between 1961 and 1966. From 1951 to 1960 he attended between 9 and 39 percent of the meetings. Compiled from Committee on Education and Labor, *Minutes* 1951-66. There are no data for 1953-54 and 1957.

3. This count excludes the twenty-two days Powell was in Europe at a meeting of the International Labor Organization.

4. See Committee on Education and Labor, *Activities and Accomplishments*, 87th-89th Cong. These committee publications contain lists of all subcommittees and discussions of what each accomplished in each session.

5. See Hickey and Edwin (1965, 285-88) for a more thorough discussion of Powell's delaying tactics.

6. See Sorenson (1965, 340); Hardeman and Bacon (1987, 455); Powell (1971, Chap. 10); and Puryear (1979, 132).

7. This incident was described to the author in an interview with a former committee member. It is also cited by Hickey and Edwin (1965, 133), MacNeil (1963, 311-12), and Puryear (1979, 110). Puryear cited the Greensboro *Daily News*, July 22, 1955, as one of his sources.

8. Unless otherwise noted, information in this section was drawn from the following sources: Powell (1971, 159-84); *In re Adam Clayton Powell* 1967; *Congressional Quarterly Almanac* (1966, 519-24); Jacobs (1973); and Hickey and Edwin (1965, 280-85). Hamilton (1991, 313-25, 406-45) also treats Powell's legal difficulties in detail.

9. See Jacobs 1973 for a discussion of the contemplated proceedings against Powell.

Chapter 5. The Committee during the Perkins Years

1. Representative William Clay (D-MO) was an exception from this region, coming from an urban, labor district in St. Louis.

2. Statements to this effect surfaced in several interviews conducted for this study. That the committee is a hardship post for Republicans was not necessarily true in 1989. In an interview, a Republican member said that Representative Thomas J. Tauke (R-IA) transferred to another committee and had to fight to get back on Education and Labor. The Democrats, however, were having trouble filling their vacancies. They resorted to using temporary appointees in recent years and had eight in the 100th Congress (1987-88). Over the years Chairman Perkins frequently used his personal influence to recruit new Democrats, who generally were not clamoring for Education and Labor seats.

3. The Democrats arranged for Representative Timothy J. Penny (D-MN) to be assigned elsewhere in the 101st Congress because he consistently voted with the Republicans. This strategy was recounted by a member in an interview and was supported by subsequent interviews with other members and staff.

4. According to committee staff members interviewed for this study, the majority leader sat on the committee as a temporary, allegedly to counteract the influence of Edith Green (D-OR), who was acting more and more like a Republican in those days and aggravating the more liberal Democrats.

5. The 1973 Democratic Caucus rules limited party members to service on one exclusive committee (Rules, Appropriations, or Ways and Means), or one major and one nonmajor committee, or two nonmajor committees. See *Congress and the Nation* 4:752; and Sheppard (1985, 236).

6. The "Subcommittee Bill of Rights" allowed each committee's majority members to choose subcommittee chairmen, to establish subcommittee jurisdictions and set the party ratios to reflect that of the full House, to provide subcommittee budgets, and

to set the number of subcommittees the full committee would have. See *Congress and the Nation* 4:746; and Smith and Deering (1990).

7. Committees had been directed to exercise "continuing watchfulness" over administrative agency execution of the laws under their jurisdiction by the Legislative Reorganization Act of 1946 (P.L. 79-601). See *Congress and the Nation* 1965, 1418.

8. House *Rules* 1979, rule 11 cl. 2 (m) (1), H. Res. 988, 93d Cong., p. 34470. Previously, only a few committees were permitted to issue subpoenas.

9. The data on House and caucus reforms are drawn from Deering and Smith (1981, 264; *Congress and the Nation* vols. 3 and 4; and Sheppard (1985). Education and Labor reform data are drawn from the printed rules of the committee. The dates refer to the time of enactment of similar rules (or practices), if applicable, on the committee if different from the year of the House or caucus reforms.

Chapter 6. The Chairmanship of Carl Perkins

1. This remark was made in the author's presence at Chairman Perkins's funeral by Connie Frederick Crosby.

2. The amount of the fee was printed in Perkins's obituary in the *New York Times*, written by Marjorie Hunter. The story came from staff members who heard it told often.

3. Glickman (1972) gave the salary as $59.60 per month.

4. This comment about Perkins's academic record was made by a later president of Lees Junior College to a committee staff member.

5. The description of Perkins as a bumpkin surfaced repeatedly in interviews conducted with members and staff as part of this study. Gladieux and Wolanin also describe his image as "something of a country bumpkin" (1976, 170).

6. This incident was recounted many times to Education and Labor staff members by Sam Ezelle, former secretary-treasurer of the Kentucky AFL-CIO.

7. Andrew Jackson May, chairman of the House Military Affairs Committee, and John Langley both represented Floyd County, Kentucky, an area in Perkins's Seventh District.

8. The author overheard remarks to this effect at Perkins's funeral on Aug. 7, 1984.

9. He did lose in 1984 on portions of a bill to ensure "equal access" to public school facilities by religious groups. The leadership, not in favor of the bill, sent it instead to Judiciary, where it was certain to be defeated.

10. According to staff, before he had made up his mind on how to vote on some issues, Perkins had his office staff call the office of Representative M. Caldwell Butler (R-VA), in whose judgment Perkins put great stock, to find out how he was going to vote (interviews).

11. Chairman Wilbur Mills (D-AR) of Ways and Means was another who avoided sanctions for the most part. See Manley (1967, 1969).

12. For example, she denied one member's request for travel money because she suspected that he wanted to conduct official business for another committee.

13. Some variant of this comment surfaced repeatedly in interviews with members and staff.

14. For example, Senator Sam Nunn (D-GA), chairman of the Senate Armed

Services Committee, and former representative Wilbur Mills (D-AR), chairman of Ways and Means, each is an expert based on his knowledge of the subject matter under his committee's jurisdiction. See Manley (1967, 1969) for a discussion of "expert power" as it applied to Chairman Mills.

15. This conference is treated in great detail in Gladieux and Wolanin (1976, 161-205). Some of the strategies were summarized in an interview for this study with one of the authors.

16. The "Blue Books" are the prints of the legislation taken to conference. They include the House bill beside the Senate bill and the differences between the two versions.

17. Some variant of this expression surfaced in several interviews with members and staff.

Chapter 7. Leadership and Development on Education and Labor

1. The opinion that others thought he was not sophisticated enough was expressed several times in interviews with other members and with staff members. Most people who knew him knew better.

2. Dr. Robert Martin, former president of Eastern Kentucky University and former state official (commissioner of finance, superintendent of state public instruction, and state senator) told this several years ago to Benjamin F. Reeves, assistant to the chairman of the Committee on Education and Labor, who related it to the author.

References

Abram, Michael, and Joseph Cooper. 1968. The Rise of Seniority in the House of Representatives. *Polity* 1:1 (Fall):52-85.

Advisory Commission on Intergovernmental Relations. 1966. *Intergovernmental Relations in the Poverty Program*. (A-29). Washington, D.C.: GPO.

———. 1980. *The Federal Role in the Federal System: The Dynamics of Growth: Federal Involvement in Libraries*. (A-84). Washington, D.C.: The Commission.

———. 1981a. *The Federal Role in the Federal System: The Dynamics of Growth: Intergovernmentalizing the Classroom: Federal Involvement in Elementary and Secondary Education*. (A-81). Washington, D.C.: The Commission.

———. 1981b. *The Federal Role in the Federal System: The Dynamics of Growth: The Evolution of a Problematic Partnership: The Feds and Higher Ed.* (A-82). Washington, D.C.: The Commission.

———. 1981c. *Significant Features of Fiscal Federalism, 1980-81 Edition*. (M-132). Washington, D.C.: The Commission.

Anderson, James E. 1966. *Politics and the Economy*. Boston: Little, Brown and Co.

———. 1967. Poverty, Unemployment, and Economic Development: The Search for a National Antipoverty Policy. *Journal of Politics* 29:1 (Feb.):70-93.

Anderson, Lee F., Meredith W. Watts, Jr., and Allen R. Wilcox. 1966. *Legislative Roll-Call Analysis*. Evanston, IL: Northwestern University Press.

Asher, Herbert B., and Herbert F. Weisberg. 1970. Voting Change in Congress: Some Dynamic Perspectives on an Evolutionary Process. *American Journal of Political Science* 22:2 (May):391-425.

Bach, Stanley. 1984. Membership, Committees, and Change in the House of Representatives. Paper presented at the annual meeting of the American Political Science Association. Washington, D.C., Aug. 30-Sept. 2.

———. 1986. Suspension of the Rules, the Order of Business, and the Evolution of Legislative Procedure in the House of Representatives. Paper presented at the annual meeting of the American Political Science Association. Washington, D.C., Aug. 28-31.

Barber, James David. 1972. *The Presidential Character: Predicting Performance in the White House.* 2d ed. Englewood Cliffs, NJ: Prentice-Hall.

Barden, Graham A. Papers. Duke University Library, Durham, NC.

Barnes, Bart. 1984. Rep. Carl Perkins of Education Panel Dies. *Washington Post*, Aug. 4, B4(1).

Barone, Michael, Grant Ujifusa, and Douglas Matthews. 1977. *The Almanac of American Politics, 1978.* New York: Dutton.

Baumer, Donald C., and Carl E. Van Horn. 1985. *The Politics of Unemployment.* Washington, D.C.: CQ Press.

Bendiner, Robert. 1964. *Obstacle Course on Capitol Hill.* New York: McGraw-Hill.

Berg, John. 1978. The Effects of Seniority Reform on Three House Committees in the 94th Congress. In *Legislative Reform: The Policy Impact*, ed. Leroy N. Rieselbach, 49-59. Lexington, MA: Heath.

Bibby, John, and Roger Davidson. 1967. *On Capitol Hill: Studies in the Legislative Process.* New York: Holt, Rinehart and Winston.

———. 1972. *On Capitol Hill: Studies in the Legislative Process.* 2d ed. Hinsdale, IL: Dryden Press.

Bibby, John F., Thomas E. Mann, and Norman J. Ornstein. 1980. *Vital Statistics on Congress, 1980.* Washington, D.C.: American Enterprise Institute for Public Policy Research.

Biographical Directory of the American Congress, 1774-1971. 1971. Washington, D.C.: GPO.

Bolling, Richard. 1966. *House Out of Order.* New York: Dutton.

———. 1968. *Power in the House: A History of the Leadership of the House of Representatives.* New York: Dutton.

Brady, David W. 1972. Congressional Leadership and Party Voting in the McKinley Era: A Comparison to the Modern House. *Midwest Journal of Political Science* 16:3 (Aug.):439-59.

———. 1978. Critical Elections, Congressional Parties and Clusters of Policy Change. *British Journal of Political Science* 8:79-99.

———. 1982. Congressional Party Realignment and Transformations of Public Policy in Three Realignment Eras. *American Journal of Political Science* 26:2 (May):333-60.

Brady, David W., and Charles S. Bullock. 1983. Party and Factional Organization in Legislatures. *Legislative Studies Quarterly* 8:4 (Nov.):599-654.

Brady, David W., Joseph Cooper, and Patricia A. Hurley. 1979. The Decline of Party in the U.S. House of Representatives, 1887-1968. *Legislative Studies Quarterly* 4:3 (Aug.):381-407.

Brady, David W., and Barbara Sinclair. 1984. Building Majorities for Policy Changes in the House of Representatives. *Journal of Politics* 46:1033-60.

Branch, Taylor. 1988. *Parting the Waters: America in the King Years, 1954-63.* New York: Simon and Schuster.

Brenner, Phillip. 1974. Committee Conflict in the Congressional Arena. *Annals of the American Academy of Political Science* 411:87-101.

Brown, George Rothwell. 1922. *The Leadership of Congress.* Indianapolis, IN: Bobbs-Merrill.

Brown, Mike. 1988. Prodigal Son: Perkins Could Be Losing His Grip on Father's Rich Political Bequest. Louisville *Courier-Journal*, Sept. 25, p. 1.

Brown, William Holmes, ed. 1979. *Constitution, Jefferson's Manual, and Rules of the House of Representatives of the United States, 96th Congress*. Washington, D.C.: GPO.

Brown v. *Board of Education of Topeka*. 347 U.S. 483 (1954).

Brown v. *Board of Education of Topeka, II*. 349 U.S. 294 (1955).

Burks, Edward C. 1969. Perkins Asks 5 Years More for Poverty Drive. *New York Times*, March 25.

Burns, James MacGregor. 1978. *Leadership*. New York: Harper and Row.

Carroll, Holbert N. 1958. *The House of Representatives and Foreign Affairs*. Pittsburgh: University of Pittsburgh Press.

Casstevens, Thomas W. 1970. Linear Algebra and Legislative Voting Behavior: Rice's Indices. *Journal of Politics* 4:32 (Nov.):769-83.

Cater, Douglass. 1964. *Power in Washington*. New York: Random House.

Cherryholmes, Cleo H., and Michael J. Shapiro. 1969. *Representatives and Roll Calls*. Indianapolis, IN: Bobbs-Merrill.

Chiu, Chang-Wei. 1928. *The Speaker of the House of Representatives since 1896*. New York: Columbia University Press.

Clapp, Charles L. 1963. *The Congressman: His Work as He Sees It*. Garden City, NY: Doubleday.

Clark, Joseph S., ed. 1965. *Congressional Reform: Problems and Prospects*. New York: Crowell.

Clausen, Aage R. 1973. *How Congressmen Decide: A Policy Focus*. New York: St. Martin's.

Clausen, Aage R., and Richard B. Cheney. 1970. A Comparative Analysis of Senate-House Voting on Economic and Welfare Policy: 1953-64. *American Political Science Review* 64:1 (March):138-52.

Clausen, Aage R., and Carl E. Van Horn. 1977. The Congressional Response to a Decade of Change: 1963-72. *Journal of Politics* 39:3 (Aug.):625-66.

Clubb, Jerome M., and Sandra Traugott. 1977. Partisan Cleavage and Cohesion in the House of Representatives, 1861-1974. *Journal of Interdisciplinary History* 7:375-402.

Cnudde, Charles F., and Donald J. McCrone. 1966. The Linkage between Constituency Attitudes and Congressional Voting Behavior: A Causal Model. *American Political Science Review* 60:1 (March):66-72.

Cohen, Matthew C. 1978. Decision Making in a Committee Context: The House Education and Labor Committee Deliberations of the Elementary and Secondary Act Extension of 1974. Ph.D. diss., Carnegie-Mellon University.

Collie, Melissa P. 1984. Voting Behavior in Legislatures. *Legislative Studies Quarterly* 9:1 (Feb.):3-50.

———. 1988. The Rise of Coalition Politics: Voting in the U.S. House, 1933-1980. *Legislative Studies Quarterly* 13:3 (Aug.):321-42.

Committee on Education and Labor. *Calendar*. 80th-98th Congresses.

Congress and the Nation, 1945-1964. 1965. Washington, D.C.: CQ Service.

Congress and the Nation, vol. 2, *1965-1968*. vol. 3, *1969-1972*. vol. 4, *1973-1976*.

vol. 5, *1977-1980*. vol. 6, *1981-1984*. Washington, D.C.: Congressional Quarterly.

Congressional Directory. 1950-84. 81st-96th Congresses. Washington, D.C.: GPO.

Congressional Quarterly Almanac. 1951-84. Washington, D.C.: CQ Press.

Congressional Quarterly Weekly Report. 1951-92.

Cooper, Joseph. 1970. *The Origins of the Standing Committees and the Development of the Modern House*. Houston, TX: Rice University Press.

———. 1971. The Study of Congressional Committees: Current Research and Future Trends. *Polity* 4:4 (Fall):123-33.

———. 1975. Strengthening the Congress: An Organizational Analysis. *Harvard Journal of Legislation* 12:307-68.

———. 1977. Congress in Organizational Perspective. In *Congress Reconsidered*, ed. Lawrence C. Dodd and Bruce I. Oppenheimer. New York: Praeger.

———. 1981. Organization and Innovation in the U.S. House of Representatives. In *The House at Work*, ed. Joseph Cooper and G. Calvin Mackenzie, 319-55. Austin: University of Texas Press.

Cooper, Joseph, and David W. Brady. 1981a. Institutional Context and Leadership Style: The House from Cannon to Rayburn. *American Political Science Review* 75:2 (June):411-25.

———. 1981b. Toward a Diachronic Analysis of Congress. *American Political Science Review* 75:4 (Dec.):988-1006.

Cooper, Joseph, David William Brady, and Patricia A. Hurley. 1977. The Electoral Basis of Party Voting: Patterns and Trends in the U.S. House of Representatives, 1887-1969. In *The Impact of the Electoral Process*, ed. Louis Maisel and Joseph Cooper. Vol. 3, Sage Electoral Studies Yearbook. Beverly Hills: Sage Publications.

Copeland, Gary W. 1987. Seniority and Committee Transfers: Career Planning in the Contemporary House of Representatives. *Journal of Politics* 44:2 (May): 553-64.

Daley, Ron. 1984. Congressman Carl D. Perkins, Dead at 71: Thousands Attend Funeral. Knott County, KY, *Troublesome Creek Times*, Aug. 4, p. 1.

Davidson, Roger H. 1972. *The Politics of Comprehensive Manpower Legislation*. Baltimore: Johns Hopkins University Press.

———. 1974. Representation and Congressional Committees. *Annals of the American Academy of Political and Social Science* 411:48-62.

———. 1981a. Congressional Leaders as Agents of Change. In *Understanding Congressional Leadership*, ed. Frank H. Mackaman, 135-56. Washington, D.C.: CQ Press.

———. 1981b. Subcommittee Government: New Channels for Policy Making. In *The New Congress*, ed. Thomas E. Mann and Norman J. Ornstein, 99-133. Washington, D.C.: American Enterprise Institute for Public Policy Research.

———. 1986. The Legislative Work of Congress. Paper presented at the annual meeting of the American Political Science Association. Washington, D.C., Aug. 28-31.

Davidson, Roger H., and Walter Oleszek. 1976. Adaptation and Consolidation: Structural Innovation in the U.S. House of Representatives. *Legislative Studies Quarterly* 1:1 (Feb.):37-66.

Deckard, Barbara Sinclair. 1976. Political Upheaval and Congressional Voting: The Effects of the 1960s on Voting Patterns in the House of Representatives. *Journal of Politics* 38:2 (May):326-45.

Deering, Christopher J., and Steven S. Smith. 1981. Majority Party Leadership and the New House Subcommittee System. In *Understanding Congressional Leadership*, ed. Frank H. Mackaman, 261-92. Washington, D.C.: CQ Press.

———. 1984. Subcommittees in Congress. In *Congress Reconsidered*, 3d ed., ed. Lawrence C. Dodd and Bruce I. Oppenheimer, 189-210. Washington, D.C.: CQ Press.

Derrickson, Russell C. 1961. Background and Organization. An unpublished manuscript on the Committee on Education and Labor. Files of the Committee on Education and Labor, Washington, D.C.

Dionisopolous, P.A. 1970. *Rebellion, Racism, and Representation: The Adam Clayton Powell Case and Its Antecedents*. Dekalb, IL: Northern Illinois University Press.

Dodd, Lawrence C. 1972. Committee Integration in the Senate: A Comparative Analysis. *Journal of Politics* 34:4 (Nov):1135-71.

———. 1979. The Expanded Roles of the House Democratic Whip System: 93rd and 94th Congresses. *Congressional Studies* 7 (Spring):27-56.

Dodd, Lawrence C., and Bruce I. Oppenheimer. 1989. Consolidating Power in the House: The Rise of a New Oligarchy. In *Congress Reconsidered*, 4th ed., ed. Lawrence C. Dodd and Bruce I. Oppenheimer, 39-64. Washington, D.C.: CQ Press.

Dodd, Lawrence C., and John C. Pierce. 1975. Roll Call Measurement of Committee Integration: The Impact of Alternative Methods. *Polity* 7:3 (Spring):386-401.

Dodd, Lawrence C., and Terry Sullivan. 1981. Majority Party Leadership and Partisan Vote Gathering: The House Democratic Whip System. In *Understanding Congressional Leadership*, ed. Frank H. Mackaman, 227-60. Washington, D.C.: CQ Press.

Donovan, John C. 1973. *The Politics of Poverty*. New York: Bobbs-Merrill.

Downs, Anthony. 1967. *Inside Bureaucracy*. Boston: Little, Brown and Co.

Dyson, James W., and John W. Soule. 1970. Congressional Committee Behavior on Roll Call Votes: The U.S. House of Representatives, 1955-1964. *Midwest Journal of Political Science* 14:4 (Nov.):626-47.

Edstrom, Eve. 1969. Poverty Hearings Open with Sharp Wrangling. *Washington Post*, March 25.

Eidenberg, Eugene, and Roy D. Morey. 1969. *An Act of Congress*. New York: Norton.

Elazar, Daniel J. 1984. *American Federalism: A View from the States*. 3d ed. New York: Harper and Row.

Entin, Kenneth. 1973. Information Exchange in Congress: The Case of the House Armed Services Committee. *Western Political Quarterly* 26:427-39.

Erikson, Robert S. 1971. The Electoral Impact of Congressional Roll Call Voting. *American Political Science Review* 65:4 (Dec.):1018-32.

Eulau, Heinz. 1969. Introduction: On Units and Levels of Analysis. In *Micro-Macro Political Analysis*, ed. Heinz Eulau, 1-22. Chicago: Aldine.

Eulau, Heinz, and Vera McCluggage. 1984. Standing Committees in Legislatures: Three Decades of Research. *Legislative Studies Quarterly* 9:2 (May):195-270.

Evans, C. Lawrence. 1986. Influence in Senate Committees: The Role of Formal Leadership. Paper presented at the annual meeting of the American Political Science Association. Washington, D.C., Aug. 28-31.

———. 1991. *Leadership in Committee: A Comparative Analysis of Leadership Behavior in the U.S. Senate.* Ann Arbor: University of Michigan Press.

Farnsworth, David N. 1961. *The Senate Committee on Foreign Relations.* Urbana: University of Illinois Press.

Feig, Douglas G. 1979. The Stability of Congressional Committees. *Political Methodology* 6:311-41.

———. 1981. Partisanship and Integration in Two House Committees: Ways and Means and Education and Labor. *Western Political Quarterly* 34:3 (Sept.):426-37.

Fenno, Richard F. 1962. The House Appropriations Committee as a Political System. *American Political Science Review* 56:2 (June):310-24.

———. 1965. The Internal Distribution of Influence: The House. In *The Congress and America's Future*, ed. David B. Truman, 52-76. Englewood Cliffs, N.J.: Prentice-Hall.

———. 1966. *The Power of the Purse: Appropriations Politics in Congress.* Boston: Little, Brown and Co.

———. 1969. The House of Representatives and Federal Aid to Education. In *New Perspectives on the House of Representatives*, 2d ed., ed. Robert L. Peabody and Nelson W. Polsby, 281-323. Chicago: Rand McNally.

———. 1973. *Congressmen in Committees.* Boston: Little, Brown.

———. 1978. *Home Style: House Members in Their Districts.* Boston: Little, Brown.

———. 1989. *The Making of a Senator: Dan Quayle.* Washington, D.C.: CQ Press.

Ferejohn, John A. 1974. *Pork Barrel Politics: Rivers and Harbors Legislation, 1947-1968.* Stanford, CA: Stanford University Press.

Fiedler, Fred E. 1967. *A Theory of Leadership Effectiveness.* New York: McGraw-Hill.

Fiorina, Morris P. 1974. *Representatives, Roll Calls, and Constituencies.* Lexington, MA: Heath.

———. 1975. Constituency Influence: A Generalized Model and Its Implications for Statistical Studies of Roll-Call Behavior. *Political Methodology* 2:249-66.

Flinn, Thomas, and Harold Wolman. 1966. Constituency and Roll Call Voting: The Case of Southern Democratic Congressmen. *Midwest Journal of Political Science* 10:192-99.

Follett, Mary Parker. 1896. *The Speaker of the House of Representatives.* New York: Longmans, Green.

Fox, Douglas M., and Charles H. Clapp. 1970. The House Rules Committee and the Programs of the Kennedy and Johnson Administrations. *Midwest Journal of Political Science* 14:4 (Nov.):667-72.

Franklin, Grace A., and Randall B. Ripley. 1984. *CETA: Politics and Policy, 1973-1982.* Knoxville: University of Tennessee Press.

French, Burton L. 1915. Subcommittees of Congress. *American Political Science Review* 9 (Feb.):68-92.

Froman, Lewis A. 1967. *The Congressional Process.* Boston: Little, Brown and Co.

———. 1968. Organization Theory and the Explanation of Important Characteristics of Congress. *American Political Science Review* 62:2 (June):518-26.

Froman, Lewis A., and Randall B. Ripley. 1965. Conditions for Party Leadership: The Case of House Democrats. *American Political Science Review* 59:1 (March): 52-63.

Furguson, Ernest B. 1984. Carl Perkins: Kentucky Mourns a Man Who Knew What Government Is For. *Baltimore Sun*, Aug. 12, 26(1).

Galloway, George B. 1953a. *The Legislative Process in Congress*. New York: Crowell.

———. 1953b. *Congress at the Crossroads*. New York: Crowell.

———. 1956. *Congressional Reorganization Revisited*. College Park: Bureau of Governmental Research, College of Business and Public Administration, University of Maryland.

———. 1959. Leadership in the House of Representatives. *Western Political Quarterly* 12:2 (June):417-41.

Garrow, David J. 1986. *Bearing the Cross: Martin Luther King, Jr., and the Southern Christian Leadership Conference*. New York: Vintage.

Gladieux, Lawrence E., and Thomas R. Wolanin. 1976. *Congress and the Colleges: The National Politics of Higher Education*. Lexington, MA: Heath.

———. 1978. Federal Politics. In *Public Policy and Private Higher Education*, ed. David W. Breneman and Chester E. Finn, 197-230. Washington, D.C.: Brookings Institution.

Glickman, Lora Jane. 1972. *Carl D. Perkins: Democratic Representative from Kentucky*. Ralph Nader Congress Project, Citizens Look at Congress, Aug. Washington, D.C.: Grossman Publishers.

Goldman, Eric F. 1969. *The Tragedy of Lyndon Johnson*. New York: Knopf.

Goodwin, George, Jr. 1959. The Seniority System in Congress. *American Political Science Review* 53:2 (June):412-36. Reprinted in *Congressional Reform: Problems and Prospects*, ed. Joseph S. Clark, 178-206. New York: Crowell, 1965.

———. 1962. Subcommittees: The Miniature Legislatures of Congress. *American Political Science Review* 56:3 (Sept.):596-604.

———. 1970. *The Little Legislatures: Committees of Congress*. Amherst: University of Massachusetts Press.

Green, Harold P., and Alan Rosenthal. 1963. *Government of the Atom: The Integration of Powers*. New York: Atherton.

Green, Mark J., James M. Fallows, and David R. Zwick. 1972. *Who Runs Congress?* New York: Grossman.

Gunther, Lenworth, III. 1985. Flamin' Tongue: The Rise of Adam Clayton Powell, Jr., 1908-1941. Ph.D. diss., Columbia University.

Haas, J. Eugene, and Thomas E. Drabek. 1973. *Complex Organizations: A Sociological Perspective*. New York: Macmillan.

Hall, Richard L. 1986. Participation in Committee Decision Making. Ph.D. diss., University of North Carolina.

———. 1987. Participation and Purpose in Committee Decision Making. *American Political Science Review* 81:1 (March):105-27.

———. 1989. Committee Decision Making in the Postreform Congress. In *Congress Reconsidered*, 4th ed., ed. Lawrence C. Dodd and Bruce I. Oppenheimer, 197-223. Washington, D.C.: CQ Press.

Hamilton, Charles V. 1991. *Adam Clayton Powell, Jr.: The Political Biography of an American Dilemma*. New York: Atheneum.

Hammond, Susan Webb. 1989. Congressional Caucuses in the Policy Process. In *Congress Reconsidered*, 4th ed., ed. Lawrence C. Dodd and Bruce I. Oppenheimer, 351-71. Washington, D.C.: CQ Press.

Hardeman, D. B., and Donald C. Bacon. 1987. *Rayburn: A Biography*. Austin: Texas Monthly Press.

Harrington, Michael. 1962. *The Other America: Poverty in the United States*. New York: Macmillan.

Harris, Fred R., and Paul L. Hain. 1983. *America's Legislative Processes: Congress and the States*. Glenview, IL: Scott, Foresman and Co.

Henderson, Thomas A. 1970. *Congressional Oversight of Executive Agencies: A Study of the House Committee on Government Operations*. Gainesville: University Presses of Florida.

Hickey, Neil, and Ed Edwin. 1965. *Adam Clayton Powell and the Politics of Race*. New York: Fleet.

Hinckley, Barbara. 1969. Seniority in the Committee Leadership Selection of Congress. *Midwest Journal of Political Science* 13 (Nov.):613-630

———. 1970. Congressional Leadership Selection and Support: A Comparative Analysis. *Journal of Politics* 2:32 (May):268-87.

———. 1971. *The Seniority System in Congress*. Bloomington: Indiana University Press.

———. 1975. Policy Content, Committee Membership, and Behavior. *American Journal of Political Science* 19:3 (Aug.):543-57.

Horn, Stephen. 1970. *Unused Power: The Work of the Senate Committee on Appropriations*. Washington, D.C.: Brookings Institution.

Huitt, Ralph K. 1954. The Congressional Committee: A Case Study. *American Political Science Review* 48:2 (June):340-65.

———. 1961. Democratic Party Leadership in the Senate. *American Political Science Review* 55:2 (June):331-44.

———. 1965. The Internal Distribution of Influence: The Senate. In *The Congress and America's Future*, ed. David B. Truman, 77-101. Englewood Cliffs, NJ: Prentice-Hall.

Hunter, Marjorie. 1984. Rep. Carl D. Perkins Dies at 71; Led the Fight for Social Programs. *New York Times*, Aug. 4, sec. 1, p. 28, col. 1.

In re Adam Clayton Powell: Report of Select Committee Pursuant to H. Res. 1. 1967. 90th Cong., 1st sess. Feb.

Inter-University Consortium for Political and Social Research. 1984. *Voting Scores of Members of Congress (1945-1982)*. ICPSR Study 7645

Inter-University Consortium for Political and Social Research. *Roster of United States Congressional Officeholders and Biographical Characteristics of Members of the United States Congress, 1789-1985 Merged Data*. ICPSR Study 7803. Ann Arbor.

Jacobs, Andy. 1973. *The Powell Affair: Freedom Minus One*. Indianapolis, IN: Bobbs-Merrill.

Jewell, Malcolm E., and Chu Chi-hung. 1974. Membership Movement and Committee Attractiveness in the U.S. House of Representatives, 1963-1971. *American Journal of Political Science* 18:2 (May):433-41.

Jewell, Malcolm E., and Samuel C. Patterson. 1966. *The Legislative Process in the United States*. New York: Random House.

Johnson, Lyndon Baines. 1964. State of the Union Address. Jan. 8.
———. 1971. *The Vantage Point: Perspectives of the Presidency, 1963-1969.* New York: Holt, Rinehart and Winston.
Jones, Charles O. 1962. The Role of the Congressional Subcommittee. *Midwest Journal of Political Science* 6:4 (Nov.):327-44.
———. 1968. Joseph G. Cannon and Howard W. Smith: An Essay on the Limits of Leadership in the House of Representatives. *Journal of Politics* 30:3 (Aug.):617-46.
———. 1974. Between Party Battalions and Committee Suzerainty. *Annals of the American Academy of Political and Social Science* 411:158-68.
———. 1981. House Leadership in an Age of Reform. In *Understanding Congressional Leadership,* ed. Frank H. Mackaman, 117-56. Washington, D.C.: CQ Press.
———. 1984. *An Introduction to the Study of Public Policy.* 3d ed. Monterey, CA: Brooks/Cole.
Kaiser, Fred M. 1977. Congressional Change and Foreign Policy: The House Committee on International Relations. In *Legislative Reform: The Policy Impact,* ed. Leroy N. Rieselbach, 61-71. Lexington, MA: Heath.
Kaplan, Lewis. 1968. The House Un-American Activities Committee and Its Opponents: A Study in Congressional Dissonance. *Journal of Politics* 30:3 (Aug.):647-71.
Kellerman, Barbara, ed. 1984. *Leadership: Multidisciplinary Perspectives.* Englewood Cliffs, NJ: Prentice-Hall.
Kempton, Murray. 1960. The Payoff. *New York Post,* June 20.
Kershaw, Joseph A. 1970. *Government against Poverty.* Washington, D.C.: Brookings Institution.
Key, V. O. 1961. *Public Opinion and American Democracy.* New York: Knopf.
Kingdon, John W. 1977. Models of Legislative Voting. *Journal of Politics* 39:3 (Aug.):563-95.
———. 1981. *Congressmen's Voting Decisions.* 2d ed. New York: Harper and Row.
Kliever, Douglas E. 1965. *Vocational Educational Act of 1963: A Case Study.* Washington, D.C.: American Vocational Association.
Kozak, David C. 1982. Decision-Making on Roll Call Votes in the House of Representatives. *Congress and the Presidency* 9:51-79.
Kuklinski, James H., and Richard C. Elling. 1977. Representational Role, Constituency Opinion, and Legislative Roll-Call Behavior. *American Journal of Political Science* 21:1 (Feb.):135-47.
Lees, John. 1967. *The Committee System of the United States Congress.* New York: Humanities Press.
Levitan, Sar A. 1973. *Federal Aid to Depressed Areas: An Evaluation of the Area Redevelopment Administration.* Baltimore: Johns Hopkins University Press.
Lewis, Anne L. 1978. Floor Success as a Measure of Committee Performance in the House. *Journal of Politics* 40:2 (May):460-67.
Lewis, Claude. 1963. *Adam Clayton Powell.* Greenwich, CT: Fawcett.
Lijphart, Arend. 1971. Comparative Politics and the Comparative Method. *American Political Science Review* 65:3 (Sept.):682-93.
Little, Thomas Hamilton. 1991. How Should Leaders Lead?: A Study of Individual and Institutional Needs and Expectations of Legislative Leaders. Ph.D. diss., Ohio State University.

Loftus, Joseph A. 1966a. Challenger Sees Defeat of Powell. *New York Times*, Sept. 17, p. 1.

———. 1966b. 13 on House Unit Approve Stripping Powell of Power. *New York Times*, Sept. 21, p. 1.

———. 1966c. House Strips Powell of Powers by a 27-1 Vote, and He Hails Decision. *New York Times*, Sept. 23, p. 1.

Loomis, Burdette A. 1981. The "Me Decade" and the Changing Context of House Leadership. In *Understanding Congressional Leadership*, ed. Frank H. Mackaman, 157-79. Washington, D.C.: CQ Press.

Lowell, A. Lawrence. 1902. The Influence of Party upon Legislation in England and America. *Annual Report of the American Historical Association for 1901*. Vol. 1. Washington, D.C.: GPO.

Lyons, Richard L. 1972. Adam Clayton Powell, Apostle for Blacks. *Washington Post*, April 6, B5.

McConachie, Lauros G. 1898. *Congressional Committees*. New York: Crowell.

McCormick, James M. 1985. The Changing Role of the House Foreign Affairs Committee in the 1970s and 1980s. *Congress and the Presidency* 12:1 (Spring):1-20.

MacCrae, Duncan, Jr. 1956. Roll Call Votes and Leadership. *Public Opinion Quarterly* 20:543-58.

———. 1958. *Dimensions of Congressional Voting: A Statistical Study of the House of Representatives in the Eighty-first Congress*. Los Angeles: University of California Press.

———. 1965. Method for Identifying Issues and Factions from Legislative Votes. *American Political Science Review* 59:909-26.

Mackenzie, G. Calvin. 1981. Coping in a Complex Age: Challenge, Response, and Reform in the House of Representatives. In *The House at Work*, ed. Joseph Cooper and G. Calvin Mackenzie. Austin: University of Texas Press.

MacNeil, Neil. 1963. *Forge of Democracy: The House of Representatives*. New York: David McKay Co.

Malbin, Michael. 1980. *Unelected Representatives: Congressional Staff and the Future of Representative Government*. New York: Basic Books.

———. 1981. Delegation, Deliberation, and the New Role of Congressional Staff. In *The New Congress*, ed. Thomas E. Mann and Norman J. Ornstein, 134-77. Washington, D.C.: American Enterprise Institute for Public Policy Research.

Mangum, Garth L. 1968. *MDTA: Foundation of Federal Manpower Policy*. Baltimore: Johns Hopkins University Press.

Manley, John. 1965. The House Committee on Ways and Means: Conflict Management in a Congressional Committee. *American Political Science Review* 59:4 (Dec.):927-39.

———. 1967. The House Committee on Ways and Means: 1947-1966. Ph.D. diss., Syracuse University.

———. 1969. Wilbur D. Mills: A Study in Congressional Influence. *American Political Science Review* 63:2 (June):442-64.

———. 1970. *The Politics of Finance: The House Committee on Ways and Means*. Boston: Little, Brown and Co.

March, James G., and Herbert A. Simon. 1967. *Organizations*. New York: Wiley.

Marwell, Gerald. 1967. Party, Region and the Dimensions of Conflict in the House of Representatives, 1949-1954. *American Political Science Review* 61:2 (June): 380-99.

Masters, Nicholas A. 1961. Committee Assignments in the House of Representatives. *American Political Science Review* 55:345-57. Reprinted in *New Perspectives on the House of Representatives*, 2d ed., ed. Robert L. Peabody and Nelson Polsby, 227-252. Chicago: Rand McNally, 1969.

Matsunaga, Spark M., and Ping Chen. 1976. *Rulemakers in the House*. Urbana: University of Illinois Press.

Matthews, Donald R. 1973. *U.S. Senators and Their World*. New York: Norton.

Matthews, Donald R., and James A. Stimson. 1970. Decision-Making by U.S. Representatives: A Preliminary Model. In *Political Decision-Making*, ed. S. Sidney Ulmer, 14-43. New York: Litton.

———. 1975. *Yeas and Nays: Normal Decision-Making in the U.S. House of Representatives*. New York: Wiley.

Miles, Robert H. 1980. *Macro Organizational Behavior.* Santa Monica, CA: Goodyear.

Morrow, William L. 1969. *Congressional Committees*. New York: Scribner's.

Munger, Frank J., and Richard F. Fenno. 1962. *National Politics and Federal Aid to Education*. Syracuse, NY: Syracuse University Press.

Murphy, James T. 1974. Political Parties and the Porkbarrel: Party Conflict and Cooperation in House Public Works Committee Decision Making. *American Political Science Review* 68:1 (March):169-85.

Murphy, Jerome T. 1973. The Education Bureaucracies Implement Novel Policy: The Politics of Title I of ESEA, 1965-1972. In *Policy and Politics in America*, ed. Allan P. Sindler, 161-98. Boston: Little, Brown and Co.

Murphy, Thomas P. 1978. *The Politics of Congressional Committees: The Power of Seniority*. Woodbury, NY: Barron's.

Murray, Charles. 1984. *Losing Ground: American Social Policy, 1950-1980*. New York: Basic Books.

Murray, Michael A. 1969. The House Education and Labor Committee and the 1967 Poverty Controversy: A Study of Congressional Avoidance. Ph.D. diss., University of Illinois at Urbana-Champaign.

Nelson, Garrison. 1977. Partisan Patterns of House Leadership Change. *American Political Science Review* 71:3 (Sept.):918-39.

Neustadt, Richard E. 1960. *Presidential Power*. New York: Wiley

———. 1990. *Presidential Power and the Modern Presidents: The Politics of Leadership from Roosevelt to Reagan*. New York: Free Press.

Norton, Bruce. 1970. The Committee on Banking and Currency as a Legislative Subsystem of the House of Representatives. Ph.D. diss., Syracuse University.

Oppenheimer, Bruce I. 1977. The Rules Committee: New Arm of Leadership in a Decentralized House. In *Congress Reconsidered*, ed. Lawrence C. Dodd and Bruce I. Oppenheimer, 96-116. New York: Praeger.

———. 1981. The Changing Relationship between House Leadership and the Committee on Rules. In *Understanding Congressional Leadership*, ed. Frank H. Mackaman, 207-25. Washington, D.C.: CQ Press.

Ornstein, Norman J. 1974. Towards Restructuring the Congressional Committee System. *Annals of the American Academy of Political and Social Science* 411:147-57.

Ornstein, Norman J., and Shirley Elder. 1978. *Interest Groups, Lobbying and Policymaking.* Washington, D.C.: CQ Press.

Ornstein, Norman J., Thomas E. Mann, Michael J. Malbin, and John F. Bibby. 1982. *Vital Statistics on Congress, 1982.* Washington, D.C.: American Enterprise Institute for Public Policy Research.

Ostrom, Donald. I. 1972. The House Education and Labor Committee: An Alternative Strategy. Ph.D. diss., Washington University, St. Louis.

——. 1979. Consensus and Conflict in the House: A Revised Look at the Ways and Means and Education and Labor Committees. *Polity* 11:3 (Spring):430-39.

Parker, Glenn R. 1977. The Evaluation of House Committee Leaders. Paper presented at the annual meeting of the Midwest Political Science Association, Chicago. April 21-23.

——, ed. 1985. *Studies of Congress.* Washington, D.C.: CQ Press.

Parker, Glenn R., and Suzanne L. Parker. 1979. Factions in Committees: The United States House of Representatives. *American Political Science Review* 73:1 (March):85-102.

——. 1985. *Factions in House Committees.* Knoxville: University of Tennessee Press.

Patterson, Samuel. 1963. Legislative Leadership and Political Ideology. *Public Opinion Quarterly* 27 (Fall):399-410.

Peabody, Robert L. 1966. The Ford-Halleck Minority Leadership Contest, 1965. In *Eagleton Cases in Practical Politics.* New York: McGraw-Hill.

——. 1974. Committees from the Leadership Perspective. *Annals of the American Academy of Political and Social Science* 411:133-46.

——. 1976. *Leadership in Congress: Stability, Succession, and Change.* Boston: Little, Brown and Co.

——. 1981. Senate Party Leadership: From the 1950s to the 1980s. In *Understanding Congressional Leadership*, ed. Frank H. Mackaman, 51-115. Washington, D.C.: CQ Press.

——. 1985a. House Party Leadership: Stability and Change. In *Congress Reconsidered*, 3d ed., ed. Lawrence C. Dodd and Bruce I. Oppenheimer, 253-71. Washington, D.C.: CQ Press.

——. 1985b. Leadership in Legislatures: Evolution, Selection, and Functions. In *Handbook of Legislative Research*, ed. Gerhard Loewenberg, Samuel C. Patterson, and Malcolm E. Jewell, 239-71. Cambridge, MA: Harvard University Press.

Perkins, Lynette P. 1980. Influence of Members' Goals on Their Committee Behavior: The U.S. House Judiciary Committee. *Legislative Studies Quarterly* 5:373-92.

Peters, B. Guy. 1982. *American Public Policy.* New York: Franklin Watts.

Plessy v. Ferguson. 163 U.S. 537 (1896).

Politics in America: The Politics and Issues of the Postwar Years. 1969. 3d ed. Washington, D.C.: CQ Service.

Polsby, Nelson. 1968. The Institutionalization of the U.S. House of Representatives. *American Political Science Review* 62:1 (March):144-68.

Polsby, Nelson, Miriam Gallaher, and Barry Spencer Rundquist. 1969. The Growth of the Seniority System in the U.S. House of Representatives. *American Political Science Review* 63:3 (Sept.):787-807.

Powell, Adam Clayton, Jr. 1945. *Marching Blacks.* New York: Dial Press.
——. 1971. *Adam by Adam.* New York: Dial Press.
Pressman, Jeffrey L. 1966. *House vs. Senate: Conflict in the Appropriations Process.* New Haven: Yale University Press.
Price, David E. 1972. *Who Makes the Laws? Creativity and Power in Senate Committees.* Cambridge, MA: Schenkman Books.
——. 1978. Policymaking in Congressional Committees: The Impact of "Environmental" Factors. *American Political Science Review* 72:2 (June):548-74.
Price, Hugh Douglas. 1962. Race, Religion, and the Rules Committee: The Kennedy Aid-to-Education Bills. In *The Uses of Power: 7 Cases in American Politics,* ed. Alan F. Westin, 1-72. New York: Harcourt, Brace and World.
Puryear, Elmer. 1979. *Graham A. Barden: Conservative Carolina Congressman.* Buies Creek, NC: Campbell University Press.
Puryear, Paul J. 1973. Graham A. Barden and the Struggle over Federal Aid to Elementary and Secondary Schools, 1949-1960. M.A. thesis, University of North Carolina.
Rapoport, Daniel. 1975. *Inside the House: An Irreverent Guided Tour Through the House of Representatives, from the Days of Adam Clayton Powell to those of Peter Rodino.* Chicago: Follett
Ray, Bruce. 1982. Committee Attractiveness in the U.S. House, 1969-1981. *American Journal of Political Science* 26:609-13.
Reeves, Benjamin F. 1977. Letter to Adron Doron, March 30. From the files of Benjamin F. Reeves. Bethesda, MD.
——. 1984. Obituary of Carl Dewey Perkins for the memorial service program. Sept. 11. Author's personal files, Huntsville, AL.
Regents of the University of California v. *Bakke.* 438 U.S. 265 (1978).
Rep. Carl Perkins Mourned as Champion of Worker Goals. 1984. *AFL-CIO News,* Aug. 11, p. 3.
Rice, Stuart. 1928. *Quantitative Methods in Politics.* New York: Knopf.
Rieselbach, Leroy N. 1975. Congressional Reform: Some Policy Implications. *Policy Studies Journal* 4:2 (Winter):180-88.
Rieselbach, Leroy N., and Joseph K. Unekis. 1981-82. Ousting the Oligarchs: Assessing the Consequences of Reform and Change on Four House Committees. *Congress and the Presidency* 9:1 (Winter):83-117.
Ripley, Randall B. 1967. *Party Leaders in the House of Representatives.* Washington, D.C.: Brookings Institution.
——. 1969. *Majority Party Leadership in Congress.* Boston: Little, Brown and Co.
——. 1974. Congressional Party Leaders and Standing Committees. *Review of Politics* 36: (July):394-409.
——. 1975. *Congress: Process and Policy.* New York: Norton
——. 1978. *Congress: Process and Policy.* 2d ed. New York: Norton.
Robertson, Nan. 1966. Powell Faces House Move to Strip Him of Powers. *New York Times,* Sept. 16, pp. 1, 4.
Robinson, James A. 1963. *The House Rules Committee.* Indianapolis, IN: Bobbs-Merrill.
Rohde, David W. 1974. Committee Reform in the House of Representatives and the

Subcommittee Bill of Rights. *Annals of the American Academy of Political and Social Science* 411:39-47.

Rohde, David W., and Kenneth Shepsle. 1987. Leaders and Followers in the House of Representatives: Reflections on Woodrow Wilson's "Congressional Government." *Congress and the Presidency* 14:2 (Autumn):111-33.

Saloma, John S., III. 1969. *Congress and the New Politics.* Boston: Little, Brown and Co.

Scher, Seymour. 1960. Congressional Committee Members as Independent Agency Overseers: A Case Study. *American Political Science Review* 54:4 (Dec.):911-20.

Schneider, Jerrold E. 1979. *Ideological Coalitions in Congress.* Westport, CT: Greenwood.

Schuck, Peter H. 1975. *The Judiciary Committees.* Ralph Nader Congress Project. New York: Grossman.

Sheppard, Burton D. 1985. *Rethinking Congressional Reform: The Reform Roots of the Special Interest Congress.* Cambridge, MA: Schenkman Books.

Sinclair, Barbara. 1977a. Determinants of Aggregate Party Cohesion in the U.S. House of Representatives. *Legislative Studies Quarterly* 2:155-75.

———. 1977b. Party Realignment and the Transformation of the Political Agenda. *American Political Science Review* 71:3 (Sept.):940-53.

———. 1978a. From Party Voting to Regional Fragmentation: The House of Representatives, 1933-1956. *American Politics Quarterly* 6:125-46.

———. 1978b. The Policy Consequences of Party Realignment—Social Welfare Legislation in the House of Representatives, 1935-1954. *American Journal of Political Science* 22:83-105.

———. 1981. Majority Party Leadership Strategies for Coping with the New U.S. House. In *Understanding Congressional Leadership,* ed. Frank H. Mackaman, 181-205. Washington, D.C.: CQ Press.

———. 1982. *Congressional Realignment, 1925-1978.* Austin: University of Texas Press.

———. 1983. *Majority Leadership in the House.* Baltimore: Johns Hopkins University Press.

———. 1985. Agenda, Policy, and Alignment Change from Coolidge to Reagan. In *Congress Reconsidered,* 3d ed., ed. Lawrence C. Dodd and Bruce I. Oppenheimer, 291-314. Washington, D.C.: CQ Press.

———. 1989. House Majority Party Leadership in the Late 1980s. In *Congress Reconsidered,* 4th ed., ed. Lawrence C. Dodd and Bruce I. Oppenheimer, 307-29. Washington, D.C.: CQ Press.

Smith, Gilbert E. 1982. *The Limits of Reform: Politics and Federal Aid to Education, 1937-1950.* New York: Garland.

Smith, Steven S. 1986. The Central Concepts in Fenno's Committee Studies. *Legislative Studies Quarterly* 11:1 (Feb.):5-33.

Smith, Steven S., and Christopher J. Deering. 1984. *Committees in Congress.* Washington, D.C.: CQ Press.

Smith, Steven S., and Christopher J. Deering. 1990. *Committees in Congress,* 2d ed. Washington, D.C.: CQ Press.

Sorenson, Theodore C. 1965. *Kennedy.* New York: Harper and Row.

Stewart, John G. 1971. Two Strategies of Leadership: Johnson and Mansfield. In

Congressional Behavior, ed. Nelson W. Polsby, 61-92. New York: Random House.

Stogdill, Ralph M. 1974. *Handbook of Leadership: A Survey of Theory and Research*. New York: Free Press.

Strahan, Randall. 1990. *New Ways and Means: Reform and Change in a Congressional Committee*. Chapel Hill: University of North Carolina Press.

Sundquist, James L. 1968. *Politics and Policy: The Eisenhower, Kennedy, and Johnson Years*. Washington, D.C.: Brookings Institution.

Tacheron, Donald G., and Morris K. Udall. 1966. *The Job of the Congressman: An Introduction to Service in the U.S. House of Representatives*. Indianapolis, IN: Bobbs-Merrill.

Thomas, Norman C. 1975. *Education in National Politics*. New York: David McKay Co.

Truman, David B. 1951. *The Governmental Process: Political Interests and Public Opinion*. New York: Knopf.

———. 1959. *The Congressional Party: A Case Study*. New York: Wiley.

Turner, Julius. 1951. *Party and Constituency: Pressures on Congress*. Baltimore: Johns Hopkins University Press.

Turner, Julius, and Edward V. Schneier. 1970. *Party and Constituency: Pressures on Congress*. Rev. ed. Baltimore: Johns Hopkins University Press.

Udall, Morris K. 1972. *Education of a Congressman*. Edited by Robert L. Peabody. Indianapolis, IN: Bobbs-Merrill.

Unekis, Joseph K. 1978a. From Committee to the Floor: Consistency in Congressional Voting. *Journal of Politics* 40:3 (Aug.):761-69.

———. 1978b. The Impact of Congressional Reform on Decision-Making in the Standing Committees of the House of Representatives. Paper presented at the annual meeting of the Southern Political Science Association, Atlanta. Nov. 9-11.

———. 1979a. The Impact of Policy Content and Member Goals on Decision Making in House Congressional Committees (1971-1978). Paper presented at the annual meeting of the Southwestern Political Science Association, Fort Worth. March 28-31.

———. 1979b. Reform Inspired Change in Committee Decision-Making: Consequences for Partisanship, Floor Success, and Committee Prestige in House Committees of the Modern Reform Era (1971-1978). Paper presented at the annual meeting of the Midwest Political Science Association, Chicago. April 19-21.

———. 1984. The Conservative Coalition in House Committees: Structure and Strength. Paper presented at the annual meeting of the Southern Political Science Association. Savannah, GA. Nov. 1-3.

Unekis, Joseph K., and Leroy N. Rieselbach. 1983. Congressional Committee Leadership, 1971-1978. *Legislative Studies Quarterly* 8:2 (May):251-70.

———. 1984. *Congressional Committee Politics: Continuity and Change*. New York: Praeger.

U.S. Bureau of the Census. 1969. *Statistical Abstract of the United States: 1969*. 90th ed. Washington, D.C.: GPO.

———. 1980. *Statistical Abstract of the United States: 1980*. 101st ed. Washington, D.C.: GPO.

U.S. Congress. 1971. *Biographical Directory of the American Congress: 1774-1971.* Washington, D.C.: GPO.

U.S. Congress. House. 1979. *Rules of the House of Representatives.* 96th Congress. Washington, D.C.: GPO.

———. Committee on Education and Labor. 1951-84. *Minutes.* Unpublished.

———. Committee on Education and Labor. 1957-84. *Rules.* Committee prints.

———. Committee on Education and Labor. 1961-67. *Activities and Accomplishments.* 87th-89th Congresses. Committee prints.

———. Committee on Education and Labor. 1968-84. *Summary of Major Legislative Action.* 90th-98th Congresses. Committee prints.

———. Committee on Education and Labor. 1984. *Report on the Activities.* 98th Congress. Committee Print.

U.S. Department of Commerce, Bureau of the Census. 1963. *Congressional District Data Book, Districts of the 88th Congress: A Statistical Abstract Supplement.* Washington, D.C.: GPO.

Uslaner, Eric M. 1974. *Congressional Committee Assignments: Alternative Models for Behavior.* Beverly Hills: Sage.

Valenti, Jack. 1975. *A Very Human President.* New York: Norton.

Vineyard, Dale. 1968. The Congressional Committees on Small Business: Pattern of Legislative Committee-Executive Agency Relations. *Western Politics Quarterly* 21:3 (Sept.):391-99.

Vogler, David J. 1974. *The Politics of Congress.* Boston: Allyn and Bacon.

Waldman, Sidney. 1980. Majority Leadership in the House of Representatives. *Political Science Quarterly* 95:373-93.

Westefield, Louis P. 1974. Majority Party Leadership and the Committee System in the House of Representatives. *American Political Science Review* 68:4 (Dec.): 1593-604.

Westerfield, H. Bradford. 1955. *Foreign Policy and Party Politics.* New Haven: Yale University Press.

Wilson, James Q. 1960a. Two Negro Politicians: An Interpretation. *Midwest Journal of Political Science* 4: 4(Nov.):436-69

———. 1960b. *Negro Politics: The Search for Leadership.* Glencoe, Il.: Free Press

Wilson, Rick K., and Calvin Jillson. 1989. Leadership Patterns in the Continental Congress: 1774-1789. *Legislative Studies Quarterly* 14:1 (Feb.):5-37.

Wilson, Woodrow. 1885. *Congressional Government: A Study in American Politics.* Baltimore: Johns Hopkins University Press.

Wolfinger, Raymond E., and Joan Heifetz. 1965. Safe Seats, Seniority, and Power in Congress. *American Political Science Review* 59:2 (June):337-49.

York, Michael. 1984. Congressman Proud of Work for District. Knott County, KY, *Troublesome Creek Times,* Aug. 8, p. 19.

Zarefsky, David. 1986. *President Johnson's War on Poverty: Rhetoric and History.* University: University of Alabama Press.

Index

www.ingramcontent.com/pod-product-compliance
Lightning Source LLC
Chambersburg PA
CBHW020403100426
42812CB00001B/185